Teresa of Avila

Also by Shirley du Boulay

BEYOND THE DARKNESS:
A BIOGRAPHY OF BEDE GRIFFITHS

THE ROAD TO CANTERBURY:
A MODERN PILGRIMAGE

TUTU:
VOICE OF THE VOICELESS

THE GARDENERS

THE WORLD WALKS BY
(with Sue Masham)

CICELY SAUNDERS:
FOUNDER OF THE MODERN HOSPICE MOVEMENT

Teresa of Avila

An Extraordinary Life

Shirley du Boulay

BlueBridge

Cover design by Per-Henrik Gurth
Cover art: François Gérard (1770–1837). *Saint Teresa of Avila* (detail).
Erich Lessing/Art Resource, New York.
Interior design by ediType
Map by Tzyh Ng

Library of Congress Cataloging-in-Publication Data
available upon request.

ISBN 0-9742405-2-4

Published by

BlueBridge

An imprint of United Tribes Media Inc.
240 West 35th Street, Suite 500
New York, NY 10001
www.bluebridgebooks.com
Printed in the United States of America

For John

Contents

Teresa's Bookmark

Nada te turbe,
Nada te espante,
Todo se pasa,
Dios no se muda,
La paciencia
Todo lo alcanza;
Quien a Dios tiene
Nada le falta;
Sólo Dios basta.

Let nothing disturb you
Let nothing frighten you
All things pass away:
God never changes.
Patience obtains all things.
He who has God
Finds he lacks nothing;
God alone suffices.

(Found in the breviary Teresa was using at the time of her death.)

Foundations of Discalced Carmelite Women's Convents by Teresa of Avila

Avila — St. Joseph's	1562
Medina del Campo	1567
Malagón	1568
Valladolid	1568
Toledo	1569
Pastrana	1569
Salamanca	1570
Alba de Tormes	1571
Segovia	1574
Beas de Segura	1575
Seville	1575
Caravaca	1576
Villanueva de la Jara	1580
Palencia	1580
Soria	1581
Burgos	1582

SPAIN
FRANCE
Pyrenees
Bilbao
León
Burgos
Palencia
Rio Ebro
Zaragoza
Barcelona
Valladolid
Rio Duero
Soria
Medina del Campo
Salamanca
Segovia
Avila
Pastrana
Alba de Tormes
Alcalá
Madrid
Toledo
Rio Tajo
PORTUGAL
Valencia
Palma
Villanueva de la Jara
Rio Guadiana
Malagón
Caravaca
Beas de Segura
Córdoba
Rio Guadalquivir
Murcía
Seville
Ecija
Granada
Málaga
Almería
ATLANTIC OCEAN
MEDITERRANEAN SEA

1

Castilian Childhood
1515–1536

They say in Spain that to understand Teresa of Avila one must look at Castile. Its wind-swept plains, its granite boulders, its bitter winters and sun-scorched summers were the womb that nourished the "undaunted daughter of desires" of Richard Crashaw's poem. A gentler landscape would not have produced a woman of such courage and determination.

Apart from its famous cities and towns — Madrid, Toledo, Valladolid and Segovia — Castile is a bleak and desolate region. It is monotonous, the barren landscape seldom softened by mist or rain. Yet this very monotony, this quality of endlessness, is curiously exciting. It speaks of hardship and danger, of struggle and tenacity, of time and eternity, of life and death. The light is diamond bright, the climate at the mercy of violent changes in temperature. So dry is the land that much of it is still uncultivated; today, even where it has been watered, sunflowers struggle to reach a pathetic two feet in height. This is central Spain, a land not of patios, fountains, and orange blossom, but harsh, ascetic, extreme. *Todo o nada* (all or nothing). Castile does not compromise.

At the foot of the Gredos mountains, some sixty miles to the northwest of Madrid, stands Avila, its towers and turrets rising proud from the bare Castilian plain. "Avila of the Knights," for many years at the center of the struggle between Christians and Moors, was finally won for Christianity at the end of the eleventh century, when King Alfonso VI built its impregnable walls. It was a city not only of martial traditions but also of ancient myth. Hercules, worshipped by the Romans as the god of victory, was reputed to have been its founder; Jimena Blasquez, its most famous heroine, was proudly remembered in song and dance. The legends tell how, in the absence of her husband, the governor, Jimena defended the city against the Moors. She gathered the women together, dressed them in false beards and large hats to disguise them as warriors, and led them to victory.

Avila, a city of churches and convents, palaces and plazas, is set on a windswept plateau over three thousand feet high. Its famous medieval walls, the *murallas,* still stand, supported by eighty-eight semicircular towers and nine gates. One of them, the Puerta del Puente, leads to the bridge across the river Adaja. The granite cathedral, begun in the twelfth century, is fortified like a castle, its apse forming a part of the city's defenses.

En Avila cantos y santos (in Avila stones and saints), the saying went. And chivalry too, a chivalry that put God first, demanded loyal service to the king and, in war, death rather than flight. Chivalry permeated life: the truth must always be spoken, the poor succored, the old venerated, ladies defended and provocation never given without cause. Violating the *pondonor* (the point of honor) could lead to fierce quarrels, even to death.

In Spain in the early sixteenth century this gallantry and courage were finding their outlet not only at home but in daring exploits overseas. Christopher Columbus had arrived in America in 1492 (though he was from Italy, he had been financed by

Ferdinand and Isabella of Spain, the Catholic Monarchs) and the Spaniards Hernan Cortez and Francisco Pizarro were poised to conquer Mexico and Peru; at home the Catholic Monarchs had conquered Granada, the last Moorish possession in Spain. Gold and silver would soon flow across the ocean in immense quantities. The world was expanding and Spain was riding high. It was a time of noble deeds, austerity, and sometimes fanaticism, witnessing brutal conversions or the expulsion of countless Muslims and Jews all across Spain. Now national pride, fueled by religious fervor and with more than a hint of racism, was intense. The true Spaniard must be able to boast pure blood, untainted by whiff of Jew or Moor. And over everything loomed the specter of the Inquisition.

Into this world, at dawn on March 28, 1515, Teresa Sánchez de Cepeda y Ahumada was born.

She was of noble birth, accustomed to comfort. Her father, Don Alonso Sánchez y Cepeda, was a rich and respected man who loved splendor, bought his ruffs from Paris and his saddles from Rouen, and owned magnificent estates. He was also a great reader and a devout, compassionate man. In an age when it was normal for someone of his rank to have slaves, he refused to do so. Teresa records that, even when a slave-girl of his brother's was staying in his house, he treated her like one of his own children. "He used to say that it caused him intolerable distress that she was not free."[1] She adds that he was extremely truthful, never swore or spoke slanderously and that he was "most rigid in his chastity."

Don Alonso was, however, of mixed blood, a fact about which the family were disinclined to speak freely and was never mentioned by Teresa in her autobiography, the *Vida*, or *Life*. That his father, Juan Sánchez, was Jewish was not known by Teresa's biographers until 1947, when an article appeared quoting a contemporary record of a lawsuit brought in 1519[2] and revealing the unpalatable truth: the family was not of pure blood, the treasured *limpia sangre,* but of tainted stock.

In racial fanaticism sixteenth-century Spain was comparable to Hitler's Germany: the merest hint of Jewish ancestry could lead to deprivation, humiliation, and exile. At the age of five Don Alonso had witnessed his father's degradation during a penitential procession in Toledo. Juan Sánchez was a *converso,* a Jew who had, at the insistence of the Inquisition, adopted Christianity; in obedience to an edict published by the Inquisitors he had admitted offenses against the Holy Catholic Church. This could have meant simply that he had continued to practice some harmless Jewish custom like refusing to eat pork. Nevertheless he, along with several hundred others, was whipped, forced to parade half naked around the Toledo churches, and disqualified from holding any high office. Juan's attempts to start a new life after this humiliation took him to Avila, where he was so successful in the silk and wool trade that he was able to purchase a certificate attesting to his noble, though completely fictitious, birth. He also took care to ensure that his children were brought up in the Christian faith.

Alonso married twice, his first wife dying after three years of marriage, leaving him three children. At the age of thirty he married a beautiful, though frail, young girl of fourteen, Doña Beatriz de Ahumada. Surely now his tainted Jewish past was purged? Beatriz was from one of the noblest families of Castile, in fact the very name "Ahumada" attested to their gallantry. The story was that, while fighting the Moors, one of her ancestors and his three sons were trapped in a tower, which the Moors surrounded and set on fire. Miraculously the flames produced smoke of such density that the warriors were able to escape. The family were from then on known as "Ahumada" from *humo* (smoke); further they were granted armorial bearings depicting a tower surrounded by flames.

After a wedding of such magnificence that the people of Avila remembered it for years, the couple returned to Don Alonso's house just inside the city walls, a splendid rambling mansion with patios and gardens, busy with servants washing, sewing, spinning, digging, planting, grooming the horses and branding the sheep. It was a devout household, and Christian practices were observed with scrupulous regularity. The day began with morning prayer, there was daily Mass, the Angelus was rung three times a day, grace was said before meals, and extracts from the lives of the saints were read aloud.

Already stepmother to two boys and a girl, Beatriz bore Alonso nine more children, all boys except for Teresa, her third child, and Juana, the last, born when Teresa was thirteen. The large family was a happy, high-spirited bunch, whose mother's presence was, however, remote. Teresa remembers her as a woman of remarkable beauty, though "she never showed the least signs of setting any store by it," modest, meek, virtuous and intelligent, but constantly sick and even as a young woman dressing in a manner beyond her years. Her one pleasure was in secretly reading tales of chivalry, something of which her austere husband, who preferred weightier matter such as Boethius's *Consolations of Philosophy* or the devotional poems of Pérez de Guzmán, entirely disapproved.

Teresa was fond of all her brothers and sisters, and they of her, but her special favorite was Rodrigo, four years her senior. As they read the lives of the saints together Teresa longed to die like them. She knew this was not for love of God, but because she was fearful of the torments of hell, impatient to experience the joys which she had read were laid up in heaven. Even in her comfortable circumstances, illness, hardship, and death were all around her: her mother was sick; when Teresa was only three years old, there was a serious threat of famine; and the following year the Great Plague took the lives of thousands all over Spain. The brevity of life was all too apparent. So the questions came early. What lay beyond death? Would it be the pain of hell or the bliss of heaven? The children had been told that pain and bliss would last forever, a thought that astonished them. They would discuss this curious idea, chanting *para siempre, siempre, siempre*... (forever and ever and ever...). Perhaps, if they followed the example of the saints, they would reach heaven quicker? Then they would live in endless bliss rather than risk endless pain?

Always one to act on her instincts, Teresa persuaded Rodrigo to travel to the land of the Moors with her, so that they might be beheaded and become martyrs. Aware of the dangers of travel, aware too that having parents was "a very great hindrance," early one morning they set out, Teresa aged seven and Rodrigo eleven, carrying a few crusts of bread, prepared, when these ran out, to beg their way. They crossed the bridge over the river Adaja and started along the road to Salamanca only to find that other members of the family could be a hindrance too; less than a quarter of a mile from home, at the monument of the Four Columns, they met their Uncle Francisco and were ignominiously taken home. Don Alonso and Doña Beatriz knew their children, and it was Teresa who was held responsible and duly reprimanded.

Her attempt at martyrdom having come to nothing, Teresa decided to become a hermit. Once again she co-opted Rodrigo and together they tried to build hermits' cells from the stones lying around in the orchard. But no sooner had they erected a little pile, large enough to allow their small bodies to squeeze in, than the entire edifice collapsed. Again she was thwarted. So she had to be content with saying her Rosary, something she had often seen her mother do, and leading the other girls in playing at nunneries. She, of course, was the prioress.

When Teresa was thirteen, her mother died. At a time when young girls most need a mother, even one as remote as Doña Beatriz, she was motherless. Her elder siblings, the children of Don Alonso's first marriage, were grown up. At eighteen and seventeen Hernando and Rodrigo were occupied with manly pursuits. The six other children were too young to give her the companionship she needed. Teresa, on the verge of womanhood, was a very lonely girl. Deeply distressed, she went to an image of Our Lady, traditionally thought to be the image now in the cathedral of Avila, and begged her to become her mother. Though she acted in childish innocence, she felt she benefited from it, "for whenever I have turned to the supreme Virgin I have always been conscious of her aid."

Teresa's account of her early life is permeated by a sense of sin and guilt. She was aware of her own gifts and of her good fortune in her parents, she felt her brothers and sisters took after them in their excellent characters, yet distress at her own shortcomings surfaces again and again. She repeatedly says she is the least virtuous of her family and that she failed to learn from the modesty and goodness of her elder sister; indeed the very first words of her *Life* are "If I had not been so wicked. . . ." Poignantly, she felt she used her very gifts to offend against God.

It is hard today to see her as sinful; indeed, her constant self-abasement and humility are, until the reader is perforce convinced of her sincerity, irritating. But how did others see her? How did she appear to the world? From her own words and from contemporary descriptions a vivid portrait emerges.

Too honest to indulge in coy modesty, she knew that she was her father's favorite, she was aware of "the natural graces with which the Lord endowed me" and that "the Lord gave me the grace of pleasing wherever I was."[3] Others corroborate and amplify these simple statements. All accounts agree that she was a beautiful girl, indeed it was said locally, "Teresa of Avila? She will marry whomsoever she pleases." In appearance she was short, well-built, and graceful in movement, pale-skinned with good color in her cheeks; her eyes were black and expressive, her mouth full, her chestnut hair luxuriant and curly. She had a lively, constantly changing expression, and the vivacity of her manner was enhanced by the frequency of her laughter and by three small dimples.

Her pleasing appearance was matched by her gifts. Her natural talent as a writer emerged early: when very young, she and Rodrigo even wrote a book together, which they read to their mother, but burnt before their exacting father could see it. She was good at chess, a bold horsewoman and a graceful dancer. After her mother's death she ran the household with smooth efficiency, and was an excellent cook and a skilled embroiderer — an exquisitely worked towel, used on Maundy Thursdays and still treasured at the Convent of the Incarnation, bears witness to this talent. Her father, unusually in those days, insisted that all his children should be able to read by the time they were seven, and Teresa took to this pastime with enthusiasm. "I was so enthralled by it that I do not believe I was ever happy if I had not a new book." Ironically her father became so annoyed by this passion — probably because she went through a stage of enjoying the tales of chivalry which had so occupied her mother's attention — that she had to keep it secret from him. Teresa herself was ambivalent about her addiction, on the one hand feeling it did not seem wicked, on the other saying that it began to "chill her desires" and to lead her astray.

Though some of her reading might not have been suitable for a young girl, her sense of guilt was so pervasive that it is hard to distinguish the real from the imaginary, particularly as she is tantalizingly vague about the form these sins actually took. As a grown woman she looked back with shame at behavior that would be considered normal in an attractive young girl. "I began," she wrote, "to deck myself out and to try to attract others by my appearance."[4] Her catalogue of youthful sins includes such innocent activities as "wearing finery," taking care of her hands and hair, and using perfumes and jewelry. Years later, thanking one of her brothers for a gold medallion, she writes that "if it had come in the days when I wore gold ornaments, I would have coveted it dreadfully, for it is extremely pretty."[5] So, too, she looked back with horror at her friendship with some cousins who often came to the house. She talked and gossiped with them, heard of their friends and pastimes, learned of their "affections and follies, which were anything but edifying." The influence of these cousins was strong enough to make her feel "so changed that I lost nearly all my soul's natural disposition to virtue." There has even been speculation that she was close to marrying one of them. Apart from a fondness for solitude and an exaggerated sense of guilt, she was an ordinary, healthy young girl with the instincts, petty vanities, and sentimentalities entirely appropriate to her age.

If these constant references to her unworthiness alienate the modern reader, and would indeed be considered pathological today, it is impossible not to be drawn by her ready affection and love for people. But even this she regards as a sin:

> I had a very serious fault, which led me into great trouble. It was that if I began to realize that someone liked me, and I took to him myself, I would grow so fond of him that my memory would feel compelled to revert to him and I would always be thinking of him; without intentionally giving any offense to God, I would delight in seeing him and think

about him and his good qualities. This was such a harmful thing that it was ruining my soul.[6]

But, whether she liked it or not, for many years of her life this need to receive love, as well as to give it, colored her very being. It was typical of her open nature too that, when she was hurt, she did not try to conceal it. "I am surprised," she wrote as a mature woman, "at your neglect of me, when you know how many troubles I have."[7] Indeed, it is not because she was talented, beautiful, and saintly, but because she was so impulsive, so open, and so human that through the ages people have felt able to respond to her. Who could not warm to someone who says ruefully that "when it came to doing anything wrong I was very clever,"[8] who acknowledges that "my own temperament is such that, when I desire anything, I do so with impetuosity," or can admit her fallibility so freely as to say "the Devil sends so offensive a spirit of bad temper that I think I could eat people up." Most profoundly of all she was caught in a painful war of opposites. While this tension is part of the human condition, in her the contradictions were writ large. She did not merely incline this way and that, but was pulled passionately in diametrically different directions.

Her conflict began after the wedding of her older half-sister, María. It was not considered suitable for Teresa to stay at home with neither a mother nor an elder sister, and at sixteen, in 1531, she was sent as a boarder to the Convent of Our Lady of Grace, Santa María de Gracia, run by Augustinian nuns, and just outside the walls of Avila. There were in those days no places of higher education for girls, but Our Lady of Grace, one of the most prestigious convents in town, took the wealthy daughters of distinguished families. They were not expected to acquire much academic education beyond reading and writing; rather they were encouraged to be virtuous, to become familiar with the catechism, to keep accounts, embroider, spin, make lace, and play a musical instrument. A training, in fact, for marriage.

At first she was desperately unhappy at Our Lady of Grace. It was not so much that she disliked the life of the convent, more that she had a shrewd suspicion she was being sent away to protect her from the company of her cousins and to discourage her from the frivolous lifestyle to which she was becoming addicted. She did not really believe that her father knew of her behavior, for she was so concerned for her good reputation — especially in his eyes — that she had concealed it from him, but she knew she could have no secrets from God. She was already tiring of her "wrong-doing," but felt the devil was still tempting her, indeed that she was the most depraved girl in the convent, a conviction not helped by the attempts of her old friends to smuggle messages through to her. However, this was soon stopped and in less than a week she had settled down, finding she was even happier than she had been in the family home. More relevantly, she was deeply impressed by the nuns, particularly by one whom she regarded as both sensible and saintly; as she listened to her she began to feel again the desires she used to have for eternal things when she and Rodrigo would intone, "Forever and ever and ever. . . . "

She stayed in the convent for eighteen months, battling with the opposing voices within her. She was frankly hostile to the thought of becoming a nun, yet she admired and envied those around her, particularly those she saw weeping as they prayed. Her own heart, she insists, was so hard "that even if I had read the whole Passion through I should not have shed a tear." She began to pray and ask people to pray for her that she might know what to do with her life. Gradually her dread of taking the habit lessened. It seems curious that she even persisted in the idea, so strong was her aversion, yet there were really only two choices for a woman of her background and time: to enter a convent or to be married. She still had no enthusiasm for becoming a nun, and she certainly did not have what would today be called a "vocation," yet she was afraid of marriage too. She had, after all, seen her mother live in total submission to her husband, seen her die after so much child-bearing. Years later she wrote to some of her nuns, telling them how fortunate they were to have been spared being in total subjection to a man and risking an early death through endless confinements. It was not sex that she feared, but submission, the thought of not even being able to express an opinion before her husband.

When, intermittently, she did consider entering a religious order, there was only one thing of which she was sure: that she would not go to Our Lady of Grace, where she found the devotional practices excessive, but to the Convent of the Incarnation, La Encarnación, where her friend Doña Juana Suárez was a nun. But, tossed between the world and God, between fear of marriage and uncertainty about religious life, she simply could not decide.

Eventually this inner conflict made her ill. Or, as she later saw it, God sent her a serious illness in order that she could have leisure to consider what she should do with her life. The illness meant she had to return to her father's house to recover; she then went to convalesce with her half-sister María and her husband, Martín Guzmán, at their home in the country not too far from Avila. On the way they passed the village of Hortigosa, where she broke the journey for a few days to stay with an uncle, Don Pedro. It was he who provided the turning point in her indecision.

Don Pedro was a devout elderly widower, who later gave up all his possessions and became a friar. He was a voracious reader and liked to talk about God and the vanity of the world. Teresa, always anxious to please, fell in with his wishes, pretending to enjoy the books he asked her to read to him. She was rewarded by finding the truths of her childhood ringing with renewed force:

once again her heart resounded to the thought that all is nothing and the things of this world soon pass. She began to fear that, if her illness had been mortal, she would have gone to hell. Still she did not want to take the habit, but she was becoming convinced that, even if it was not what she wanted, it was the safest thing to do. Admitting that her motivation was "servile fear rather than love," she decided to force herself to become a nun.

For three months she fought this battle, given courage by reading the letters of St. Jerome, that reclusive, controversial fourth-century monk who suffered from ill health, endured strong temptations of the flesh, and was famous for his translation of the Bible. The arguments flew to and fro in her mind. Could she, after such a comfortable life, endure the rigors of convent life? That would be nothing compared to the sufferings of Christ. In any case, the trials of religious life could not be greater than those of purgatory. And if she endured purgatory in this world, then surely she would have earned her place in heaven? She was forcing herself to embark on an interior struggle as dangerous and as exciting as that which tempted the young men of Avila, including many of her own family, to go overseas to fight wars and win territory. The difference was in weaponry. She was armed with prayer and an overwhelming desire to reach heaven; they with swords and an eagerness to prove their courage.

Eventually she decided to tell her father of her resolve. This would amount to taking the habit, for her gritty Castilian determination would never allow her to go back on her word. *Determinación* (determination) is a word she used constantly. Once she had decided on a course of action, especially if she was convinced it was what God wanted of her, she would not be thwarted. In Don Alonso, though, she met her first outer hurdle. He was adamant that she must not go; the most he would agree was that she could do as she wanted after his death. She now feared for her own resolve. She must act quickly, lest she lose her newfound courage. It was no longer a matter of her own comfort or even of her father's happiness; the salvation of her soul was at stake.

She persuaded her younger brother Antonio, who soon afterward became a Dominican, to accompany her — to go alone was too much even for her — and in November 1536, early one morning, they stole out of the family home, and walked out of the city gate and down the hill to the Convent of the Incarnation. She was in "such dreadful distress that the pain of death itself cannot be worse." She had no love of God to subdue her love for her father and relatives, no certainty that she was doing the right thing, no support from the father she loved so much. It is hardly surprising that she felt as though "every bone in my body seemed to be wrenched asunder."

2

The Convent of the Incarnation
1536–1543

The decision made, the ambivalence resolved, Teresa was overcome by a relief that filled her with energy and joy. Never again would she let fear prevent her from acting, never would she forget "the Lord's favors . . . to those who use force with themselves in his service." The lethargy of inaction was replaced by the vigor of knowing her goal: The resolution to serve God as a nun gave her confidence that she had ensured the safety of her soul. Though at the time she could not (and did not) claim to have a vocation in the usual sense of the word, and though she had done violence to herself in making the decision, now she had a heroic role to play which both suited her temperament and reflected the spirit of her age.

Having mixed or even downright opportunistic motives for taking the habit was not unusual for women in those days. Widows, uncertain how to face life alone, would seek solace within convent walls; girls disappointed in love or simply too poor to survive in the world were among those applying for admission. Convents abounded in sixteenth-century Spain; Teresa had plenty of choice. In finding herself drawn to the Carmelite Convent of the Incarnation, she was not following in the footsteps of a favorite saint — thus far the Carmelites had not been particularly distinguished and had not produced too many notable saints or theologians — it was largely her friendship with Doña Juana Suárez which had led her there. However, the Order's beginnings in the Holy Land appealed to her imagination.

Mount Carmel, honored as "the most sacred of all mountains," is in Israel, across the bay from Acre, near the city of Haifa. It has a long history as a place of worship, and medieval Carmelites even claimed continuity with Elijah and the group known as "the sons of the prophets." What is not in doubt is that they are descended from a group of hermits who settled near "the fountain of Elijah" in the thirteenth century and to whom Albert, Patriarch of Jerusalem at the time, gave a short, simple rule so spiritual, so unlegalistic, so overwhelmingly concerned with love that it has been called "the rule of mysticism." In 1425 the Carmelites were given papal approval to receive women, later to be called Second Order Carmelites, and soon the Order spread through France, Italy, and Spain.

The Convent of the Incarnation was founded in 1479 as a home for ladies who were under vows, but not fully professed. In 1515, the year of Teresa's birth, it was turned into a Carmelite convent. The primitive rule of St. Albert had been mitigated in 1432 and much of the contemplative spirit lost. Of course the nuns spent many hours in chapel, were expected to make their confession at least once a fortnight and to take the "discipline" (a scourge of knotted cords used as an instrument of penance) three times a week; they wore the coarse serge habit of the time and fasted regularly. However, in many ways the 180 nuns lived an easygoing life of surprising freedom. They were allowed to wear padded skirts, colored sashes, and jewelry: they could accept presents and those who could afford to kept pets and had personal servants; they were referred to as "ladies," addressed as "Madam," and could entertain friends and relatives in the *locutorio* or parlor; they were even allowed to spend long periods away from the convent on visits. There was blatant discrimination between the rich and the poor. Those who brought small dowries or nothing at all slept in dormitories, wore clogs, and used earthenware dishes; while those whose families could pay good dowries lived in correspondingly greater comfort, wearing high-heeled shoes and drinking from silver cups. Had it not been for a few devout nuns, it would have been more like a guest house for single ladies with a taste for religion than a monastic community.

Even so, the conditions were hardly what Teresa de Cepeda y Ahumada, daughter of a wealthy, aristocratic family, had known. The house had no rich sponsor and there was a constant struggle to obtain funds. The nuns would knit stockings and make sweets, which they would sell at the gate. The daily food ration, outside fasting periods, was 150 grams of bread and 115 grams of meat for lunch and supper, with a little milk and honey for breakfast. Such was their poverty that the nuns were encouraged to go out and eat with their families, thus leaving more food for those who remained in the convent. Though her ambivalent motives cannot have given her much strength, to her own surprise Teresa was delighted by everything about the life. Not for a moment did she miss the comforts of her luxurious home or the hours previously spent on her personal indulgence and adornment; sweeping the stone floors of the convent seemed an excellent exchange and gave a far deeper freedom. She was filled with a new joy, which amazed and puzzled her, for she could not account for it. Several years later she wrote that she had been brought to "a state so secure" and that she found there "a joy so great that it has never failed me to this day, and God converted the aridity of my soul into the deepest tenderness."[1]

She could hardly have experienced such happiness if she had been living in the knowledge of her beloved father's disapproval. In fact, Don Alonso accepted the situation with good grace; he knew his daughter and would not have expected her to change her mind after such a dramatic gesture. He signed the necessary documents, giving her the sort of dowry that, with her background, she might have expected. He promised to give the convent an annual gift of either twenty-five measures of grain from his estate at Gotarrendura or two hundred gold ducats; further he undertook to provide Teresa with clothes, a bed, and bedclothes; to give every nun a new coif; and to pay for a supper for the whole community on the day his daughter made her profession. Teresa, for her part, formally renounced all claims to the family estate.

Don Alonso's generosity meant that Teresa was among those living in considerable comfort, and it is curious that, though later she was to insist on equality, she never mentions the disparity of the nuns' living conditions. She appears either not to have noticed or to have thought that such inequality was quite acceptable. Apart from her cell, Don Alonso's daughter had a guest room, a kitchen and her own oratory, where she could celebrate the feast of her favorite saint and which she was allowed to decorate with her own pictures and statues. After the death of her father, she was even allowed to have her younger sister, Juana, stay with her. But it is clear from the way she writes of this period that physical conditions were irrelevant. Her words have the ringing certainty of someone who has found the right path. Whatever the difficulties and problems ahead, she would be tackling them safe in that knowledge, from that secure base.

Problems there were. She suffered long periods of unrest about matters which, in themselves, she considered of little importance. She could not bear being blamed for things that were not her fault — a penance often demanded of young nuns. She delighted in the good opinion of others and hated appearing ridiculous, hence her shame in often needing guidance in chapel; talented though she was, she was not good at singing. She instinctively considered her fastidiousness a virtue, yet felt it led her to follow "what I knew to be wrong and neglect what was good."

She was not worried by the simple life or the inadequate diet occasioned as much by poverty as by deliberate abstinence, nor by the penances practiced by the more devout; these were part of the heroic sacrifice, and the young postulant willingly accepted them as such. She took the discipline, scourged herself with nettles, and ate simply and little. She even learned to speak little and behave with a decorum that cannot have come naturally to one of her ebullient temperament. Sometimes, and it must be said untypically, she lost all sense of proportion and common sense. Her French biographer Marcelle Auclair describes how one day she "came into the refectory crawling on all fours, a mule's pack saddle loaded with stones on her back, dragged along like a beast by a sister who was pulling at the halter which Teresa had put round her neck."[2] She found encouragement and inspiration in the example set by some of the other nuns, for whom she quickly developed a deep respect. Even so, the life was fundamentally unsatisfying because these deprivations were not balanced by a real contemplative life.

The postulants were instructed in the history of their Order and the Rule, and there were, of course, the regular celebrations of the liturgy. But long hours in the chapel were not complemented by regular periods of mental prayer and contemplation: spiritual life at the Convent of the Incarnation lacked vitality, in fact the idealistic rule of St. Albert was honored more in the breach than in the observance. She had given up the world, but she had not found the inner compensation for which, whether she knew it at the time or not, she longed. Thus the guilt which had pervaded her since childhood still went unassuaged. The other nuns, often finding her in tears, would assume she was missing her old life, and she did not disabuse them. But in reality she was haunted by shame at the sins she felt she had committed in the past, by her present shortcomings, and with hindsight as she wrote of it, by the sinful way in which she would continue to live. On November 3, 1537, a year and a day after her unorthodox arrival at the convent, she made her final profession. But, remembering it as a mature woman, she does not recall it as the sparkling social occasion it was, with all the *caballeros* (noblemen) of Avila and their families watching her process up the aisle to the music of the "Veni, Creator Spiritus," but looked back at it with searing pain. She writes of "the great determination and sacrifice with which I made it [her profession] and the betrothal I contracted with Thee," but there she almost breaks down. "I cannot speak of this without tears, and they ought to be tears of blood, and my heart ought to break, and even that would be showing no great sorrow for the offenses which I afterward committed against Thee."[3]

What was the nature of these sins? Some of her biographers[4] have suggested that they were sexual, but the lack of hard evidence coupled with her own tantalizing vagueness make certainty impossible. Indeed, if contemporary accounts are to be believed, she seemed hardly to have experienced sexual temptation at all. Ribera, her first biographer, writing in 1590, tells how, as a mature woman, she had answered an inquiry on the subject by saying, "Daughter, I understand none of these things, indeed the good God gave me grace that throughout my life I have never allowed anything of this kind to enter my mind."[5] Another nun, giving evidence for her canonization, recalls how she asked Teresa's advice about chastity and was told she should look for someone else, as "the Lord had given her the grace never to have any temptation on that score." While this absence of desire in a normal young woman is unlikely and while the possibility of the nun's memory being selective must be taken into account, Teresa herself is so evidently honest that it is hard to doubt her words, and it is she herself who wrote, "I never felt the inclination to do anything much that was wrong."

What she did is not really the point. Sexual irregularities, even illegitimate children, were not unusual in sixteenth-century Spain; indeed her own brother fathered a love-child to whom Teresa was devoted. Even given the greater disapproval leveled at women's sexual aberrations than men's, the depth of her guilt is not in proportion to the suggested offense. Despite her passionate temperament, from what is known of her early life it is hard to believe that she had committed any really serious sins. The interest lies in why her guilt was so profound, so pervasive, so hard to allay. She often writes as if she was guilty in the core of her being.

Was it an overdeveloped sense of responsibility that led her to assume personally the sinful nature of man? Again, at an archetypal level, did the knowledge of her Jewish ancestry, at a time when racism was rampant, infuse her whole personality with a guilt beyond her control? Did she feel she had let down her father? A psychological explanation might suggest that the cause lay more with her mother. A remote, cold mother inevitably leaves a child feeling unloved. Soon it feels not only unloved, but unlovable. Why? What has it done wrong to make it unlovable? Mother is good, she must be. It must be the child's own fault, its guilt, its sinfulness.

Another possible explanation is that the higher the ideal, the more painful the comparison. To compare oneself with others is to invite dissatisfaction, and that is what she continually did. She compared herself with her family, with friends, and with the other nuns — and always to her own detriment. She continually castigates herself for mysterious sins of whose exact nature we are never quite certain, but particularly for misusing the gifts with which she knew she had been endowed. In a passage of untypical complexity she laments: "On granting me all the graces Thou hast bestowed on me already, why has it not seemed well to Thee, not for my advantage but for Thy honor, that this habitation wherein Thou hast had continually to dwell should have become so greatly defiled?"

Beyond all those she knew on earth, it was her comparison of herself with God, of whose goodness and love she was utterly sure, that led her into torrents of self-abasement. Though she frequently says she had not committed any mortal sin and that she had little inclination to do wrong, she perceives herself intrinsically as the most wicked and sinful woman, constantly bewailing her great sins and offenses against God and saying she "fully deserved to be in hell." By 1562, when she wrote her *Life,* she realized that her guilt had much to do with her keen perception of the contrast between her own human frailty and God's perfection. "We can deduce our own unworthiness by imagining a state of real virtue. This accounts for my tears and vexation when I took stock of my own feelings."[6] It is their very sanctity that makes holy people aware of their sinfulness before God. This, however, would not have been how she saw it, and nothing appears to have offered her much consolation, for her sense of sinfulness was to preoccupy her for most of her life.

These powerful feelings of guilt led her not only to frequent confession but also to penitential acts of all sorts, from secretly darning the sisters' old cloaks to volunteering to care for a nun so ill that the other nuns were afraid to be near her. She had open sores on her stomach exuding pus and excrement, she could not eat, and she was dying. Teresa looked after her until her death, feeling not fear but "only great envy of her patience." So much did she long for patience, indeed for all "eternal blessings," that no sacrifice was too great. She begged God that he would send her an illness, so that she could follow the dying nun's example. Barely a year after she had made her solemn profession as a nun, her prayer was answered and she herself fell seriously ill.

Throughout her life illness was to be Teresa's constant companion. There are no medical records to determine the exact nature of her ailments, but from her own writings and from her early biographers a long list emerges. If they are to be believed (and allowance must be made for the state of medical knowledge at the time), she suffered, at various times, from heart disease, palsy, paralysis, trembling, epilepsy, sickness, sore throats, intense headaches, tuberculosis, quartan ague (fever occurring every fourth day), quinsy (inflammation of the throat), malaria, consumption, noises in the head, and fainting fits. While illness was common among the nuns — Teresa's letters are full of inquiries as to her correspondents' state of health and gently recommended cures — she unquestionably suffered far more than most. Various suggestions have been made as to why she had such exceptionally poor health. Was it entirely physical? Did it all spring, as has been claimed, from malaria? Today, when psychology makes so many connections between bodily and mental health, suggestions have been made that she was a hysteric, but her own attitude to her ill health, her exasperation with it, the way she refused, as far as possible, to let it restrict her activities, does not support this argument. Vita Sackville-West, writing in the early 1940s, claims that "obviously the majority of her afflictions arise from what we should call neuropathic causes." Yet she also contributes, tentatively, some sympathetic suggestions:

> To what extent were her disorders physical or pathological? Were they due to a combination of genuine physical infirmity aggravated by the nervous tension of her most peculiar temperament? The truth probably lies in this hypothesis. The mental and the physical are in some cases inexplicably mixed up; inexplicably, that is, to the incomplete attainments of our so-far knowledge. Are we perhaps putting the cart before the horse in ascribing the mental disturbance to physical causes, and would it not be truer to say that a mental composition of such excessive sensibility produced so severe a strain that the body inevitably paid? Or was it that a low physical resistance impaired the control and balance of the mind? Impaired is perhaps not the right word, since the spiritual gain of such unspeakable benefit could not be purchased at too high a price.[7]

Teresa herself, as we shall see, came to have a perceptive understanding of the possible psychosomatic dimensions to her ill health, but of her complete breakdown in 1538 she simply says she had heart trouble, her fainting fits became more numerous, and "I also had many other ailments." Her condition became increasingly serious until she was hardly ever fully conscious; indeed she sometimes lost consciousness altogether. Her father arranged for the best doctors in Avila to see her, but they were not able to cure or even help her. All they could suggest was that she should return home and that a better diet might aid in restoring her health. It is not likely she would have agreed to that, and Don Alonso, desperate to do something for his beloved daughter, who seemed to be fading away before his eyes, arranged for her to see a *curandera,* a female healer recommended by her older half-sister, María.

So, with Juana Suárez for company, he took her, in late 1538, to stay with María and her husband in the foothills of the Gredos mountains, not far from the home of the *curandera,* who lived in the small town of Becedas.

On the way they stayed, as they had five years earlier, with Don Alonso's brother, Don Pedro, who once again was to have a decisive influence on Teresa's inner life. And yet again it was to be through a book, this time *The Third Spiritual Alphabet* by Osuna.

Francis of Osuna, like Ignatius of Loyola, was a soldier as well as a mystic and had been in Tripoli when the town was taken by the Spaniards in 1510. He later became a Franciscan and in 1527 *The Third Spiritual Alphabet* (*El tercer abecedario*), a crucial book in Spanish mysticism, was published in Toledo. It was seminal because it was written at a time when the breach between one group of believers, the *alumbrados,* practicing total and ecstatic abandonment of the soul to God, and the *recogidos,* followers of a way of perfection based on recollection, was at its widest. Osuna numbered many *alumbrados* among his followers, so this long book, in which he allied himself firmly with the *recogidos* and advocated mental concentration and active directing of the mind, became controversial.

Teresa fell on it with delight. She claims that at the time she did not know how to practice prayer or how to recollect herself; at the time her only form of prayer was vocal, prayers of thanksgiving, praise, and petition. She determined to follow this way of prayer "with all my might." Her copy of Osuna's work is preserved in the sacristy of the first convent she founded, St. Joseph's in Avila, with her favorite passages marked with a cross, a heart, or a pointing hand. It is easy to imagine her pleasure when in the first chapter she read, "Friendship and communion with God are possible in this life of exile. This friendship is not remote but more sure and more intimate than ever existed between brothers or even between mother and child." Accustomed to words, though aware of their limitations, her excitement must have been immense when she came across this passage:

> The highest part of the soul is lifted more purely and affectionately to God on the wings of desire and pious affection strengthened by love. The greater our love the fewer words we use . . . for genuine love does not know how to cast about for roundabout, complex argumentation, but becomes silent and achieves great things.[8]

At the time she was unable to pray without a book, for "My soul was as much afraid to engage in prayer without one as if it were having to go and fight against a host of enemies." However, she found that as soon as she started reading, her thoughts would become collected and "the book acted like a bait to my soul. Often the mere fact that I had one by me would be sufficient." With *The Third Spiritual Alphabet* beside her she found a novel way of praying. "I used to think of Jesus Christ, our Good and our Lord, as present within me, and it was in this way that I prayed."[9] She was at the beginning of the path that was eventually to lead to extraordinary heights of mystical experience.

The herbs needed for the cure would not be ready for gathering until the spring, so Don Alonso left Teresa and Juana Suárez with María for the winter and returned home. During this period Teresa formed a relationship which had a profound effect on her; she wrote about it at length in her autobiography, admitting that it unsettled her, though the outcome was good.

The person in question was a priest of good family and keen intelligence, to whom she began to make her confession. The priest was very attracted by Teresa and, although the friendship seems to have been innocent enough, she realized his affection for her was too strong to be appropriate between a nun and her confessor. What troubled her more, since she felt well able to cope with an ardent priest, was that their roles imperceptibly began to change and he began to confide in her, telling her that for seven years he had been living with a local woman. This was well known in the village, members of his household saying, as if excusing him, that the woman had cast a spell over him by giving him a little copper figure to wear around his neck. No one had been able to persuade him to part with this, but Teresa, who, while not believing in spells, realized the significance of the gift, succeeded where others had failed. In order to please her, the priest gave her the figure, which she immediately asked a friend to throw in the river. At once "he became like a man awakening from a deep sleep. . . . He was amazed at himself and grieved at this lost condition and he began to hate the woman who had led him to it." He gave up seeing the woman, and when only a year later he died, it was "very devoutly."

Eventually spring came and the cure began. The remedies were drastic. For three months Teresa endured severe tortures without even the solace of improving health. The pain in her heart became worse, so bad that she felt "as if sharp teeth had hold of me, and so severe was the pain they caused that it was feared I was going mad." She grew thinner and weaker, could take nothing but liquid, and was in a continual fever. Daily purgatives contracted her nerves, and she was in intolerable agony night and day.

At the end of July her father took her home and once again called in the Avila doctors. They held out no hope, saying that, in addition to everything else, she was consumptive. She asked to make her confession, but her father, fearing it would sap her will to live, forbade it. He was soon to regret this mistaken kindness, for on the night of August 15 Teresa suffered what she calls "a fit," but has been variously referred to as a "syncope" and "an attack of catalepsy." As she lay unconscious, the family took turns watching at her bedside. On one occasion Lorenzo fell asleep and nearly allowed his sister to burn to death when a guttering candle set her bedclothes ablaze. A priest administered Extreme Unction; her family recited the Creed, "as though," Teresa adds, "I could have understood any of it." While she lay unconscious a bell was tolled at the Incarnation and a grave was dug. At another Carmelite monastery the rites for the dead were performed for her. She would have been buried had her father not insisted that she was alive. He was right. Eventually, after four long days, she woke to find wax on her eyes — her body was being prepared for burial. Indeed, she felt she had been raised from the dead, but, despite the gratitude of her soul, her body was still tormented by pain:

> My tongue was bitten to pieces; nothing had passed my lips: and because of this and of my great weakness my throat was choking me so that I could not even take water. All my bones seemed to be out of joint and there was a terrible confusion in my head. As a result of the torments I had suffered during these days, I was all doubled up, like a ball, and no more able to move arm, foot, hand or head than if I had been dead, unless others moved them for me. I could move, I think, only one finger of my right hand.[10]

She was eager to return to the Incarnation, so, barely alive and so weak that she had to be carried on a sheet held at each corner, she was taken back, and stayed for many months in the convent's infirmary. The slightest touch was agonizing; she was delirious; she could not lie full length, but lay curled up with her knees to her chin in a fetal position which once again leads to speculation as to her state of mind. For eight months she was acutely paralyzed. It was three years before she could cautiously move about on her hands and knees.

Teresa bore her sufferings with remarkable resignation, even with joy. She had, after all, prayed for illness and part of her was resigned to God's will, even if her health was never to improve. She was, though, only twenty-five, and it would hardly have been natural for her to have become totally resigned to the life of an invalid. She longed to be well enough at least to enjoy some solitude, something quite impossible in the infirmary; she believed, too, that she could serve God better if she were healthy. So, as medicine could not help her, she decided to seek a cure from "heavenly doctors." She had Masses said for her — strictly in accordance with the church's teaching, for she had no patience with unorthodox ceremonies — and she commended herself to someone who was to become her favorite saint, St. Joseph. Strong-willed by temperament, yet determined to be obedient, she found she could submit to the image of one to whom Christ himself was subject on earth. She attributed her improvement — it could not be called a cure, because she was at no time completely well — entirely to him and never ceased to commend him to others. She would make requests of him every year on his festival, claiming that they were always granted, even that "if my petition is in any way ill directed, he directs it aright for my greater good."

Eventually her health so much improved that it was accounted by many to be nothing short of miraculous. Teresa's way of life became such that she would later look back on it with horror and shame:

> I began, then, to indulge in one pastime after another, in one vanity after another and in one occasion of sin after another.

> Into so many and such grave occasions of sin did I fall, and so far was my soul led astray by all these Vanities, that I was ashamed to return to God in the intimate friendship which comes from prayer.

Once again today's reader, accustomed to daily accounts of muggings, murder, drug abuse, and sexual depravities, can look in vain for evidence of sin as our secular time understands it. Her shortcomings were venial, even trivial, in the eyes of the world; the worst that can be said is that they were inappropriate in a convent.

Anxious though she is to confess every peccadillo, she admits that she did nothing without leave, never (as by implication others did) "talking to people through crevices or over walls by night." She was so meticulous in never speaking ill of people behind their backs that she earned the complete trust of the community. But still there is this irritating elusiveness about her sins; they seem, even in her own mind, to be less sins of commission than sins of omission. "I had this unfortunate characteristic that, if the Lord gave me grace to do anything good, the way I did it was full of imperfections and extremely faulty."[11] The only shortcomings one can perceive are her vanity and her desire to be well thought of in matters esteemed by the society in which she lived. But underpinning everything — and probably the cause of much of her guilt — is her awareness that her spiritual life was lived on a superficial level, that the outer appearance was not matched by a corresponding inner conviction and depth.

Though she frequently sought solitude and appeared to be praying, despite the influence of Osuna's *Third Spiritual Alphabet*, she was only praying vocally, almost automatically. She read a great deal and liked to speak about God, but she was not experiencing him. She decorated her oratory with religious pictures, but it was all external — a surface, rather than a lived, religion. She had been caught up in the attitude so common in the religious houses of sixteenth-century Spain, where outer observance was superficial and inner spiritual vitality the exception rather than the norm.

Teresa was aware of this and decries the freedom they were given. Because of her outward piety, her charm, and the good opinion she made sure the nuns had of her (one of the aspects of her vanity), she was given as much liberty as the oldest nuns, who in any case welcomed the presents brought by Teresa's numerous friends and relations. She came to the conclusion that she would have been far better in an enclosed convent. It seemed to her very dangerous for nuns to have such freedom: "for those who want to be wicked it is not so much a remedy for their weakness as a step on the way to hell." Indeed (the Spanish idea of honor surfacing again), she felt it would be better for girls to marry beneath them than to put them in convents where the obligations of nuns were so inadequately understood.

While she was aware of the risks of too much freedom, gatherings in the convent parlor were so normal a part of her life at this time that she did not appreciate the dangers they held for her. She tells of an instance which both sums up these dangers and which acted as a catalyst to a change in her behavior.

She was, she wrote, in the company of a "certain person" (the Spanish word *persona* does not reveal the sex of her friend) when "Christ revealed Himself to me, in an attitude of great sternness, and showed me what there was in this that displeased Him." This experience made such an impression on her that she still remembered it years later and immediately decided she never wanted to see that person again. However, her resolve began to weaken. She enjoyed the friendship; she was also assured that her good name would be enhanced by such a contact, a factor that was still important to her. It did not suit her to believe that this came from God, far easier to attribute it to her imagination or to the devil. There was no one with whom she felt able to discuss the matter, and eventually she gave into her own wishes and the demands of the person in question: they agreed to meet again. This time the warning was crude, indubitably owing more to imagination than divine intervention. They saw a great toad crawling "much more quickly than toads are wont to do" across the parlor floor. It is curious that this incident should have held such significance for her. Presumably her conscience was alert to any sign that she was disobeying the firm injunction she had already received. This, too, she never forgot and was convinced it had a hidden meaning.

The social whirl of the convent parlor continued on its lively, worldly religious, shallow course and Teresa's shame deepened. In fact, her feeling that she dared not approach God in prayer reached the point where she gave up prayer completely, a state which she felt nearly brought about her ruin. Yet she had a strong desire to encourage and help others, in her words "a common temptation in beginners"; for some time she lived the curiously painful paradox of teaching others to follow a path she was no longer following herself.

A further paradox was that her father-daughter relationship with Don Alonso was reversed as she became his teacher, encouraging him in prayer and lending him books. She could not bear to deceive him about herself, so she led him to believe it was her health that had stopped her praying, that it was all she could do to attend the choir offices. So, at this time, it was he who "reached such a high state of prayer he used not to stay with me for so long, but after he had seen me would go away, saying that he was wasting his time." One wonders which made him sadder, that his daughter was too ill to pray or that, for reasons he cannot have fully understood, her inner state of mind made it impossible.

While father and daughter were living this unsatisfactory relationship, he became seriously ill. Teresa went home to look after him, striving to conceal her grief from him as she realized he was dying. For three days he was almost unconscious, regaining consciousness only on the day of his death, Christmas Eve 1543. Halfway through reciting the Creed he died, looking "like an angel." Once again Teresa felt "as it my very soul was being torn from me."

3

"That Stormy Sea" 1543–1555

Little is known of Teresa's outer life during her thirties, probably because it was largely uneventful. On the surface things continued much as they had since her entry into the convent when she was twenty-one. Apart from the social life of the parlor, meals, and recreation periods, most of the day was spent in church. Teresa did her share of the cleaning and adornment of the altars, and of the organizing of processions inside the convent. There were personal devotions overseen by individual nuns — Teresa, for instance, was particularly concerned that St. Joseph's feast should be observed with loving devotion. Then there were various pious practices such as the recitation of the Rosary, the Angelus and the Way of the Cross, and the celebration of feast days and the major festivals of Lent, Easter, and Christmas. Punctuating the day, continuously impregnating it with prayer, was the regular singing of the canonical hours. The day started in the hours before dawn with Matins, Lauds, and Prime. As the sun rose the nuns would be hearing Mass; during the course of the day there would be Terce, Sext, and None; in the evening Vespers and Compline. It was a demanding and, many would say, boring routine, though Teresa never complained or even referred to it.

All that is known of her contacts with the world during this period is that, following her father's death, Teresa found herself caught up in financial matters and personal feuds. Despite his moral integrity, Don Alonso had died in debt, and more than fifty creditors began pressing their claims to his estate. Even more painfully, the children of his two wives disputed their shares of his will. Teresa, who was an executor, would have preferred to settle the matter out of court, but, much against her will, litigation procedures were started. Predictably, the only people to gain were the lawyers, as by the time the case was over there was hardly anything left to distribute between the various contenders.

Once these business affairs were concluded, the family dispersed, the younger brothers joining those who had already gone to seek fame and fortune in the Americas. Their role in Spain's conquest of the New World was both gallant and tragic. Four of the brothers fought in the famous battle on the plains of Inaquito, in Ecuador, in 1546, where Antonio lost his life; Fernando, Agostino, and Teresa's favorite accomplice, Rodrigo, were all later to die on the battlefield. Of the sisters, María was already married and Juana, the youngest, was only fifteen when she was left an orphan and went to live with Teresa at the Incarnation. Later she married Juan de Ovalle.

Though Teresa was, for the most part, able to appear calm, even cheerful, beneath the surface she lived in torment. Her writings show clearly that her inner life was deeply troubled and difficult. In fact she describes the first twenty years at the Convent of the Incarnation as a time when she constantly failed God and was buffeted on "that stormy sea, often falling in this way each time rising again, but to little purpose, as I would only fall once more."

She was generous and scrupulously honest in her writing, and it is this firsthand knowledge of her inner life, particularly during this period, which enables us to identify with her as a fellow human being and as a woman. She experienced spiritual apathy, aridity in prayer, and a sense of failure common to so many. Had we only known her as the recipient of extraordinary experiences, as a mystic as gifted in prayer as was Rembrandt in art, Beethoven in music, or Shakespeare in literature, we would not be able to identify with her so closely, nor would she have touched so many lives.

While these years were spiritually a lonely time for Teresa, she did find one person able to help her. Among the few good things to emerge from the distressing events surrounding Don Alonso's death was that, through her constant attendance at his bedside, she came to know his confessor, the respected Dominican theologian Vicente Barrón. He was one of the few priests who approved of the growing vogue for mental prayer and, when she made her confession to him and told him of her problems, admitting that she had given up prayer, his prescription was simple. He urged her to take communion once a fortnight (at the time frequent communion was not customary) and to return to the practice of mental prayer. She followed his advice and from that moment, whatever difficulties she encountered, she never abandoned prayer again, saying that it was not in her power to do so, because "He who desired me for His own in order to show me greater favors held me Himself in His hand." Though she felt herself under God's guidance, this was far from being the end of her problems. Indeed, her sufferings increased, "because by means of prayer I learned more and more about my faults."

From one already so aware of her failings this is an arresting statement. Could someone whose judgment of herself was so merciless that she saw even her virtues as faults find her sins etched in yet clearer and harsher lines? As her knowledge of God's goodness deepened, did her sins become darker in comparison with his light? What is clear is that she was becoming increasingly aware of the contradictory tensions in her own nature. The stormy sea on which she was tossed was not only the sea of prayer, fraught with problems and highlighting her sense of sin, but also of her richly complex personality. In her, to a rare extent, the opposites met, fought out their various claims and were, eventually, reconciled.

At the most basic level she had to contend with the problems of being a woman with what were then regarded as strong masculine characteristics. This polarity, actively challenged and often successfully met in our own time, was especially acute in sixteenth-century Spain, where men were generally the sole achievers and doers, while women were expected to be content with submission, domestication, and passivity. Though part of Teresa's appeal is the extent to which she was in many ways such an ordinary woman, loving and longing to be loved, motherly, practical and skilled in the feminine arts around the house, blessed with down-to-earth common sense, she also had the independence of mind, efficiency, and capability in those days normally associated with men. The tension between what she was and what society allowed her to be led her to dislike her body, and she constantly expresses a disparaging view of women, referring to them as weak, self-loving, silly, and timorous, frequently (perhaps sometimes tongue-in-cheek?) writing of her sex as unlearned and unlettered. She once admitted that "the mere thought that I am a woman makes my wings droop."

The problem of allowing her masculine and her feminine characteristics to mingle and complement each other was enhanced for Teresa by her personal circumstances. On the one hand her mother, frail and silent in life, fading into an early death, left her with no model of femininity and, indeed, pushed her at thirteen into maternal responsibilities. On the other hand masculine images surrounded her: her brothers were able to be and do much that she could not, while she lived under the loving protection of her father, to whom she was devoted. It is not hard to imagine the frustration this produced in a woman who eventually defied the conventions of her time and proved herself more capable and energetic than most men.

Her difficulty in reconciling the masculine and feminine in her own personality also contributed to other dichotomies. For instance, how, in prayer, should she balance receptivity and action? She knew she must make the initial effort of approaching God; she must give time to prayer and conquer the inattention and boredom which pervaded her early attempts, yet she knew too that God was in charge and that she must be open to receive. Even more pervasively, there was the question of obedience. As a woman, she was accustomed to be obedient, considering religious obedience a blessing and giving it a high priority in her teaching, but, when her superiors gave her contradictory commands, what then? Worse, she did not always feel that the instructions of her earthly masters coincided with God's will. Who then should she obey?

The contradictions in her nature ranged across all human characteristics; she epitomized the conflicts that tear many apart. Delighting in human relationships, she yearned to abandon herself solely to God; commending poverty, she was fastidious; loving and gregarious, she needed solitude; concerned with the things of God, her upbringing would never let her forget worldly etiquette and honor; and, wanting nothing more than to be alone with God, she knew she had practical tasks on earth. Being who she was, she longed for spiritual perfection, yet she did not forget that we have earthly bodies and that they too have needs. She expressed this forcefully: "To want to become angels while we are still on earth, and as much on earth as I was, is ridiculous."[1] She knew that virtues have their corresponding vices, and her own moods vacillated between joy and torment. But most poignant of all was the conflict which beyond all obsessed her throughout those years at the Incarnation: she was torn between God and the world.

Even as a child she felt equally strongly both the call to virtue and the temptations of the world. Later, as a young nun, she recalls, "When I was among the pleasures of the world, I was saddened by the memory of what I owed to God, and my worldly affections disturbed me when I was with God." And again:

> On the one hand, God was calling me. On the other, I was following the world. All the things of God gave me pleasure, yet I was tied and bound to those of the world. It seemed as if I wanted to reconcile these two contradictory things, so completely opposed to one another — the life of the spirit and the pleasures and joys and pastimes of the senses.[2]

Though she was talking as much about good and evil as about God and the world, and though it was, above all, the conflicting claims of human and divine relationships which so troubled her, today, when Christians actively try to find God *in* the world, and do not see the two as "completely opposed to one another," Teresa's problem may seem rather exaggerated. Yet, for her, this presented torments which pervaded every waking moment and added to the overwhelming problems she was finding in her attempts to pray.

Anyone who has ever tried to pray will have experienced difficulties, yet there tends to be an unspoken assumption that for saints and mystics prayer is easy. The open and totally honest way in which Teresa admits to her own problems in prayer is one of her valuable legacies; that she, too, found prayer difficult is not only endearing but also immensely reassuring. For years, despite her longing to reach God in prayer, she suffered from a condition that has been referred to as a kind of spiritual apathy: "I suffered great trials in prayer, for the spirit was not master in me, but slave. I could not, therefore, shut myself up within myself (the procedure in which consisted my whole method of prayer) without at the same time shutting in a thousand vanities."[3]

She was not yet able to offer herself to God in her totality, faults and all; sins and distractions were, in the language of her time, "assaults of the devil," to be resisted, not incorporated. This battle between her idealism and the aridity common to ordinary men and women produced such tension that she was barely able to pray at all. She writes frequently of aridity in prayer, comparing distracting thoughts to "flighty moths" and "having a madman in the house." Later in life, though, she was to commend it, for instance writing to her niece: "As to the aridity you are suffering from, it seems to me Our Lord is treating you like someone He considers strong: He wants to test you and see if you love Him as much at times of aridity as when He sends you consolations. I think this a very great favor for God to show you."[4]

If this advice is too austere for most people, there is no problem in identifying with the way she writes of her early trials:

> Over a period of several years, I was more occupied in wishing my hour of prayer were over, and in listening whenever the clock struck, than in thinking of things that were good. Again and again I would rather have done any severe penance that might have been given to me than practice recollection as a preliminary to prayer. . . . Whenever I entered the oratory I used to feel so depressed that I had to summon up all my courage to make myself pray at all.[5]

She felt imprisoned and alone, unable to believe her confessors, who treated so lightly the shortcomings in her prayer life which she knew, in her heart, were a failure in her obligation to God. But one of the ways in which she is set apart from most people is in the courage and determination with which she persevered; she battled and fought against her problems in prayer as fiercely as any soldier fights his enemy. With no one offering her the help she needed — a fact she frequently laments and was not beyond criticizing — she simply persisted. Through her twenties and thirties she endured boredom, aridity, frustration, disappointment, and an acute sense of failure. This period, too often glossed over, is the soil from which the flower of her mysticism was to grow. It should never be forgotten that it lasted from her novitiate until she was about forty years old.

It was probably in 1555 (though the exact date is arguable) that the turning-point came. It was unexpected, as these moments so often are, and it came at a time when Teresa was tired from her long struggle and longing for rest. No doubt her exhaustion contributed to her receptivity: she herself says that she had by then quite lost trust in herself and was placing all her confidence in God.

One day, as she went into the oratory to pray, she saw an image of Christ that had been borrowed by the convent for a particular festival. Tradition has it that it was an *Ecce Homo* still venerated at the Incarnation today, though it could have been a representation of Christ bound to the column with Mary Magdalene weeping at his feet. What is certain is that it represented Christ sorely wounded — the Spanish excel at stark realism — and that it moved Teresa to the depths of her being:

> So great was my distress when I thought how ill I had repaid Him for those wounds that I felt as if my heart was breaking,

> and I threw myself down beside Him, shedding floods of tears and begging Him to give me strength once and for all so that I might not offend Him. . . . I believe I told Him then that I would not rise from that spot until He had granted me what I was beseeching of Him.[6]

This was her *fiat,* the moment when she gave herself totally to Christ. She was still a step away from resolving her problem over personal relationships, but there was no longer any doubt as to the direction of her life or who was at its center.

Despite the fact Teresa at the time had no living people to confide in, no confessor who really met her needs, she read widely and often found help in the great spiritual writers of the past. Now it was St. Augustine with whom she could identify. She had always felt drawn to him, both because she had lived in a convent run by nuns of his Order and also because he had considered himself as grave a sinner as she believed herself to be. His *Confessions* had recently been translated into Spanish, and she was given a copy. Reading it, she seemed to be seeing her own experience mirrored in his. When she reached Augustine's account of his conversion and read of how he heard a voice in the garden, "It seemed exactly as if the Lord were speaking in that way to me, or so my heart felt. I remained for a long time dissolved in tears, in great distress and affliction."[7]

These two experiences, so vivid and important that they are often referred to as her "second conversion," quickened Teresa's spiritual life and gave fresh vitality to her prayer. The nuns saw a change in her as they noticed she was no longer interested in the social chatter of the parlor and saw her spend long hours praying before the Blessed Sacrament. In her *Life* she simply says, "I began to improve," but it is clear from the way she writes about her prayer life that she was entering a new phase. She was never to be entirely free from aridity, but the long years of effort were beginning to bear fruit.

She then devised a method of prayer that suited her own temperament. She claimed not to be able to reason with her mind or to be able to make pictures in her imagination as an aid to recollection. Nor, she says, could she see heavenly things or anything sublime. She compares herself to someone who is blind or in the dark, quite sure that someone is there, but unable to see. So she would make pictures of Christ *inwardly.* This distinction may seem at first rather arbitrary, but, in the light of the experiences she was to have, it is important. There is, after all, a great difference between forming a picture of someone as regards their height, size, coloring, and expression, and thinking about their qualities and attributes, their suffering and joy. So Teresa would start her prayer by imagining Christ's feelings rather than his physical presence, preferring to dwell on those times in his life when he was most alone. She was particularly attached to the prayer in the Garden of Gethsemane, where she would keep him company, think of the affliction he endured there and long to wipe the sweat from his face. This she dared not do, the knowledge of her sins prevented her, but the fact that he was "alone and afflicted, like a person in need, made it possible for me to approach Him."[8] As so often, her humility dictated her approach.

She still found it helpful, indeed for many years essential, to have a book nearby when she began to pray. Although she might not even open it, its presence was enough to help her toward recollection. She also liked to look at a field, at water, or at flowers. "These reminded me of the Creator — I mean, they awakened me and thus served me as a book."[9]

Sometimes, when praying thus, she would unexpectedly become conscious of the presence of God in a way that was in no sense a vision and of which she says rather doubtfully: "I believe it is called *mystical theology*." Using the Augustinian distinction between will, memory, and understanding, she wrote: "The soul is suspended in such a way that it seems to be completely outside itself. The will loves; the memory, I think, is almost lost; while the understanding, I believe, though it is not lost, does not reason—I mean that it does not work, but is amazed at the extent of all it can understand."[10]

Now she knew that she could not doubt that God was within her and that she was "totally engulfed in Him." Her ship had weathered a long and fierce storm, but she could hardly have guessed either the mystical heights to which she would rise or the accusations and obloquy to which she would be subjected by the world.

4

"Another and a New Life" 1555–1559

In her early forties Teresa's inner life acquired a totally fresh dimension: She was no longer in control. She expresses it tentatively but unambiguously:

> From this point onward, I am speaking of another and a new book — I mean of another and a new life. Until now the life I was describing was my own; but the life I have been living since I began to expound these matters concerning prayer is the life which God has been living in me — or so it has seemed to me.[1]

Before writing these lines in her *Life* Teresa had digressed for some twelve chapters to explain four stages of prayer, and it is to these pages we must look to discover what point she had reached on her journey. Finding it impossible to express herself directly, she uses, most beautifully, a metaphor dear to her heart, that of water; more specifically, the watering of a garden. (The image has, of course, even more significance when one remembers the scarcity of water in the dry, barren land of Castile.)

Her analogous garden is already planted (prayer life has begun), but the plants will die unless they are tended and watered carefully. This can be done in four ways. There is the laborious work of drawing water from the well; the slightly easier method of using a water-wheel and buckets; a stream running through the garden, saturating the ground from beneath, lightens the gardener's load further; but best of all is rain, the natural source of water and one which entails no work at all on the part of the gardener.

The beginner in prayer toils to and fro, fetching water from the well. The effort is entirely his, for sometimes the well is empty and he cannot fill the bucket, but he persists, because he loves his flowers and cannot bear to see them die. Every drop of water contributes to life, and the privilege of tending the garden compensates for the grueling work. This is mental prayer, which has to embrace much hardship and aridity. The beginner should be humble, asking little and wary of elation. He must be content that he has the desire for growth.

If, however, the gardener uses a water-wheel and buckets, he can draw more water with less effort, and long hours do not prove wearisome. The will is content to be God's prisoner, but the memory and understanding come and go, over-eager to help, "like doves which are not pleased with the food given them by the owner of the dovecote, without their having worked for it, and go in search of food elsewhere, but are so unsuccessful that they return."[2] Teresa uses this stage of her analogy to describe the beginning of contemplation, passive recollection followed by the Prayer of Quiet. Effort is still necessary, but the place of receptivity is better understood. "For even if we wear ourselves to pieces with penances and prayers and all kinds of other things, we can acquire but little if the Lord is not pleased to bestow it."[3] This second stage is a time of trial, a time for weeding and pruning, and taking out weak and unnecessary plants. And because the higher stages are still unknown, there is a temptation to cling to periods of joy and peace, and to encourage them. This is ultimately self-defeating. "for, hard as we may try to make the fire burn in order to obtain this pleasure, we seem only to be throwing water on it to quench it."[4] To avoid becoming trapped at this stage — something which in Teresa's experience happens to many — the beginner must not search for words even of penitence or gratitude, but must "go softly and make no noise." The flowers are growing strongly and are almost ready to bloom. Why disturb them?

In the third stage God is active, providing water by a spring or stream running through the garden. There is now no question of turning back, the delight is too sweet, it is "a glorious folly, a heavenly madness in which true wisdom is acquired." In this state, which Teresa calls "the sleep of the faculties, which are neither wholly lost nor yet can understand how they work," the will is quiet at last, the soul is free from all worries and content to be idle. God is now the gardener, and the supply of water is infinite. This is not complete union with God, though until she tried to set it down on paper, even Teresa herself was uncertain of the precise difference. The distinction, she eventually decided, was that in this third stage the faculties are not so absorbed as to cease entirely from action, but at least they only concern themselves with the things of God. Martha and Mary, action and contemplation, are in perfect harmony, though not yet entirely absorbed into God. Worldly distractions are, at last, irrelevant; even eating and sleeping seem unnecessary distractions. There is simply a deep need to give voice to joy, just as the flowers begin to open and send out their fragrance

When she reaches the fourth stage, where the garden is watered by rain and the gardener has nothing to do but watch the flowers grow, Teresa at first claims to be lost for words. This is an appropriate reaction to the Prayer of Union, of which she says "if it [the soul] can communicate, then it is not union." Nevertheless, immediately after an experience of union, there is the possibility of communication, and she tries hard to remember how she felt and to express herself:

> There is no feeling, only rejoicing, unaccompanied by any understanding of the thing in which the soul is rejoicing. It realizes that it is rejoicing in some good thing, in which are comprised all good things at once, but it cannot comprehend this good thing. In this rejoicing all the senses are occupied, so that none of them is free or able to act in any way, either inwardly or outwardly.[5]

Union, brought about by "this rain from heaven," is a state which comes when the gardener is least expecting it and rarely lasts long. Teresa says that half an hour would be a long time and that she herself never experienced union for as long as that. While she stresses that, as "the soul becomes conscious that it is fainting almost completely away, in a kind of swoon," it cannot be aware of what is happening, she is precise about what happens to the senses: They are completely suspended. If the eyes are open, they see almost nothing; the ears understand nothing of what they hear; speech is impossible. However, there is the sensation of "an exceeding great and sweet delight."

In the absence of bodily senses, what is the faculty that experiences this joy? The word Teresa uses most often is "soul," but she is perplexed by the problems inherent in language. It comes almost as a relief to realize that there are some aspects of mystical experience which defy even her acute analysis. She admits not understanding, for instance, what is meant by "mind," or the difference between "mind," "soul," and "spirit." She attributes this confusion to her own lack of learning, favoring the word "soul" and, as so often, in describing it, lets metaphor come to her rescue:

> They all seem the same to me, though the soul sometimes issues from itself, like a fire that is burning and has become wholly flame. This flame rises very high above the fire, but that does not make it a different thing; it is the same flame which is in the fire. This, with all your learning, Your Reverences will understand: there is nothing more that I can say of it.[6]

Though Teresa's directness enables her to state quite simply that union is "two things becoming one," she tussles continually with the distinction between will, memory, and understanding. In this fourth state, the state of union, she affirms that at last all three are suspended: "The memory is now burning its wings and can no longer fly. The will must be fully occupied in loving, but it cannot understand how it loves; the understanding, if it understands, does not understand how it understands."[7]

If description of the state of union defeats even her, Teresa has much to say about its benefits. After this type of prayer she found herself in a state of overwhelming tenderness, bathed in tears of joy; in fact, sometimes it was only these tears, something she valued deeply, which convinced her she had not been dreaming. She felt humble, full of courage, able to make heroic promises and was beginning to abhor the world. In the face of these favors her sense of unworthiness increased, "for in a room bathed in sunlight not a cobweb can remain hidden." So, too, was there a desire to share the fruits of this prayer and a burgeoning of love, for in this experience the soul has met God. "It is alone with Him: what is there for it to do but to love Him?" Fascinated though she is by her own experience, beyond all evaluation and analysis of mystical states lay her relationship to God. Love was what it was about; her life of prayer was the story of an intimate friendship with God.

This was the point Teresa had reached on her long spiritual journey when she wrote that God "began to grant me quite frequently the Prayer of Quiet, and often, too, the Prayer of Union." But her joy in the sweetness of these experiences was tarnished by fear. Why, she wondered, should she, a sinner, be granted such spiritual consolations? Was she deluded in thinking they came from God? Could it not be the devil suspending her faculties and convincing her it was good? How could she know she was indeed on the right path?

Her fears were well founded, for not only was the Inquisition suspicious of the kind of experiences Teresa was having, but there had been many cases of people, particularly women, who claimed to have received mystical graces and were eventually denounced. There had been devout women known as *beatas* (religious women either living in a community without being professed or living under a rule in their own homes), like the Beata of Piedrahita, who claimed to have long, intimate conversations with heavenly companions and who would, on entering a room, make way for the Virgin Mary, whom she seemed to regard as her mother-in-law. There was the case of Juana de la Cruz, so determined to flaunt her family's opposition to her becoming a nun that she disguised herself as a man in order to escape; her prophetic utterances caused her to be venerated by some, but denounced by many more. There were ecstatics who prophesied the conversion of all Moors and Jews, lamented the corruption of the church, and promised reform. Most recently there had been the case of Magdalena de la Cruz de Córdoba, a Franciscan nun who, on the instructions of her confessor, wrote a long account of the mystical graces she claimed to have received. Her devotees were numerous and eminent, and included the Inquisitor himself and the Queen, Isabella of Portugal, who had asked her to make the christening robe for the child who was to become Philip II. The consternation was great when, as the nun lay dying, she asked for exorcism, confessing that her holy life had been a complete fraud and that any supernatural powers she might have were the result of a pact she had made with the devil when she was five years old. This revelation came in 1546, some years before Teresa's "second conversion."

So Teresa, always doubtful about the truth of her experiences, knew she needed advice, but where could she go? Ignatius of Loyola had recently founded the Society of Jesus, and there were already Jesuit priests in the College of San Gil in Avila. Though Teresa did not know them, she was already attracted by their prayer and lifestyle, but she did not consider herself either "worthy to speak to them or strong enough to obey them." She was also unwilling for the other nuns to know that she was consulting the Jesuits. Rumors were rife about her strange experiences; malicious tongues were wagging, and comparisons with Magdalena de la Cruz were being made. She had no wish to add fuel to the fire. Thus she went to see a distant relative, Don Francisco de Salcedo, a devout, prayerful man who lived a life "as nearly perfect as his married state permits." Indeed he was known as the *Caballero santo* (the holy gentleman). He introduced Teresa to Gaspar Daza, a learned priest of Avila, who was acquiring a reputation for spiritual direction. At first she found she was helped by him; in fact she became so dependent upon him that, if she did not see him for a few days, she became restless, thinking it was her "wickedness" that kept him away. However, when she tried, haltingly, to tell him of her experiences in prayer (it was only later she was able to be articulate on the subject), he warned her that it could be an evil spirit at work, though he was not sure.

Profoundly troubled, she turned to books. Eventually she found her own prayer life mirrored in the *Ascent of Mount Zion* (*Subida del Monte Sión*) by a Franciscan lay brother, Bernardino de Laredo. He described the union of the soul with God and how in such prayer it was impossible to think of anything. She marked relevant passages and gave it to Daza and Salcedo. If, after twenty years of prayer, she was deluded, perhaps she had better give up prayer altogether? But she knew what her life was like without prayer; she had tried it. "I was like a person who has fallen into a river: whatever the direction she takes, she is afraid the danger will be greater and yet she is almost drowning." Apprehensively she waited for their verdict. A few days later it came: Her experiences were from the devil, and she was in serious peril.

These were the words she had dreaded. Her worst fears were confirmed. She was in such distress and fear that she did not know what to do; she could only weep. But not for long. They had told her she should find a spiritual director and suggested she should consult one of the Jesuit priests. She overcame her scruples, took their advice, and began to prepare her general confession. Even more distressed at finding so much that was bad and so little that was good, she went to her first Jesuit confessor, Diego de Cetina.

He was only in his twenties at the time, and his superiors had dismissed him as someone who "preaches indifferently, hears confessions, is no use for anything else." Yet he was able to understand and help Teresa, coming to a very different conclusion from that reached by Daza and Salcedo. He was sure she was being led by God, although he felt she was not working on a sure spiritual foundation. Nor, he continued, did she appear to understand the nature of mortification — a judgment with which Teresa entirely agreed, admitting she barely understood the meaning of the word. He advised her on no account to give up prayer, and suggested she should center her prayer round one of the incidents in

Christ's Passion, thinking only of his humanity and resisting any desire toward supernatural states.

This verdict was confirmed by a more authoritative source, Francis Borgia, once duke of Gandia, then Commissary of the Society of Jesus in Spain, later canonized in 1671. He was passing through Avila and, at the suggestion of Diego de Cetina, he came to see Teresa. He not only supported the young priest both in his diagnosis and in his prescription, but he also went further, saying that as long as she followed this advice concerning prayer (which was probably based on the famous Ignatian Exercises) it was no longer advisable or necessary for her to resist any experience that followed.

However, Teresa was never to be allowed spiritual peace for long. Her young confessor was transferred elsewhere, and once again she became disconsolate and fearful, feeling that her soul was "as if in a desert." A relative arranged for her to go and stay for a few days with a devout young widow from an illustrious Spanish family who lived nearby, and thus Teresa met the beautiful and, at the time, frivolous Doña Guiomar de Ulloa, who was to become one of her dearest friends. Profiting from the easygoing life at the Incarnation, Teresa spent most of the next three years in Doña Guiomar's house and describes their friendship as closer than sisters. It was there that she met her second Jesuit confessor, the vice-rector of San Gil, Juan de Pradanos.

This confusion of confessors, the conflicting advice, and the turbulence in which she had been living acted as a catalyst. Over the following three years Teresa began to have curious experiences, at once wonderful and frightening. It was as if, in the battering waves of gossip and judgment, she had found the eye of the storm, her center. It was not yet a still center; struggles and darkness were to accompany her for many more years, but she could not have been the recipient of such mystical graces had she not in some way been in touch with the deepest parts of herself. Later Teresa was to clarify the differences between these experiences; at this stage she merely recounts what happened to her.

The first experience was "locution" — hearing an inner voice — and it came almost as a reprimand from God. She had been reciting one of the Psalms and had stopped to reflect on a verse, wondering how a just God could give favors to her rather than to some of her fellow nuns, in her opinion infinitely worthier. Quite unprepared, she heard a voice: "Thou didst answer me, Lord, saying, 'Serve thou Me, and meddle not with this.' This was the first word which I ever heard Thee speak to me and so it made me very much afraid."[8]

The second of these experiences involved sacrifice of a particular, though rather vague, nature. By then she had yet another confessor; Juan de Pradanos had fallen ill and, after being tenderly nursed by Teresa and Doña Guiomar, had, like Diego de Cetina, been transferred elsewhere. His successor was also a Jesuit, Baltasar Álvarez. Young and inexperienced when he first met Teresa in 1559, he was to be her confessor for many years and was to prove one of the best she ever had. With enormous skill and sensitivity, he gently encouraged her to give up certain friendships which he considered unsuitable. Since her "second conversion" she had to some extent resolved the tensions between human and divine relationships, but new resolutions cannot be immediately implemented, nor old friendships instantly severed. In any case, she saw no harm in them. Indeed to abandon them completely seemed to her to sin through ingratitude. It is not clear what these relationships were or with whom, but they probably took her into secular realms which did not sit easily with her spiritual aspirations. At all events, Álvarez urged her to commend the matter to God and to recite the hymn "Veni, Creator Spiritus." Always eager to obey her confessors, she spent a whole day in prayer and then began the hymn:

> While I was reciting it, there came upon me a transport so sudden that it almost carried me away: I could make no mistake about this, so clear was it. This was the first time that the Lord had granted me the favor of any kind of rapture. I heard these words: "I will have thee converse now, not with men, but with angels."[9]

She was amazed and frightened, yet the words came from the depths of her spirit, and at the same time she felt comforted. Friendships, even close friendships, would always be important to her, but they ceased to come between her and God. Her choice was made. Human relationships had their place, but there was no longer a conflict. That particular pair of opposites, her lifelong struggle with inappropriate or excessively emotional human friendships at God's expense, was resolved. She had said yes to God, and her "second conversion" was truly sealed. From that moment God was the sole, unrivalled center of her life; she would never again be able to sustain an affectionate relationship with anyone whose first concern was not with God and with prayer.

Teresa had been deprived of many of her friendships, and found she could manage quite well, if not better, without them. Now the Inquisition was to deprive her of another solace, and again she was to find compensation. In 1559 the Grand Inquisitor of Spain published an *Index of Forbidden Books,* prohibiting the reading of many devotional works in Spanish, including some of her favorites, like Osuna's *Third Spiritual Alphabet.* Teresa had no Latin and she was very dependent on books; she was desolate. But she heard the voice of God saying to her, "Be not distressed, for I will give you a living book." At first she had no idea what this meant, but a few days later she understood—she had her first vision:

> I was at prayer on the festival of the glorious Saint Peter when I saw Christ at my side — or, to put it better, I was conscious of Him, for neither with the eyes of the body nor with those of the soul did I see anything. I thought He was quite close to me and I saw that it was He who, as I thought, was speaking to me. Being completely ignorant that visions of this kind could occur, I was at first very much afraid, and did nothing but weep, though, as soon as He addressed a single word to me to reassure me, I became quiet again, as I had been before and was quite happy and free from fear.[10]

She was much troubled by this vision—any idea that mystical graces lead to an easy life are soon dispelled by Teresa's account of her experiences—and went straight to Álvarez. Sensitive though he was to his extraordinary penitent, on this occasion her attempts to get him to understand make one wonder how she bore the frustration.

First he asked her in what form she had seen Christ. She said she had not *seen* him at all. How then did she know it was Christ? She did not know how, but she knew that he was beside her; it was quite clear to her. She attempted to draw comparisons, but they did not help. It was not like being in the dark or being blind and knowing there was someone else in the room, because the person's presence can be detected by the other senses, touch, hearing, smell. No, she could not use the analogy of darkness, when the knowledge was "brighter than the sun." It could not even be compared to the presence of God experienced in the Prayer of Quiet or the Prayer of Union — that is a wonderful favor, but it is not a vision. She tried suggesting that it was as if food had been put into the stomach without one's eating it or even knowing how it got there. The only comparison which came near to satisfying her was that knowing Christ was present in a vision was like finding oneself in possession of all knowledge without having learned the alphabet.

Her confessor, no doubt struggling to understand as much as she was to communicate, asked her who told her it was Christ? He told her himself, she replied, though she knew before he did so. It was no more possible to doubt it than it would be to doubt the evidence of her eyes. "God and the soul understand each other, simply because this is His Majesty's will, and no other means are necessary to express the mutual love of these two friends."[11]

Though the baffled Jesuit dismissed her brusquely, we must sympathize with the young man, only too aware of false mystics and the skeptical Inquisitors. There is, however, a footnote to this encounter which, if true, gives it an ironic twist. A nun, who claimed to have been told this by Teresa herself, said that a few days later Álvarez himself saw a vision of Christ and confided it to Teresa. With typical, if rather rough, humor, she laughed it away — it could not have been Christ! The Jesuit assured her he was not mistaken, and gave many good reasons for his belief. "Now you see, Father," Teresa concluded. "This is how it appears to you. But to others it may appear to be whatever they say it is."[12] She herself confirms that her confessor's attitude to her changed; in fact, he was to become one of the first to defend her against those who thought she was on the road to perdition.

Another man who was to corroborate her experience and defend her against her critics was the Franciscan Peter of Alcántara (Pedro de Alcántara) who was canonized in 1669. He became known as a reformer of his order, encouraging the friars to return to a life of poverty and austerity. Teresa's love and admiration for him was boundless: "The world is not yet in a fit state to bear such perfection," she wrote of him. He was a man of strict asceticism, who lived in a cell less than five feet long, eating only once in three days; for forty years he slept for only an hour and a half a night, his head propped up against a piece of wood fixed to the wall. Whatever the weather, he wore nothing on his head or his feet and on his body only a habit of sackcloth, worn next to the skin as tightly as he could bear. For twenty years he wore a shirt of tinplate. Teresa says he was so weak that "he seemed to be made of nothing but the roots of trees." He assured her that her vision was one of the highest kinds possible, the one in which the devil has the least power.

Peter of Alcántara had a remarkable reputation as a spiritual director, so it is no surprise that she valued his support so highly. She needed the encouragement of such men, because, though God now seemed to be unequivocally on her side, she had to bear the taunts and sneers of many who pronounced her possessed. However, more than support, she needed to understand. As mystical experiences flooded over her, she had to try to analyze them, to try to understand what was happening to her.

5

Delectable Torments

Just as Teresa had been tossed for so long on "that stormy sea" of aridity and doubt, so in her mid-forties she was buffeted by waves of mystical graces. In the years between 1558 and 1562, indeed for much of the rest of her life, she received innumerable experiences of God in the form of visions, raptures, and locutions.

Mysticism, in which an immediate knowledge of God is attained through personal, direct experience, is found in all religions. In Christianity attitudes to it range from impatient dismissal, through fascination (in the literal sense of simultaneously being attracted and repelled) to wistful admiration. It has been suspected for its possible pantheistic associations and for its apparent links with the second-century Gnostics, who were reviled and considered heretical by the church. Phenomena such as visions and trances, which frequently accompany mystical experience, have produced even stronger reactions of fear, wonder, skepticism, and perhaps a measure of envy. They have been denounced by medical science as pathological states bordering on madness, as nervous disorders similar to catalepsy, or as akin to somnambulism. Philosophers have argued that ecstasy is immoral, contrary to nature and a renunciation of human liberty. The church itself has approached mystical phenomena with great caution, insisting that, while mystical experiences are, by their very nature, independent of doctrines and institutions, the insights gained from them should never be isolated from dogma. Further, that the language of mystics, if it is to be taken seriously, must express the commonly accepted truths of faith.

While there is no doubt that these mystical states exist (it is a matter of history, widely confirmed and tested) nor of the value to Christian understanding of the insights contributed by the men and women who have experienced them, they are in no way essential to faith or insight; on occasion they have been considered a hindrance. Nor do such favors lead, on their own, to canonization. The mystics have affirmed that the genuineness of the experience is seen through its effects, for instance in increased humility and love. Ecstasy is no proof of sanctity; it is the sanctity of the one who receives mystical graces which must show the ecstasy to be divine. As Matthew's Gospel has it, "Ye shall know them by their fruits."

In sixteenth-century Spain there was a schism between mystics and intellectuals, the *espirituales* and the *letrados.* One result of this was that almost all the major spiritual writers of the time such as Osuna, Peter of Alcántara, and Francis Borgia (*espirituales*) were distrusted by the church (*letrados*), and their writings were included in the list of prohibited books issued by the Inquisition in 1559. While there will always be those who encourage and even invent mystical experience to attract attention, it is hardly likely that a balanced personality would seek out something which is almost certain to lead them into trouble with the authorities and their peers alike. Teresa's experiences, however much debate they have attracted, have rarely been denied; certainly her truthfulness and good faith have not been questioned.

We know of these experiences from Teresa herself, as, in reluctant obedience to her confessors, she wrote about them at length. To a largely skeptical twenty-first century they may seem embarrassing, curious, even the product of a neurotic and disturbed mind. To her contemporaries they were the source of admiration and wonder, but also of gossip, disbelief, and mockery. To her friend the Carmelite poet and mystic John of the Cross they were irrelevant. To Teresa, although (partly as a result of John's influence) her attitude changed as she grew older, they were simultaneously signs of God's favor, for which she was constantly grateful, and yet the cause of deep distress and pain.

Mystical graces are not something experienced by the large majority, and most of her readers have no alternative but to take her on trust, which is not hard when one appreciates the scrupulous rigor with which she analyzed and assessed everything that happened to her. In the face of such honesty, skepticism tends to give way to acceptance. If so truthful a spokeswoman says that it is so, how can it be denied? It is not possible to be more exacting with her and her experiences than she was with herself. So we must first listen to her voice. Let her tell how, gradually, she saw Christ:

> One day, when I was at prayer, the Lord was pleased to reveal to me nothing but His hands, the beauty of which was so great as to be indescribable. This made me very fearful, as does every new experience that I have when the Lord is beginning to grant me some supernatural favor. A few days later I also saw that Divine face, which seemed to leave me completely absorbed. I could not understand why the Lord revealed Himself gradually like this since He was later to grant me the favor of seeing Him wholly, until at last I realized that His Majesty was leading me according to my natural weakness.[1]

Then, one day at Mass, she saw the figure of Christ whole. In seeing Christ "just as in a picture of His resurrection body" she was not reflecting the spirit of her time. Spanish art of the period tended to favor the brutal and stark: Christ bound to the pillar, falling as he carried the cross to Golgotha, crucified in agonizing torment. Her contemporaries might have been less outraged by her visions had she seen Christ in the manner they were accustomed to. In attempting to describe this vision Teresa is at her lyrical best:

> It is not a radiance which dazzles, but a soft whiteness and an infused radiance which, without wearying the eyes, causes them the greatest delight; nor are they wearied of the brightness which they see in seeing this Divine beauty. So different from any earthly light is the brightness and light now revealed to the eyes that, by comparison with it, the brightness of our sun seems quite dim and we should never want to open our eyes again for the purpose of seeing it.... It is a light which never gives place to night, and being always light, is disturbed by nothing. It is of such a kind, indeed, that no one, however powerful his intellect, could, in the whole course of his life, imagine it as it is.[2]

Sometimes Christ took an active part in her visions. Once, when she was holding the cross of a rosary, he took it from her and, when he returned it, it had become four large, very precious stones. On the cross, with exquisite workmanship, were portrayed the five wounds. He told her that it would always look to her like that, and so indeed it did.

To others, however, the cross looked just as it had before, and sharing her vision made her more vulnerable than ever to her critics. But the more she was ordered to test her experiences and the more she tried to resist them, the more numerous they became. Trying to divert her attention from them, she prayed constantly, complaining to God that she could not bear any more.

He responded by giving her advice as to what she should say to her critics. "The arguments with which He provided me were so conclusive that they made me feel perfectly secure."

However, she still could not convince her confessor, Baltasar Álvarez. The young Jesuit was kind and courageous, standing by her and defending her in stalwart fashion, but he was clearly out of his depth. Having come to the conclusion that her visions, far from being of God, were coming from the devil, he ordered her, whenever she had a vision, to snap her fingers at it (*Dar higas* — to give figs). Teresa could not believe that her visions were satanic "even if the alternative were my being cut to pieces." Nevertheless, obedient as always, she did as she was told, weeping sorely and feeling that she was mocking Christ.

She found herself "dying with the desire to see God" and knowing no way to find him other than through physical death. Bewildered by these vehement feelings, lost in distress and joy, further confused by the instructions she was being given by her confessors to spurn her visions, Teresa received for the first time the experience which, more than any other, is associated with her: the Transverberation of her heart. Such was the impact of this vision that, in 1726, Pope Benedict XIII decreed a festival in its honor, still observed on August 26; the chapel at the Convent of the Incarnation was named after it; and it is commemorated in art and sculpture, most notably in the famous statue by Bernini, whose total preoccupation with the erotic dimension of the experience at the expense of the mystical says more about Bernini than it does about Teresa.

By the time she wrote about this vision she had clearly experienced it several times:

> It pleased the Lord that I should sometimes see the following vision. I would see beside me, on my left hand, an angel in

bodily form — a type of vision I am not in the habit of seeing, except very rarely.... It pleased the Lord that I should see this angel in the following way. He was not tall, but short, and very beautiful, his face so aflame that he appeared to be one of the highest types of angel who seem to be all afire.... In his hands I saw a long golden spear and at the end of the iron tip I seemed to see a point of fire. With this he seemed to pierce my heart several times so that it penetrated to my entrails. When he drew it out, I thought he was drawing them out with it and he left me completely afire with a great love for God. The pain was so sharp that it made me utter several moans; and so excessive was the sweetness caused me by the intense pain that one can never wish to lose it, nor will one's soul be content with anything less than God. It is not bodily pain, but spiritual, though the body has a share in it — indeed a great share. So sweet are the colloquies of love which pass between the soul and God that if anyone thinks I am lying I beseech God, in His goodness, to give him the same experience.[3]

One of her problems in assimilating this experience was that very few people can reach such heights. It must be presumed that, when they eventually met, she discussed it with John of the Cross; certainly she would have found comfort in the understanding he later showed in *The Living Flame of Love,* one of his most famous poems. To him this vision, which he called the "cauterizing of the soul," is something that "God accords to founders" and stands comparison to the five wounds of love received by Francis of Assisi and the sufferings of Job. He recognized it as the most profound experience of love: It seems to it [the soul] that the entire universe is a sea of love in which it is engulfed, for, conscious of the living point or center of love within itself, it is unable to catch sight of the boundaries of this love.[4]

At the time, though, Teresa had no one with whom to share these mystical experiences. For days afterward she was in a daze, unwilling to see anyone, unable to speak. All she wanted to do was to savor the vision with its heady mixture of pain and bliss, of erotic and mystic union, and overwhelmingly of love. But she was not to be given that solace. Her raptures began to attract increasing attention, the gossip reaching such a point that she longed only to be sent away, out of range of wagging tongues. This wish was denied her by her superiors, her confessors having, for the most part, failed her, and she was thrown back on her own resources. She would have to work out for herself what was happening to her.

Had it not been for her confessors' insistence that she record her experiences, we might well have been deprived of the most skilled analysis of mystical states ever written, for Teresa did not see herself as an author. Most of her writing was done when she was preoccupied with practical matters: she complains that it kept her from spinning and doing things about the house. She often laments her lack of learning, for she had received scant formal education; she never corrected and seldom reread what she had written, and her constant digressions and casualness over dates do not make for easy interpretation. She did not even have the most basic tools of the trade as her cell possessed neither table nor chair, so she wrote kneeling on the floor at a ledge under a drafty window. Yet her books are read all over the world and in Spain come second only to Cervantes's *Don Quixote* in popularity. What is her secret? It lies in the simplicity and directness of her style, and the charm of her images; in the depth of her love and the intensity of her experience; in her honesty and in her search for truth; in the forceful immediacy of her prose, tumbling out with the exuberance of a waterfall; and in her relationship with her reader — one moment she is addressing the confessor for whom it was written, the next she turns to some imaginary reader, then suddenly she explodes in praise to God. Her genius lies in the way her personality illuminates every page. She is not concerned to impress; she is simply telling her own story, struggling with her own thoughts. And because she is talking, as she often says, from her own experience, she never falls into dry areas of unexplored theory, but simply communicates, with astonishing directness and authority.

In charting her own progress through the seas of mystical experience Teresa has drawn a map where unfamiliar territories can be better understood. Even if their language and assumptions are different, even if the goal is never reached, the few who find themselves on a similar journey can recognize stages and landmarks; the many who do not understand can draw encouragement and inspiration.

While describing the "four waters" of prayer, Teresa has already identified the early stages and hinted at a different degree of union, a state she variously calls rapture, elevation, flight of the spirit, ecstasy, or transport. Later, fully aware that she will be read by many with no experience of such union and who may even find it all ridiculous, she affirms that there is indeed a different degree of it. In union, she says, though resistance is painful, it is possible; further, it is "the same at the beginning, in the middle and at the end." The effects of rapture are more profound. Resistance is quite impossible, as "the Lord gathers up the soul, just (we might say) as the clouds gather up the vapors of the earth." It is "a strong, swift impulse," like "an eagle, rising and bearing you up on its wings."

There are numerous accounts of how Teresa appeared to those who saw her in ecstasy. To her embarrassment, her raptures would frequently occur in public and, though she would try to conceal what was happening by claiming illness, the deception did not work. Contemporary accounts say that, while she was in ecstasy, her pulse was hardly beating, her limbs stiff and her body cold — in fact, she seemed to be dead. The nuns had seen her faint through illness, but it was not, they claimed, like that — for one thing her face was not ecstatic then.

How she appeared and how she felt were similar. She says that the most usual characteristic of rapture was that her body was light, almost weightless, sometimes she could not tell if her feet were touching the ground. Her body remained in whatever position it was in when the rapture came upon it, sitting, kneeling, hands open or shut; the subject, though usually conscious, was incapable of action and could only hear and understand "dimly, as though from a long way off." In fact, for a short time, when the rapture was at its height, it was impossible to see, hear, or understand at all. As so often, her reaction was ambivalent. She would have liked to spend the rest of her life suffering in this way, although the pain was so excessive it was hardly bearable, indeed "until the next day I have pains in the wrists, and in the entire body, as though my bones had been wrenched asunder." Sometimes, especially if she tried to resist the rapture, her whole body was affected, to the point of being raised from the ground. "It seemed as if I was being lifted up by a force beneath my feet so powerful that I know nothing to which I can compare it." These experiences of levitation happened to Teresa only rarely and caused her much distress, not least because it was impossible to conceal what was happening. She would hold on to the communion rails, ask the nuns to hold her down and later urge them not to speak of it, but it was no use. Though reports of such happenings were not uncommon in those days, soon all Avila knew of the strange events at the Convent of the Incarnation and came to hear about them, even hoping to see for themselves.

Nevertheless, Teresa knew well that such experiences were, in themselves, unimportant. They only had value if they led to greater love and a more perfect obedience to the will of God; it was the effect that mattered. She was quite clear what these effects were: fear, humility, and detachment. Fear "in such a way that the hair stands on end" at seeing one's body lifted up, but even more, humility. Humility in the face of a power so great that she could do nothing, not even keep her feet on the ground; humility — as so often with Teresa coupled with guilt — that God should draw up not only the soul but also the body of "so loathsome a worm."

She found it hard to describe the detachment she felt on these occasions. It seems to have had much to do with the fact that the body itself is, if only temporarily, separated from the earth in an enforced extreme solitude, separated too from God. She suggests that it is not meant to be comforting, but rather to emphasize that all goodness is in God. Here she identified movingly with the Psalmist: "I watch, and am as a sparrow alone upon the housetop."[5]

Alone as she was, she sought help from books, and sometimes they misled her. Among her reading she came across a school of thought, widely prevalent at the time, which counseled that, in the higher stages of prayer, contemplation must be devoted to God's divinity and that to meditate on Christ in his humanity was a hindrance to progress. Convinced that this advice came from wise and learned men, she followed it, initially finding it brought her joy; nothing would make her meditate on Christ's humanity again. Soon, however, she not only decided this advice was wrong, but was unable to recall holding such an opinion without a feeling of pain; she felt she had, in holding it even briefly, committed high treason. From then on she was certain that the way of prayer must be through Christ in his humanity and that "the Creator must be sought through the creatures." Like so much else, this was a matter she had to work out for herself; her own experience was always the touchstone of her teaching.

If she was short of advice and theoretical guides to spiritual life, Teresa never suffered from lack of experience. From the time of her first ecstasy, an experience sometimes referred to as her "spiritual betrothal," she was in constant communication with God in a relationship best described in terms of friendship. Significantly, her own definition of mental prayer was "friendly intercourse, and frequent solitary converse, with Him who we know loves us." God would appear to her in visions and speak to her in ways which left her in no doubt that it was indeed him. While it is tempting and quite easy to speculate on the similarity between her visions and the art of the time, and to postulate psychological explanations for her experiences, it is not in fact very useful. There is, after all, no answer to the ultimate question of how she knew it was God speaking and not her own inner voice, God appearing to her and not her own inner eye. Nor does the answer affect the significance of the experience, for God within is just as real as God without, and theories as to the nature and definition of God do not lead one to a closer understanding of a person who spoke so predominantly from experience.

In analyzing her visions Teresa, following traditional teaching, divides them into three groups: corporeal, imaginary, and intellectual. She never experienced a corporeal vision. Writing with untypical coyness in the third person she says this quite explicitly: "She saw nothing, nor has she ever seen anything, with her bodily eyes."[6] Most of her visions came under the category of "imaginary," though it is important not to confuse this with hallucination or invention. Nonetheless, the imaginary visions confused her, for she feared the devil's interference and found that "no sooner had the vision faded — the very moment, indeed, after it had gone — than I began to think I had imagined it." Toward the end of her life she compared the imaginary vision of God to knowing that inside a gold reliquary there is a precious stone. We have never seen it, nor can we, for the owner has the key, but we are certain of its beauty and value. Then, suddenly, the owner decides to open the reliquary—God grants a revelation of himself. Although this happens with the speed of a flash of lightning, "this glorious image is so deeply engraven upon the imagination that I do not believe it can possibly disappear."[7]

She regarded the "intellectual" vision, when she experienced the presence of Christ or intuitively understood a great truth like the mystery of the Trinity, as the safest, highest, and best. Unlike an imaginary vision, it lasted for a long time and left such humility and inward peace that there was no question of it being the work of the devil. She experienced intellectual visions only rarely, most specifically in that first vision which was the source of such misunderstanding between her and Álvarez, but on several occasions she uses the same phrase to describe the experience. The soul, she says, "is conscious that Jesus Christ our Lord is near to it, though it cannot see Him either with the eyes of the body or with those of the soul."[8] Then again, even more confusingly, she suggests that sometimes the soul "seems to see within God Himself," yet, "although I say that the soul 'sees' Him, it really sees nothing."[9]

Such high stages of mystical experience are, almost by definition, impossible to communicate, but over the matter of locutions she is more specific. She was in continual converse with God, as between two friends, receiving reassurance, chastisement, or words which seem to complement her visions—"Now thou art Mine and I am thine."[10] As with her visions, she divided them into corporeal, which she heard with the physical powers of hearing, "imaginary," and "intellectual," those so indelibly imprinted on the mind that they are mysteriously and completely understood.

She is keenly aware that locutions may be mere fancy, "from the devil," and, as always, is merciless in her attempts to discern the true from the false. She says it is like the difference between listening and speaking: in false locutions "the understanding will realize that it is not listening, but being active; and the words it is inventing are fantastic and indistinct."[11] When it is truly the voice of God, it is always unexpected and there is no choice but to listen. There is a special clarity, the words are indelibly imprinted on the mind, the effects are peaceful, and what is said does actually happen. So the supportive or reassuring words left her feeling comforted; the chastisement led her to correct her attitude; and the flashes of truth did not prove false.

Teresa's almost obsessive interest in what was happening to her, particularly at this stage of her life, was forced on her both by her temperament and by the lonely position in which she found herself in the face of uncomprehending confessors.

Despite the fact that she had a touching admiration for them and heeded their every word, few of her confessors were of any help to her. Their frequent assertions that she was being deceived by the devil led her to fear they would all desert her and she would have no one to hear her confession, let alone direct her spiritual life. Such was the distress they caused her that she would spend hours in tears. It is no surprise that her own attitude to these mystical phenomena was ambivalent. Ever fearful of deception, she felt "immediately reassured whenever God bestowed any favor on me."[12] Deeply grateful for these favors though she was, they brought her such pain and unhappiness that all she wanted was death, for how else could she be entirely with God? Desolated by loneliness, she could find no one with whom she could speak freely; even keeping body and soul together was "like a voice crying out for help to breathe."[13] While she was adamant that receiving "favors" does not make one person better than the rest, she felt that they "prepare us to be better servants of God."[14] If—and this is crucial—"if we use them aright." Ironically, it was to be her most horrific experiences which were to point the way.

Aware as Teresa was of the power of the devil, she began to have visionary experiences of the dark depths of the demonic world. Though it was cosmically appropriate that Teresa should move from heaven to hell, from God to the devil, she was, naturally enough, terrified.

The concept of the devil was familiar enough in those days—in the language of her time it was he who was to be found in all shortcomings, great and small. But actually to see him made him and all that he stood for horrifically real. As with many of her visions, his various appearances remind one of the pictures which she must have known:

> Once, when I was in an oratory, he appeared on my left hand in an abominable form; as he spoke to me I paid particular attention to his mouth, which was horrible. Out of his body there seemed to be coming a great flame, which was intensely bright and cast no shadow. He told me in a horrible way that I had indeed escaped out of his hands but he would get hold of me still.[15]

When she made the sign of the Cross, he disappeared, only to return. Flinging holy water in his direction proved, as it was often to do, more effective. He would appear in various forms: once as a hideous, tiny, black Moor, "snarling as if in despair at having lost what he was trying to gain"; on another occasion he alighted on her book as she was praying. Sometimes the other nuns were conscious of him as "a very bad smell, like brimstone" or heard sounds like heavy blows. But his most dramatic appearances were in connection with other people. Once Teresa was in a place where someone had died after leading a sinful life and without making his confession: "While his body was being wrapped in its shroud, I saw a great many devils taking hold of it and apparently playing with it and treating it roughly. I was horrified at this; they were dragging it about in turn with large hooks."[16] On another occasion she had been praying for someone of whom she was very fond, but who had given up prayer, when she saw a devil in a great fury tearing up papers. This she took to be a sign that her prayer had been granted — and indeed it proved to be so. She learned that the man had made his confession and mended his ways.

It is possible to see these demonic appearances as projections of her own feelings of guilt and sin. Though the concept of the unconscious, so important to us today, was not, indeed could not, have been known to her, this seems to be what she thought herself:

> These devils keep us in terror because we make ourselves liable to be terrorized by contracting other attachments — to honors, for example, and to possessions and pleasures. When this happens, they join forces with us — since, by loving and desiring what we ought to hate, we become our own enemies — and they will do us much harm.[17]

Most terrifying of all, however, was when she felt "plunged right into hell." Though she had known both extreme physical pain and the blissful pain of mystic union, the pains of hell were of a different order altogether and were to leave an indelible mark on her. Even writing about it several years later made her literally cold with fear:

> The entrance, I thought, resembled a very long, narrow passage, like a furnace, very low, dark, and closely confined; the ground seemed to be full of water which looked like filthy,

> evil-smelling mud, and in it were many wicked-looking reptiles. At the end there was a hollow place scooped out of a wall, like a cupboard, and it was here that I found myself in closest confinement.[18]

But what she saw was nothing in comparison with what she felt. Her soul was on fire, torn from her body, rending itself asunder. She knew despair as she had never known it before. Her bodily suffering was intolerable and, worse, she knew that it would never end. Her childish chant of *para siempre, siempre, siempre* had taken an awesome twist.

She was surprised at the strength of her reaction. Had she not read about the demonic world? Was she not familiar with warnings of the pains of hell? From that time everything "seemed light to me by comparison with a single moment of such suffering as I had to bear during that vision." She was also inspired to save others from such a fate, particularly those she referred to as Lutherans but who were probably Huguenots. Teresa's confusion is understandable, for she was only two years old when Martin Luther posted his historic ninety-five theses on the door of the castle church in Wittenberg; she had grown up with a threatening awareness that his reformation was spreading through northern Europe. Though she knew little about them or their motivation, she was convinced that the Lutherans were "bringing damnation upon themselves," and she set herself to wondering what she could do — the salvation of her own soul was not enough. The vision of hell had inspired her "with fervent impulses for the good of souls." She was not to be allowed to withdraw from the world and devote herself to her inner life; she was to travel an even harder path where contemplation and action are one.

6

St. Joseph's — Secret Preparations 1560–1562

It began very quietly. One September evening in 1560 Teresa was with several friends and relations, both nuns and lay people, chatting in her cell as they often did. As on previous occasions, they were lamenting the state of affairs at the Incarnation. There were too many people, and the large community was not conducive to intimacy. They were concerned about the prevailing tendency to form damaging cliques rather than true friendships. There was so much contact with the outside world that the nuns did not have enough solitude. It was far too easy to leave the convent, often for quite long periods. ("And I," admits Teresa, "was one who did it a great deal.") The house was unnecessarily comfortable, the life too easy. In short, the Carmelite rule was not observed in its primitive rigor: though theoretically according to the Bull of Mitigation published in 1432, in practice there was considerable laxity.

These were well-worn topics, but this day was different, for a young relative of Teresa's, María de Ocampo, took the conversation out of the theoretical and into the practical. Why should they not establish a convent where they could lead the religious life as they felt it should be led, more solitary, nearer to the ideals of the original hermits on Mount Carmel? The idea was offered lightheartedly, almost as a joke, but it fell on fertile soil—Teresa had felt the same urge herself. She talked to her friend Doña Guiomar de Ulloa, who promptly offered to contribute one thousand ducats. They agreed to commend the matter to God.

Teresa was not yet completely committed to the idea. Despite her criticisms of the Incarnation, she was content there and she well knew the problems that would face her if she embarked on such a venture. Nevertheless she was beginning to feel a disturbing, rather pleasant restlessness; in her bones she knew she was capable of doing more than she was at present. Conscious of the troubled state of the church, she longed to do penance for what she regarded as her evil deeds. Nor could she forget the searing vision of hell which was still inspiring her with an urgent desire to bring people to God, "for I really believe that, to deliver a single one of them from such dreadful tortures, I would willingly die many deaths." At forty-five, after nearly a quarter of a century living an outwardly undemanding life, she had to admit that she was ready to "digest other and stronger meat than I had been in the habit of eating." Once again a pervading ambivalence had her in thrall.

While on one level Teresa may have been confused, she had no choice but to pay attention to the voice of God. As she was wrestling with her doubts, God gave her the most explicit commands: she was to work hard to establish this convent and she would succeed. The voice told her it was to be called St. Joseph's, San José, a saint to whom she was in any case devoted, and that he and Our Lady would give it their protection. She was to talk to her confessor, telling him not to oppose or hinder her, because it was God himself who was instructing her to do this.

As she was not yet ready to turn her dream convent into reality, this command caused her much consternation. She dreaded the burden it would be, the trials that most surely lay ahead. But the Lord spoke to her again and again with such convincing arguments that she had no choice: she had to tell Baltasar Álvarez. Having learned from harsh experience how hard it was to convince her superiors of God's appearances to her, she sent him a carefully written account of everything that had happened.

In doing this she was facing poor Álvarez — his cell knee-deep in books on mystical theology as he tried to understand his demanding penitent — with yet another problem, for he could not see how such an idea could be put into practice. At the most mundane level, where was the money to come from? On the other hand he was developing a deep respect for Teresa and had no wish to be the one to stand in her way. He did what many have done before and since: he referred the matter to higher authority, telling her to talk to her superior, the Carmelite provincial. She found that the provincial favored the idea; he also knew that King Philip II, who had succeeded his father, the emperor Charles V, in 1556, would be well disposed toward anything in the life of the religious orders that tended to austerity rather than laxity. He gave the proposed house his sanction. Teresa and Doña Guiomar wrote to Peter of Alcántara, who gave them whole-hearted encouragement. At the time Peter was in the midst of his own reform of the Franciscan Order and was able to pass on practical advice about the formalities necessary for official authorization of new convents. He also gave them invaluable tips on how to encourage supporters and disarm opponents.

One piece of tactical advice he offered was that it ought to be Doña Guiomar, buttressed by her rank, who should make the initial proposal rather than Teresa. So it was she who made the first approach to the Dominican confessor they both shared at the time, the learned and respected Pedro Ibáñez. She told him of her wish to help financially, even divulging the state of her income. Teresa followed this up with a letter in which, with the diplomacy she was fast acquiring, she did not risk mentioning divine intervention, but simply gave the human reasons behind her desire for a more austere way of life.

Ibáñez was aware of the project and initially was not sympathetic toward it. However, the longer he thought, the more he was convinced it should go ahead. He was his own man. He not only encouraged them to press on with their plans, but gave them advice and said that anyone standing in their way should be referred to him. Having such an ally among the Dominicans, at the time the most powerful religious order in Spain, not only comforted the women but also encouraged the doubters. Gaspar Daza and the *Caballero santo,* Francisco de Salcedo, who had been so slow to believe in Teresa's visions, both decided to back St. Joseph's. So far, so good. But, as soon as the small world of Avila society heard of the project, they ridiculed the idea, discussing it endlessly, laughing at Teresa and wondering whether the most charitable explanation was not that she was mad. They knew about this hysterical nun, seized by raptures and hearing the voice of God. They were aware that several holy men had discussed her visions. They recognized too that they had been pronounced genuine, but, even so, why could she not stay quietly where she was at the Incarnation? What right had she, a mere woman, to imitate the Desert Fathers or other saintly ascetics?

She was even denounced from the pulpits of Avila. Teresa's niece, Teresita, has described how Teresa and her sister Juana went to the little Church of St. Thomas, opposite the cathedral, where they had to sit through a sermon denouncing nuns who left their convents to found new orders. Juana, much discomfited, turned to see how Teresa was taking it, only to find her laughing gently (*Con gran paz se estaba riendo*). After all, Teresa had said that everything seemed easy by comparison with her vision of hell;

it was ridiculous to worry about anything else. She was being as good as her word.

The antipathy spread to Doña Guiomar, who became the target of much criticism and mockery; on Christmas morning she was even refused absolution by her Jesuit confessor until she had given up the idea. The Council of Avila also voiced their objections in no uncertain terms. Women had been known to found orders, but why should Teresa de Ahumada seek to reform the Order that had nurtured her for so long, and why should the city bear the financial burden of yet another convent?

Teresa was even having trouble with her fellow nuns at the Incarnation. They were quite comfortable as they were; why should they be made to feel guilty about their pleasant lifestyle?

> The nuns said that I was insulting them; that there were others who were better than myself, and so I could serve God quite well where I was; that I had no love for my own convent; and that I should have done better to get money for that rather than for founding another. Some said I ought to be thrown into a prison cell; others came out on my side, though of these there were very few.[1]

All this was too much for Teresa's superior, who changed his mind and withdrew his support. This was a grievous blow for her, for his approval had given her the official support she needed. Predictably, it also led to Álvarez writing to her ordering her to give up the foundation and, presumably in an effort to give comfort, telling her that one day she would see that it had never been more than a dream.

So, by the end of 1560, Teresa and Doña Guiomar had lost the backing of her Carmelite provincial, an official subject to the superior general, and her Jesuit confessor, while the nuns at the

Convent of the Incarnation and the people of Avila were split into friends and foes, with considerably more of the latter. On the other hand, she had the stalwart support of Pedro Ibáñez, Peter of Alcántara, Gaspar Daza, and Francisco de Salcedo. Another priest, Julián de Avila, later her biographer and a constant companion on her travels, also numbered himself among her friends. What was she to do? What was she even to think?

On one level she felt she had done all she could and was quite prepared to give up the project; indeed she writes that she remained in her own house "quite content and happy." Nor was she perturbed by suggestions that she should have to appear before the Inquisition. This idea just made her laugh: "I knew quite well that in matters of faith no one would ever find me transgressing even the smallest ceremony of the church, and that for the church or for any truth of Holy Scripture I would undertake to die a thousand deaths."[2] She was, however, deeply troubled by Álvarez's letter. His suggestion that the idea of a convent was merely a dream led her to wonder again if her visions were illusory, the voice of God a deception. She was reassured by Ibáñez, to whom she at last confided the mystical graces she had been receiving, and also by words from God telling her to obey her confessor and do nothing for a while. For five or six months she took no further action about St. Joseph's. Then, sometime in 1561, the Lord assured her that her distress would soon be over.

She took this to mean that she was going to die, a thought which, since she saw death as a gateway to the continual company of God, delighted her. It transpired that her release from uncertainty was to lie in the appointment of a new rector of the Jesuits, Gaspar de Salazar. She found herself in spiritual harmony with him, and he had total confidence in her wish to start a new foundation. As a consequence, the timid Álvarez, encouraged by his new superior, withdrew his objections. Teresa was free to continue her work.

Though she was no longer shackled by obedience to her confessor, who had now given her permission, the dissenting voices were not all stilled, so she decided to start negotiations for a house in complete secrecy. She felt very alone: "Sometimes in my distress I would say: 'My Lord, how is it that Thou commandest me to do things which seem impossible? If only I were free, woman that I am! But being bound in so many ways, without money or means of procuring it, either for the Brief [the pope's letter on a matter of discipline to a person or community] or for anything else, what can I do, Lord?' "[3]

Finding the purchase price of a house was the first hurdle she had to overcome, because Doña Guiomar, when it came to the point, found she was heavily in debt and unable to contribute more than a jar of salt and a bolt of worsted wool. (Ironically, her funds had been depleted by giving property to Peter of Alcántara for one of his reformed Franciscan houses.) But money turned up. There was a contribution from the originator of the idea, María de Ocampo, and this, together with two dowries given in advance, was just enough to start negotiating for a site. In order to maintain secrecy, this was to be bought and furnished in the name of Teresa's sister Juana. So, in the summer of 1561, they acquired a modest house of mud and stone in the poor district of San Roche, just outside Avila's eastern wall, and Juana, her husband Juan, and their two children moved in. This ruse not only deflected any suspicions concerning Teresa's involvement, but gave her the pretext of visiting her relatives, when, in fact, she was overseeing the work being done on the house. Teresa's dream was becoming a reality.

However, as anyone who has bought a house will know, this milestone merely marked the beginning of another set of problems.

Surely the tiny house was too small — had she made the right decision? Could she cope with the practicalities? She knew little of the construction of houses or of organizing the work to be done, even though they intended to live in the utmost simplicity. More crucially, she had spent everything she had on buying the house — how was she going to pay the workmen?

Again Teresa was reassured by the raptures and visions that were sweeping over her. The Lord reprimanded her for her doubts, rather irritated by her worries about the size of the house. He reminded her that he had already told her to go ahead with her plans, adding: "Oh, the greed of mankind! So you really think there will not be enough ground for you! How often did I sleep all night in the open air because I had not where to lay my head!"[4]

St. Joseph also appeared to her, advising her to carry on and money would be provided. In December 1561, shortly after a newly built wall had collapsed and Teresa was faced with yet another bill she could not meet, two hundred ducats arrived from her brother Lorenzo, now a wealthy man living in Ecuador. St. Clare of Assisi, the thirteenth-century foundress of the Poor Clares, for whom Teresa had a particular devotion, "appeared in great beauty" promising her help. She was as good as her word: There was a convent of her Order near the site of St. Joseph's and later they did actually help maintain their new neighbors. If most of the world was against her, at least the hierarchy of the saints was proving a stalwart ally.

Teresa's most glorious vision at this time, during Mass at the Dominican monastery church of St. Thomas, Santo Tomás, where she frequently made her confession, was one in which beauty and hard practical advice were most remarkably combined; its vehemence was such that Teresa could not hear the words of the Mass. She saw herself being clothed by St. Joseph and Our Lady in a pure white garment, and was given to understand that she was now cleansed of her sins. Christ's earthly parents assured her she was not to fear failure, but that both they and God would be served in her convent. Our Lady then placed around Teresa's neck a jeweled cross of such beauty that everything earthly looked "like a smudge of soot."

She was also given clear instructions as to how she should proceed with the formalities necessary to founding a new convent. Doña Guiomar and Pedro Ibáñez had already written to Rome, requesting permission to found a house under obedience to the Carmelite Order, but when the Brief arrived it was lacking an essential clause and was invalid. By following the advice God gave to Teresa in this vision, St. Joseph's eventually came under obedience to the bishop of Avila, rather than to the Carmelite Order, an apparent formality that was to prove of tremendous importance.

During this period, when she was spending much of her time with her sister Juana and her family, two incidents reveal her curiously ambivalent attitude to life and death. The first occasion, widely regarded as miraculous, was when Juana's young son Gonzalo was badly hurt in an accident. His father, unable to revive him and fearing he was dead, rushed him to Doña Guiomar's house, where Teresa was staying. Ribera, Teresa's first biographer, tells how she took the child in her arms, lowered her veil, and for some minutes bent silently over him, their two heads almost touching. Eventually, as if waking out of sleep, the child put his hands on her face and began to play with her. Soon he was running around the room, returning from time to time to kiss his aunt.

At the time Juana was heavily pregnant and soon after this dramatic incident gave birth to another boy, who was named José, after the future convent's protector. He was a healthy baby, but his mother was alarmed when Teresa took him in her arms and chanted quietly, "If you are not to grow up a good man, I pray God, my son, to take you as you are, you little angel, before you offend him." Three weeks later the baby lay mortally ill and, as he died, Teresa fell into an ecstasy and praised God.

By the end of 1561 the work on the house was progressing, secrecy was apparently being maintained, and just enough money was coming in to pay the bills. All seemed to be going well, when Teresa was suddenly removed from the scene. It was Christmas night and, as she often did at that time, she was staying with Doña Guiomar, when a messenger arrived from the Carmelite provincial. Teresa was to go immediately to Toledo to comfort a rich noblewoman who had lost her husband earlier in the year.

Doña Luisa de la Cerda was one of the grandest and richest ladies of Spain. She was a daughter of the duke of Medinaceli, himself a direct descendant of Alfonso X; her husband had been a Toledan nobleman, a nephew of the cardinal archbishop. Since his death she had been in such despair that there were fears for her sanity. No one had been able to comfort her, not her seven children, her highborn friends, the princes of the church, or her household servants. She was desperate for a companion who had sufficient social credentials to pass muster at the palace and who could comfort her spiritually. Hearing that Teresa de Ahumada was such a person, she prevailed on her friend the Carmelite provincial to send this remarkable nun to Toledo.

Teresa had been living in constant fear that the provincial would hear of her work on St. Joseph's and order her to stop. When she was informed that she was to be sent away, she must have wondered if this were not a ruse to distract her. Certainly she was surprised and annoyed. Not only was her work in Avila to be interrupted, but how could she, knowing herself "to be so wicked," succeed in comforting the noble lady when so many had failed? She put her problem before the Lord, who was quite explicit: She was to go, she would do notable service in doing so, and in any case it would be better if she were away from Avila until the Brief arrived from Rome, because, he warned her, "the devil had organized a great plot." She need not be afraid. So, on a bitter January day, accompanied by the faithful Juana Suárez and escorted by her brother-in-law, Juan de Ovalle, she made the long journey across the Castilian plain and over the snow-clad mountains to Toledo, her grandfather's hometown.

Though Philip II had recently transferred the court to Madrid, Toledo was still the social capital of Spain, referred to by contemporary chroniclers as "the head of the kingdom and the heart of Spain." Many eminent families chose to stay in their luxurious mansions in the city which for nearly five hundred years had been the capital of Castile, and their huge households were more like courts than homes. Valets, footmen, pages, major-domos, duennas, and maids, the usual retinue of servants, ministered to the needs of the immediate noble family and their countless relatives. The local aristocracy, politicians, princes of the church, and members of religious orders paid regular homage to such families, observing strict protocol, fighting over precedence and competing for favors.

Doña Luisa's household was typical of Toledan society at the time, and it was not at all to Teresa's liking. Doña Luisa took to Teresa and "began at once to grow markedly better: she felt more comforted every day," but this did not console Teresa, because finding favor with the influential lady made her the object of jealousy in the palace. She found the grand lifestyle intolerable: "Almost everything was a cross for me: the comforts in her house were a real torment and when she made so much of me I was filled with fear."

Teresa was learning to distrust the life of the nobility. She was recognizing that worldly honor, so precious to Spaniards of the time, had no place in the spiritual life. Her relationship with God made her "feel so free and enabled me so to despise all I saw — and the more I saw the more I despised it — that I never treated these great ladies, whom it would have been an honor to me to serve, otherwise than with the freedom of an equal. From this I derived great profit, and I told my lady so." Through her affection for Doña Luisa, Teresa realized how a noblewoman was as subject to passions and weaknesses as anyone else. She learned how little regard should be paid to rank, that rank made demands, and the higher the rank, the greater the demands. Meals had to be taken when they were served, not when they were wanted; the food was determined by position, not by appetite. Servants could not be trusted and must not be favored, for then they would be unpopular below stairs. This, she roundly asserts, is slavery. She came to hate the very idea of being a great lady and to seek deliverance from "this sinful fuss."

While she was trying to cope politely with a way of life she detested, Teresa's visions and revelations became more numerous, more sublime. Whenever possible she would seek solitude in her sumptuous apartment to pray, to be quiet before God, but even here there were peeping eyes at keyholes, hoping to catch the famous nun in one of her ecstasies. There was little about this life Teresa would have sought; nevertheless the six months spent consoling Doña Luisa in Toledo were to widen her experience of life and contribute to the solid foundations of the Carmelite Reform.

It was through the people she met at Doña Luisa's palace that Teresa's life was enriched. Her attitude to meeting acquaintances, friends, and even her own family was ambivalent, one of the conflicts in her nature being her love of humankind coupled with an overwhelming desire for solitude. Around this time Teresa had begun to write the *Spiritual Relations,* also known as *Spiritual Testimonies* or *Accounts of Conscience* (*Cuentas de conciencia*), and here she writes poignantly about this need:

> Sometimes the necessity of intercourse with others causes me great distress and afflicts me so sorely that it makes me shed floods of tears. For all my yearning is to be alone; and, although sometimes I am unable to pray or read, solitude comforts me, conversation, especially that of relatives and kinsfolk, seems oppressive to me, and I feel I am in great danger except among people with whom I can speak of prayer and of the soul.[5]

This cry undoubtedly rings true, but the merest glance at her correspondence reveals an outgoing, loving, and gregarious person, delighting in her friends. Her letters abound with remarks like "I wish I were with you, for it would do me good to hear a little entertaining chatter," and her pleasure in receiving letters is boundless: "I just live for your letters," "I do not know what I should have done in this place you left me in without such consolation." Even to those less enthusiastic for human contact she encourages sociability. In *The Way of Perfection* she offers her nuns this advice:

> Try, then, sisters, to be as pleasant as you can, without offending God, and to get on as well as you can with those you have to deal with, so that they may like talking to you and want to follow your way of life and conversation, and not to be frightened and put off by virtue. This is very important for nuns: the holier they are, the more sociable they should be with their sisters. Although you may be very sorry if all

your sisters' conversation is not just as you would like it to be, never keep aloof from them if you wish to help them and to have their love. We must try hard to be pleasant, and to humor the people we deal with and make them like us, especially our sisters.[6]

Teresa was far too socially adept and loving a person not to profit from the variety of people who sat round Doña Luisa's table or chatted on her balcony. Rich and poor, religious and secular, titled and commoner, they flocked to the palace. She met wealthy, influential people such as the duchess of Medinaceli, the marchioness of Villena, Princess Juana, the duchess of Alba, and the famously beautiful princess of Eboli, who was later to be such a trial to her and her nuns. Acquaintances were made, friendships formed, such as that between Teresa and María de Salazar, one of Doña Luisa's young ladies-in-waiting. She was a charming and gifted girl of sixteen, who used to slip pious verses into Teresa's hand and tell her she would like to be a nun. At the time Teresa thought her quite unsuitable for the religious life, though later she was to accept her as a novice and, as María de San José, she became one of Teresa's most remarkable prioresses, and a dearly loved friend and correspondent.

Sometimes old friends would turn up, like García de Toledo, a priest whom Teresa had known when he was the subprior of St. Thomas's, the Dominican church in Avila. She records her surprise when, one day at Mass, she was seized with a desire to know the state of his soul; three times the urge came upon her, so finally she plucked up the courage to speak to him. She saw him as a gifted and potentially holy man who was caught up in the routine of religious professionalism. Once the floodgates were opened, they confided in each other: he learned of her spiritual trials and heard her confession, while she commended him ceaselessly to

God. In one of her intimate exchanges with God she remembers saying: "Lord, Thou must not refuse me this favor. Think what a good person he is for us to have as our friend." The meeting of their minds and Teresa's interventions to God on his behalf transformed the Dominican, both in body and soul. Teresa was so touched at the humility with which he listened to her that "he seemed to have left my soul ablaze with a new fire of longing to begin to serve the Lord all over again."

García de Toledo also played a part in encouraging Teresa to write a full account of her life, a venture that led to one of the richest pieces of spiritual autobiography ever written. It is probable that it was he who instructed her to write it, though there is also evidence to suggest that the book's origins lay with previous confessors in Avila as much as five years earlier — she already had the authorization of Pedro Ibáñez. But certainly it was at Toledo, where she had more time to write, that she finished the first draft of the *Life,* and at the end of 1565, when she had completed the final version, it was to García that she first entrusted it.

Teresa was able to see other old friends. She persuaded Doña Luisa to invite Peter of Alcántara, then an old man, to Toledo, where his tattered rags and ascetic appearance must have been in strange contrast to the magnificent surroundings. On another occasion her brother-in-law, Juan de Ovalle, came to tell her that her half-sister, María, had died. Some years before Teresa had learned in prayer that María would die without first making her confession and had been to see her at her home to persuade her to change her ways. Though María had lapsed again, to Teresa's great relief she had made her confession just a week before her death; Teresa saw in a vision that her half-sister had spent only a short time in purgatory and was now at rest.

However, the person who had most influence on the Carmelite Reform was a *beata* who had walked nearly two hundred miles specifically to see Teresa. Her name was María Yepes. She was born in Granada in 1522, had been widowed very young, and entered the Convent of the Mitigated Observance in her hometown. But, even before she was professed, she, like Teresa and at almost precisely the same time, felt the call to found a reformed house. She sold her possessions and, calling herself María de Jesús, tramped barefoot to Rome. The papacy was encouraging the reform of religious orders, and Pius IV was impressed by her determination. He allowed her to stay for a while at the Carmel in Mantua, where the primitive austerities were still scrupulously observed, then authorized her to found her own community. Nevertheless, she found even more resistance among the citizens of Granada than Teresa was finding in Avila: the outcry reached the point where she was threatened with a public whipping. It was after the failure of this first attempt that she came to see Teresa.

For a fortnight the two women talked, and Teresa was stimulated at meeting a kindred spirit and eager to learn. What she discovered both surprised her and accorded with her own instincts. Though the *beata* could not read, she knew the ancient rule by heart and Teresa, for the first time, learned that it had encouraged poverty: "I had had no idea of founding a convent without revenue, my intention being that we should have no anxiety about necessaries, and I did not think of all the anxieties which are entailed by the holding of possessions."[7] For her own part, she had never doubted the value of poverty, but had hesitated to force her commitment on others. She had seen poverty lead to distraction, "and it had not occurred to me that their distraction was not due to their poverty, but that their poverty was the result of their not being recollected."

She sought advice only to find herself involved in long disputations with learned men and faced with so many contrary arguments that she was temporarily confused. She wrote to Ibáñez, who answered in "a letter two sheets long, full of refutations and theology," telling her he had studied the subject closely and trying to dissuade her from founding in poverty. Her answer to this priest for whom she had so much respect shows her growing confidence. "I replied that I had no wish to make use of theology and should not thank him for his learning in this matter if it was going to keep me from following my vocation, from being true to the vow of poverty that I had made, and from observing Christ's precepts with due perfection." Not surprisingly, her views were unreservedly endorsed by Peter of Alcántara, who knew about poverty from long personal experience. And her prayers and conversations with God left her in no doubt. God told her she must found the convent in poverty and that money only led to confusion. She sought no more advice, but let her instincts guide her. "When I betook myself to prayer again and looked at Christ hanging poor and naked upon the Cross, I felt I could not bear to be rich."

It was as a result of this decision to embrace poverty at St. Joseph's that her attitude to the poor changed. Her fastidious nature and privileged background had made her flinch from the dirt and smell which so often accompanies extreme poverty, and she admits that until then she had no natural compassion for the poor, giving alms only for love of God. Now she could say (as always, noting her progress carefully) that the poor "cause me no repulsion, even when I mix with them and touch them. . . . I realize I have improved most notably in this."

Soon after María Yepes's visit Teresa heard that her banishment to Toledo was ended; the provincial would allow her to return to Avila whenever she wished. Her reaction to this news was ambivalent. For one thing her health had been better in the slightly kinder climate of Toledo; for another she was loath to lose the

Jesuit confessor she had found there, Fr. Domenech. But what really alarmed her was that the Convent of the Incarnation was electing a new prioress and she had heard that many of the nuns, surprisingly in view of their fierce attacks only six months earlier, wanted her to be their new superior. The thought of all the administrative work the position would entail, not to mention the effect it would have on her plans for St. Joseph's, was abhorrent to her. She shed many tears and wrote asking the nuns not to vote for her.

God was not going to let her off so lightly, however. She had asked for a cross, he reminded her; there was one awaiting her in Avila and she must return. She saw no option but obedience and, even though she assumed that her cross was to become prioress against her will, she was surprised to find that her distress was making her happy: "I was being moved by two contrary feelings: that is to say, I was rejoicing and being glad and finding comfort in what was oppressing my soul." Almost unconsciously she was reconciling the opposites in her stormy nature.

The decision made, she was anxious to implement it. The days of suspense and uncertainty had left her agitated and restless; there was no joy in her prayer. Now she had a chance, through suffering, to live a life of greater perfection — what was she waiting for? "If I had to die, let me die," she wrote with bleak determination. Her impatience to embrace the cross that she was convinced awaited her is reminiscent of her childish eagerness to seek martyrdom at the hands of the Moors. Doña Luisa put every obstacle in her way, but Teresa was resolute. Eventually the great lady gave in to the nun, and Teresa was allowed to leave Toledo.

7

St. Joseph's — Victory
1562–1563

At the beginning of July 1562 Teresa returned to Avila. The journey back was as hot and torrid as the outward trip had been piercingly cold, but she was in high spirits, eager for the suffering she was convinced lay ahead. But on the night of her arrival she was greeted not only by the bishop of Avila, Don Álvaro de Mendoza, and her beloved Peter of Alcántara but also by the proper papers from Rome authorizing the foundation of St. Joseph's.

The Brief, dated February 7, 1562, and addressed to "the two illustrious widows of Avila," Doña Guiomar and her mother, was couched in terms that delighted Teresa. The two widows were given leave to endow a Carmelite convent under the jurisdiction of "the ordinary," in this case the diocesan bishop, as opposed to the Carmelite Order, and to be further overseen by three nominated clerics. It stipulated that no authorities should attempt to hinder the foundation or lodge an appeal against it. It even warned potential critics and troublemakers that the women should not be seen as rebels or disturbed either directly or indirectly by superiors, friars, ecclesiastics, judges, or indeed by anyone at all. Teresa had received more benevolent authority for her project than she had thought possible.

All that remained was to enlist the active cooperation of the bishop of Avila. This was not easy, as he was completely opposed to the establishment of a convent without endowment. (Though this was not specified in the Brief, Teresa was now adamant on the point.) He knew all too well how the city council and the people of Avila would react to having yet another convent to support through the giving of alms. Once again Teresa was indebted to Peter of Alcántara, for it was he who tracked down the bishop and persuaded him to talk to Teresa. She, with her attractive combination of passion and tact, was able to charm him into giving his staunch support. The formalities were only just complete in time, for within a few weeks Peter of Alcántara, whose mixture of holiness and worldly wisdom had proved so essential to the enterprise, had died. Though Teresa found continuing support in visions from beyond the grave, his day-to-day advice was no longer available.

As was so often to be the case, Teresa was on a see-saw of church politics and worldly practicalities. Still working in secrecy, for she had a shrewd idea that the popular resistance to St. Joseph's was by no means stilled, she applied herself to more mundane matters such as drainage, walls, and furniture. But how was she to be safe from prying eyes? She was in luck. Her brother-in-law, Juan, fell ill. His wife was at Alba, and Teresa had a cast-iron excuse to go and look after him in the future convent. She could oversee the workmen every day without any suspicions being raised; God was continuing to intervene on her behalf. "The remarkable thing was that his illness lasted only for just the time we needed for our negotiations, and, when it was necessary for him to be better so that I could be free again and he could go away and leave the house, the Lord at once restored him to health, and he was amazed at it."[1]

Further, the election of a new prioress had come and gone with Teresa mysteriously, to her relief, not receiving a single vote. She was free to continue her work; St. Joseph's had the full weight of ecclesiastical authority. Where was the cross she had anticipated with such joyful determination?

The great day arrived. At dawn on August 24, 1562, the residents of San Roche woke to hear a curious, high-pitched bell sounding among the deeper, familiar voices of the bells of St. Anne's and the Gordillas. It was the new convent's handbell, all that Teresa could afford to announce its opening. The tiny chapel was full as friends and supporters jostled for space. There was Gaspar Daza, one-time critic of Teresa's visions, now celebrating the first Mass; Doña Guiomar, Francisco de Salcedo, Julián de Avila, who was to be the first chaplain of St. Joseph's, her sister and brother-in-law, Juana and Juan de Ovalle, and a cleric named Gonzalo de Aranda. Teresa, who attended by special permission of the Incarnation, was accompanied by three of the nuns, Doña Juana Suárez, who had first encouraged her to become a Carmelite, and two cousins, Inés and María de Tapia.

The four nuns who were to be the first pillars of St. Joseph's, and thus Teresa's Carmelite Reform, were Úrsula de Revilla y Álvarez (whose religious name became Úrsula de los Santos), a protégée of Gaspar Daza's; Antonia de Henoa (Antonia del Santo Espíritu), who, at twenty-six, was the youngest; Doña Guiomar's serving girl María de la Paz (María de la Cruz); and the chaplain's sister, María de Avila (María de San José.) Teresa, though foundress, not yet a member of the tiny community herself, later also gave up her illustrious name. They became known as Discalced, or Barefoot, Carmelites, thus expressing their vow of poverty and abstinence.

The four women took the new habits cut and sewn by Teresa herself. In keeping with their austere intentions, they were made of rough frieze rather than the fine-woven serge worn at the Incarnation. The Discalced rarely went literally barefoot, but they replaced their shoes with hemp-soled sandals known as *alpargatas*, the shoes of the poor. They covered their heads with coarse veils, signifying that they were dead to the world and professed obedience to the Primitive Rule. For Teresa "it was like being in heaven." Her dream had become reality, though she would take no credit:

> Not that I thought I had done anything of all this myself: I never thought that, nor do I now; I have always known that it was done by the Lord. The part of it which concerned me was so full of imperfections that I can see I ought to be blamed rather than thanked for it. But it was a great comfort to me to see that in such a great work as this His Majesty had taken me, wicked as I am, to be His instrument. I was so happy, therefore, that I was quite carried away by the intensity of my prayer.[2]

Her happiness was short-lived: only three or four hours later she was plunged into black despair. The questions and doubts fought for her attention as they raged in her head. Was it all a dreadful mistake? Would the nuns be happy under so strict a rule? Would there be enough to eat? Would she herself, suffering as she always was from ill-health, be able to endure the life of penance after twenty-five years in "such a large, pleasant house, where I had always been so happy"? In any case, what was she doing starting a new convent when she already belonged to one? Most crucially, had she not broken her vow of obedience to the Order by founding a convent without permission from her provincial?

It seems extraordinary that she says so casually: "It had certainly occurred to me that the provincial would be rather displeased at my having placed the convent under the jurisdiction of the Ordinary, without having first told him about it." Indeed he might and, if she herself had not realized it, why had none of her advisers pointed it out?

She was in torment. It was more than the flat anti-climax that can follow euphoria, it was like "a death agony": "Here I was, such a short time ago, thinking I would not exchange my happiness with anyone on earth and now the very cause of it was tormenting me so sorely that I did not know what to do with myself."[3] Then she remembered her desire for trials and God's promise that she would carry a cross. Now she had been given it. If she used her unhappiness to serve God, it would act as a form of purgatory; this was "the way to win merit." Where, she asked herself, was her courage? She knelt before the Blessed Sacrament, promising to ask for permission to enter St. Joseph's and to take a vow of enclosure. Minutes later she was quiet and happy, though exhausted. She had found inward peace. She needed it, for while she was at prayer the news of St. Joseph's had spread all around town and Avila was in turmoil. People were talking of little but this troublesome nun daring to found a new convent in the face of the opposition she knew very well it had created. Her trials had hardly begun.

Such was the commotion in Avila that Julián de Avila, the convent's chaplain, recounts that it was as if the city were swept simultaneously "by plague, fire, and an invading army." It is hard to see how a few women wanting to live a life of seclusion and prayer could produce such an effect, but then most of us today are unfamiliar with living so closely to the things of God as was the norm in sixteenth-century Spain; such matters were dynamite and to upset the prevailing order was to risk an explosion.

There were more practical objections too. As the bishop of Avila had foreseen, the city resented having to lose the rent which the house, under secular hands, would have yielded and to support yet another convent founded *sin renta.* Every conceivable objection was voiced; there was even a claim that the alterations to the house had endangered the city's water supply. The city authorities knew too that, though Rome had authorized the convent, the king had not. Other religious houses also feared the added competition for alms, while the nuns of the Incarnation had their personal reasons for alarm. They feared that, if the Inquisition investigated the new convent (as well they might), they too, innocent of involvement, could be endangered. They not only felt insulted at the implied criticism of their own Rule and lifestyle, but wondered if they would be forced to practice the same austerities the four new nuns had voluntarily undertaken. Perhaps also their consciences were troubled at their unwillingness to give up their easygoing lives.

Teresa was trying to catch up on several sleepless nights when she was summoned to the Incarnation by the new prioress, Doña María Cimbrón. Expecting to be put in the convent prison and rather looking forward to the solitude, she left her four nuns "terribly upset," placed Sister Úrsula in charge, and put her case first to the prioress and then to the provincial. Though by now inwardly confident that she had offended neither her God nor her Order, outwardly she was tactfully contrite. The elderly prioress, distantly related to Teresa, was soon mollified, and the provincial, Ángel de Salazar, showed, in the circumstances, considerable magnanimity. He not only let her off with a severe rebuke, but also, in a subsequent private interview, promised that, when the dust had settled, she could go and live at St. Joseph's. Finally — and possibly hardest of all — she had to give her version of the affair to the nuns.

Though Teresa was more kindly treated than she expected — a lay boarder at the Incarnation recorded that she was sent "a very fine dinner" — clearly no one quite knew what to do with this controversial nun, and while the storm raged, she was confined to her cell. So, although she recounts the uproar in some detail, she was unable to take any part in the extraordinary events that were to follow.

On August 26, two days after the opening of the new convent, the city council called an emergency meeting of representatives from all the religious Orders, two learned men from each. Only one man, a Dominican, Domingo Bañez, supported the convent and even he objected to its being founded in poverty. Some said nothing; most condemned it and would have liked to be rid of it immediately. The opposition won the day, and it was decided that St. Joseph's must be dissolved. So the magistrate, accompanied by the police, went to St. Joseph's, knocked at the door and demanded admission. The four women refused to let them in, insisting that they would stay. The blows redoubled in strength. Words having had no effect, the nuns used their only weapon and took themselves to prayer. The knocking continued, but the door of the little house proved surprisingly strong and eventually, humiliated and defeated, the authorities had to leave.

Force having failed, after two days' further debate a report was sent to the royal council in Madrid, claiming that if the convent were founded in poverty it would do grave harm to the city. So the convent became the subject of an expensive lawsuit which rumbled on for two years.

Teresa, gleaning what she could from her cell, was untouched by the defamatory things being said about her, but exhausted herself worrying about what was going to happen to the convent and the four "poor orphans" whom she had been forced to leave motherless. The prioress ordered her to have nothing more to do with the matter. The provincial held his fire, neither helping nor hindering. The only support came from the Lord, who assured her that the foundation would not be dissolved, reprimanding her for her lack of faith: "Knowest thou not how powerful I am? What dost thou fear?"

While Teresa was in enforced inactivity, her supporters made themselves thoroughly unpopular defending her, speaking up at the royal council, defending her against the accusations of the local magistrate. These stalwarts included Gonzalo de Aranda, who had been present at the inauguration of St. Joseph's, Gaspar Daza, who had given the nuns their habit, the *Caballero santo,* and Julián de Avila.

In November a compromise was suggested: the foundation could proceed if it had an endowment. The exhausted Teresa was on the point of agreeing to this, at least until the storm subsided, when the Lord took her to task again. She must not agree to any such thing, for once they had an endowment they would never be allowed to give it up. That same night Peter of Alcántara appeared to her in a vision. He reminded her severely of the advice he had given her while he was alive and asked why she would not take it. Teresa was in no doubt who to obey. She instructed her negotiators not to sign the agreement, and the lawsuit continued.

Eventually it was decided that the ultimate authority of Rome must be sought. A petition was duly sent, asking permission for the convent to continue *sin renta.* Though this was granted in a papal Rescript dated December 5, 1562, it still did not satisfy the convent's vocal opponents, and the suggestion was made that the matter be put into the hands of "learned men." Teresa was uneasy at this course, but was saved from a decision by the entirely fortuitous arrival of Pedro Ibáñez. Though he had previously been adamantly opposed to the convent's foundation in poverty, now Teresa was able to persuade him of her cause. From this moment on he defended her staunchly; indeed it was he who convinced the provincial to fully allow Teresa to leave the Incarnation and live at St. Joseph's. So, although the lawsuit dragged on until well into the summer of 1563, finally petering out in sheer apathy, by the spring of that year the foundress was able to join her four "orphan daughters" in the tiny convent whose foundation had caused them such trials.

It was for her "the happiest of days." She went first to church, where she immediately experienced a rapture and saw Christ placing a crown upon her head and thanking her for what she had done for his mother in founding the convent. Later, when she was reunited with her four sisters, she saw Our Lady clad in a white mantle, "beneath which she seemed to be sheltering us all." St. Joseph's had won, and the Reform of the Carmelites had begun.

8

"The Most Restful Years of My Life" 1563–1567

At last Teresa was able to live the life for which she had longed and for which she had fought so hard. Here she was, in her "little dovecote," her "heaven on earth," where she was to spend the next four and a half years, "the most restful years of my life."

Before Teresa went to live at St. Joseph's, she took off her shoes and went barefoot to the crypt of the beautiful old church of San Vicente, just outside the city walls, a building she would have seen daily from the Convent of the Incarnation. There she lit a candle before the shrine of the Virgen de la Soterrana and dedicated herself to the service of Christ and his mother. It was from that moment that she ceased to be Doña Teresa de Cepeda y Ahumada and became Teresa of Jesus, Teresa de Jesús.

So goes the tradition. Whether true or not, certainly giving up her aristocratic title and donning a religious name, which unquestionably dates from that time, signified a profound change in Teresa. From then on everything about her and the way of life she taught spoke of poverty, silence, and simplicity, of austerity and mortification, of solitude and prayer and love. This ascetic attitude was symbolized in her arrival at the new convent. She took a cheap straw rug, a penitential shirt of chains, and a discipline (a scourge of knotted cords used as an instrument of penance) — all her worldly wealth; she wore a rough frieze habit, a white cloak and *alpargatas*. Asceticism was evident too in the convent itself, which was so small that "it wouldn't make much noise when it fell on Judgment Day." A humble house of mud and stone, it was tucked in among other humble houses. Though today the area is more prosperous, the interior of white plaster beams, brick floors, and narrow cells furnished only with a bed, a cork mat, and a crucifix has been preserved much as it was in Teresa's day. Significantly, even the prioress's chair was making a deliberate statement. A simple stool with no back, no arms and no comfort or unnecessary decoration, it expressed humility as certainly as those used by most abbesses of the time expressed power.

As the house was small, the sisters lived as close as any family, but most of the day was spent in solitude; they were living the monastic life in the spirit of hermits. Surprisingly, they did not merely tolerate this, they positively rejoiced in it. Teresa wrote: "Their consolation was solitude; and they used to tell me that they never tired of being alone: the thought that anyone might come to see them, even their brothers and sisters, was a torment to them."[1] They prayed, read spiritual books, and did much of their work in the quiet of their cells or in the hermitages which Teresa caused to be built in the garden. They met for the liturgy, for brief though regular periods of recreation, and for meals. These meals were frugal. Not only were they enjoined to live in the spirit of poverty, with long periods of fasting and total abstinence from meat, but often there was simply no money. The nuns earned meager amounts by sewing and spinning, but it was barely enough for survival. Fish was a rare treat; sometimes a couple of eggs had to suffice for the whole convent.

They lived mostly in silence and observed strict enclosure. Visitors had to have good reason for calling, there were no purely social callers as at the Incarnation, and during visits the sisters kept their laces veiled. The solid wood revolving door, the *torno* (still in use today), meant that any callers or tradesmen were invisible voices; the large, wooden, double grille in the chapel ensured that the sisters could hear Mass without being seen. Should any outsider consider forcing an unwelcome entry or an insider think of leaving, there was a high wall round the garden to deter them. Not that leaving the convent was a serious temptation, for they were very happy. Teresa had an intense dislike of "long-faced saints that make both virtue and themselves abhorrent," and there was gaiety and laughter as well as silence and high seriousness. Feast days and special events in their uneventful lives were celebrated. Flutes, drums, and tambourines, still to be seen in the museum, bear witness to the many occasions when they would sing and dance, often to their own compositions. Many were written by Teresa herself, and one of her least eloquent efforts marks a curious occasion.

One day after matins the nuns formed a short procession. Carrying a cross and singing psalms, they walked from their cells to the chapel. There they implored God to deliver them from the lice that were infesting their rough frieze habits. Teresa then sprinkled holy water around the cells and on the pallets, singing a song with the refrain:

> Do Thou keep all nasty creatures
> Out of this frieze.

One of the witnesses at Teresa's beatification declares that from that moment the plague ceased. The cross they carried became known as the Christ of the Lice.

Another event regarded as miraculous concerned a commodity essential even to the most austere community—water. There was water in the grounds of the convent, but so deep as to be virtually inaccessible and, in any case, it was reported to be undrinkable. Against the advice of experts, who said she was throwing money away, Teresa had a well sunk. The water flowed clear and abundant. Over four hundred years later, it still exists, now known as the Samaritan's Well, and continues to provide the convent with water.

Happiness is infectious, and soon the numbers grew. Teresa might have initially intended a maximum of fifteen nuns, representing the twelve apostles, Christ, Our Lady, and St. Joseph, but settled at thirteen. Later it became necessary to increase the number to twenty, enough to enable the nuns to support themselves. New arrivals included Teresa's niece, María Cepeda y Ocampo, whose half-jesting remark a few years back had started it all and who took the name María Bautista after John the Baptist; and Doña María Dávila, a beautiful girl from one of the noblest families in Avila, who took the name of María de Santo Jerónimo. Soon all local opposition disappeared. Even those who had been most hostile found they approved of the new convent, were proud of it and prepared to give it alms. Eventually the lawsuit was abandoned and, on August 22, 1564, the provisional permission given Teresa to transfer from the Incarnation to St. Joseph's was officially confirmed by the papal nuncio.

For the first few months Teresa lived as a simple nun. In July 1563, however, at the insistence of the bishop and the provincial, she became prioress. There were to be no distinctions of background; the seductive temptations of honor and rank were left behind when the women took the habit. "Let the sister who is of the highest birth speak of her father least; we must all be equals." Just as they gave up their worldly titles, so they all shared household tasks. Teresa's fastidiousness and domestic skills together with her willingness to share in the humblest chores were appreciated by the nuns, but they must have been rather alarmed when they found her one day beside the stove, holding a frying pan, in a rapture. It was, nonetheless, in keeping with her conviction that God was in all things. One of her most famous sayings is that "God walks also among the pots and pans."

Despite rejoicing in a life filled with what she referred to from the troubled times of 1573 as "the calm and quiet of which my soul often sorely misses," she was always busy in prayer, domestic tasks, administration, or writing. While she was at St. Joseph's she finished the second version of her *Life,* amplified the Rule under which they were living in *The Constitutions,* and started and completed the first version of *The Way of Perfection.*

In 1562, when the Brief was issued for the foundation of St. Joseph's, Teresa was authorized to draw up the constitutions by which it was to be governed. When she set about this task, she took as her basis what she believed to be the original rule written by St. Albert in the thirteenth century. What she could not have known was that, though the translator had claimed it to be unmitigated, in fact later research shows it to have been subjected to slight changes by Pope Innocent IV. For instance, meat was allowed when the nuns were out of the house (given the strictness of their enclosure, this must have been rare), and the "Great Silence" was cut from fifteen hours to nine. However, even had Teresa known, it is hard to believe that she would have minded. In their combination of gentleness of spirit and extreme austerity of lifestyle her *Constitutions* are essentially Albertine.

Teresa's Reform of the Carmelite Order must be seen in the context of her times and in her awareness of "the great evils that beset the church." Throughout her life the Protestant Reformation had been spreading: she was only two years old when Martin Luther made his famous attack on indulgences and eighteen when Henry VIII broke with Rome. She understood little of the motivation and ideals behind the Reformation, but this did not prevent her holding strong views on the subject: as far as she was concerned, it was quite simply wrong. For her the church she knew and loved was Christ, and the Protestant reformers were crucifying him all over again. Identified as intimately with Christ as Teresa was, she herself experienced this anguish. She writes of her concern at "the harm and havoc that were being wrought in France by these Lutherans and the way in which their unhappy sect was increasing." With tears she besought God to remedy "this great evil." There are shades of the heroic romanticism of her childhood in her eagerness to lay down her life to save a single soul which, in her eyes, was being lost.

She would have been well aware of the Counter-Reformation and the crucial part played in it by the Council of Trent. It had opened in 1545 and was only to close in 1563, soon after she arrived at St. Joseph's. She needed to make her own contribution, but what could she, a woman and a sinner, do? Since God "has so many enemies and so few friends, these last should be trusty ones." Aware though she was of the shortcomings of the church and frustrated as she had been by its bureaucracy, she would not imitate the Protestant reformers in attacking it, even out of love. Her proudest boast was to be "a daughter of the church," and she would operate within its traditions. She would see that God had good friends at St. Joseph's; her community would honor God and pray for the church and its defenders.

Above all other aspects of religious life, Teresa valued obedience. This attribute was to be a cornerstone of her reform. For one who experienced such strange heights of mystical union, the container of the church was crucial. She was not going to kick this ladder from under her feet; indeed sometimes she honored its rules — like obedience — not only in the spirit but so literally as to be almost ludicrous. She tells with admiration, if jokingly, of a nun who pointed out a large, fat worm to a prioress. "Go and eat it then," said the prioress. The eager nun was on the point of frying and eating it, only just being prevented from doing something that might well have been dangerous. Teresa admitted this possibility, adding wryly that she was so devoted to obedience that she preferred it to be carried to excess.

Another pathetic attempt at obedience is commemorated by a patio at St. Joseph's known as the Patio of the Cucumber. Teresa asked one of the nuns to plant a small, rotten cucumber. "Upright or lengthways?" asked the nun. "Lengthways," said Teresa, watching approvingly as the sister went to plant a cucumber that would immediately shrivel and die in the hot sun. On yet another occasion she sent Úrsula de los Santos off to bed, assuring her she was ill. The obedient nun, feeling perfectly fit, did as she was told, even telling the sympathetic nuns who visited her that she was "poorly, my sisters, very poorly."

It is easy to mock obedience at this level, but these anecdotes are merely the froth bubbling over the deep waters of Teresa's conviction. Her love of obedience was deeply rooted in her theology. She was determined that nothing would be done under her aegis which ran counter to the church's teaching. In writing of her first foundation she says:

> I did nothing without asking the opinion of learned men, lest in any way whatever I should act against obedience. . . . Had they told me that there was the slightest imperfection in this, I think I would have given up a thousand convents, let alone a single one . . . if I found that the Lord would have

> been better served by my abandoning it entirely, I should have done so with complete tranquility.[2]

This spirit of obedience was to cause her continual anguish. Her insistence on obedience frequently led to her being torn apart outwardly, just as her temperament tore her apart inwardly. In cases of conflict, who was she to obey, her confessor or God? Sometimes God would change her confessor's opinion "so that he would do what He willed"; but there were occasions when the situation was not so conveniently resolved. When two courses of action presented themselves, should she follow her own insight or the teaching of the institutional church? Should she obey the Holy See or the royal council, in the Spain of her time a second source of ecclesiastical jurisdiction? Her *Constitutions* must, therefore, be read in the light of her fervent desire to provide God with friends and her determination to be obedient to the church's teachings. Teresa is at her most methodical and precise. Here there are no digressions, no spontaneous interjections; she is, quite simply, spelling out the life her nuns will live.

Prayer was, of course, the central preoccupation of the nuns' lives, and she begins by giving the precise times and manner in which the daily office is to be observed, the days on which they may receive Communion, and the spiritual books they were to read. "Of things temporal" she insists (though this was modified in some cases) they must have no income, there must be no begging and they must live on alms voluntarily given. They must have no personal possessions or even the tiniest drawer or cupboard where they might be kept. The instructions as to dress are almost military in their precision:

> The habit shall be of frieze or coarse black woolen cloth, and the smallest possible amount of material shall be used in the

> making of it. The sleeve shall be narrow and no wider at the bottom than at the top. There shall be no pleats in the habit, which must be circular, no longer behind than in front and reaching to the feet. The scapular shall be similarly made, and four inches shorter than the habit.[3]

She had learned at the Incarnation how easy it was for dress to become almost secular; she was not going to leave any opportunity for frivolity, however mild, to creep in. With enclosure there must be no opportunity for inappropriate behavior or for unsuitable relationships to arise; even inside the house there must be no special friendships. Thus only immediate family could see a nun without her veil and there must be two chaperones for interviews with the doctor, the barber, or even the confessor.

But even in these businesslike *Constitutions* there is gentleness too. Teresa specifically mentions that novices may receive visitors "for in case they [the novices] should be discontented it must be made clear that we do not want them except of their own free will, and so they must be given the chance of letting it be known if they do not wish to remain." Sick nuns should be tended with the greatest love and compassion. The prioress must be strict but should strive "to be loved so that she may be obeyed."

Mortification is not unduly stressed. According to many who knew her, Teresa inflicted severe mortifications on herself in the privacy of her cell. She also clearly admired others who followed austere practices; for instance, she wrote approvingly of an attractive woman wishing to be a nun who "would even go into an open courtyard, moisten her face, and then disfigure it by exposing it to the sun, so that offers of marriage, with which she was still being importuned, should ease." Mortification of this sort is beyond the understanding of our own time. Whatever Teresa herself thought of such individual practices freely and privately undertaken, she deprecated excessive penances as part of normal religious life. In *The Constitutions,* almost as an afterthought, she simply advocates the regular taking of the discipline, but only with twigs. "Let no one do more than this, or perform any penance, without permission."

If any rules are broken, the punishments are set down, graded into "slight faults," "faults of medium gravity," "grave faults," and the "gravest faults." A disobedient or rebellious nun who committed one of the "gravest faults" risked excommunication, imprisonment, exclusion from ecclesiastical burial, and even becoming the target of a weapon one would not have expected Teresa to use, humiliation. For instance, a nun convicted of habitual slander was given the following penance:

> At the hour of dinner, without her mantle but wearing a scapular on the back and front of which have been sewn two tongue-shaped strips of red and white cloth, one of each on either side, let her sit on the floor, in the center of the refectory, and take bread and water, as a symbol of punishment for her great sin of the tongue, and let her be taken thence to the [convent] prison, and if she ever be set free from prison let her have no voice or seat in the chapter [meeting of the members of a religious house to discuss business and other matters].[4]

Teresa had finished the second version of her *Life* during the first years at St. Joseph's, and for some time it was passed from hand to hand on a journey which was to bring it to the eyes of lay men and women, priests, confessors, and even the Inquisitors themselves. As it was not available at the time to the nuns of St. Joseph's, they entreated her to write something for them. So hardly had she laid down her pen from writing *The Constitutions* before she took it up again, this time in *The Way of Perfection* (*Camino de perfección*) to amplify, explain, and elaborate on the bare rules laid out in *The Constitutions*. Here she is once more her informal, impulsive, discursive self. She intended to write about the way of life that should be practiced at St. Joseph's, but "I shall also write of other things," she tells us with endearing inconsequence, "according as the Lord reveals them to me and as they come to my mind: since I do not know what I am going to say I cannot set it down in suitable order."

The Way of Perfection exists in two versions. The first, known as the Escorial, after the library in which it is preserved, is, even by Teresa's standards, colloquial and intimate. As the book became more widely read she feared for its homeliness. "What would happen if these lines should be seen outside this house? What would all the nuns say of me?" She wondered if they would be shocked at her using the bullfight as a metaphor, suggesting that those who watch from the grandstand "are safer than the men who expose themselves to a thrust from the bull's horns." She asked herself what people would think of her likening the contemplative life to a game of chess in which the Divine King is checkmated by Humility. Surely nuns did not play games? Were they not forbidden to do so? Fearing such reactions, she wrote a second version, the Valladolid, in a style less diffuse, more precise, the informality slightly more restrained.

Both versions of *The Way of Perfection* provide a vivid picture of life at St. Joseph's. She writes on her favorite themes: love, detachment, and (constantly) humility, which she feels embraces all the rest; prayer, the very basis of their lives; poverty, which they must not simply endure, but desire; sickness and malingering — "If once the devil begins to frighten us about losing our health, we shall never get anywhere"; and determination — "We can die, but we cannot be conquered." The nuns must never be swayed from reaching their goal whatever the trials. Nor must they heed criticisms from the world:

> Yet again and again people will say to us: "It is dangerous," "So-and-so was lost through doing this," "Someone else got into wrong ways," "Some other person, who was always praying, fell just the same," "It is had for virtue," "It is not meant for women; it may lead them into delusions," "They would do better to stick to their spinning." "These subtleties are of no use to them," "It is quite enough for them to say their Paternoster and Ave Maria."[5]

The directness of this passage suggests that these very same criticisms had been leveled at her. Certainly they are still, today, directed at those who choose the contemplative life.

Of all the themes on which Teresa reflects in this rich book, two of the most significant, running through her whole life, are the curiously connected themes of honor and friendship.

Honor was almost a disease in sixteenth-century Spain. Pride of blood, *limpia sangre* (literally "pure blood"), was accorded an importance which bordered on the absurd. To be socially acceptable a Spaniard must be untainted by Jewish or Muslim connections and must be confident that he or she was not descended from anyone once condemned by the Inquisition. Teresa, with her Jewish ancestry, could not make that claim, but even had she been able to boast the purest blood "undefiled by Jew or Moor," by this stage in her life she would have set no store by it. Her concept of honor had no room for family pride. She knew what damage could be done by family loyalties. At the Incarnation she had witnessed the destructive effect that cliques and alliances could have on community life. The only honor that mattered was God's honor, and much of the thrust of her Reform was to ensure that God was given the honor that was his due. She was deeply ashamed that at one time she herself had taken pride in her own honor and she expressed herself fiercely on the subject. Insisting on points of honor is "like children building houses of straw." It does not matter whether someone is given the title "Illustrious" or "Magnificent." Noble descent is of no use in eternity; in the kingdom of God St. Peter, a fisherman, has more authority than St. Bartholomew, the son of a king. By the time she wrote *The Way of Perfection* she was quite unambiguous on the subject:

> God deliver us from people who wish to serve Him yet who are mindful of their own honor. Reflect how little they gain from this: for, as I have said, the very act of desiring honor robs us of it, especially in matters of precedence: there is no poison in the world which is so fatal to perfection.[6]

She found the whole idea of worldly honor "enough to make one laugh — or, it would be more proper to say, to make one weep." So in her convents no one would have titles, all would share the menial tasks, all would be equal and so all could be friends. They were to be friends of God, whose honor was under threat from laxity and Lutherans, pointless precedence and sheer indifference, as well as friends with each other.

While her attitude to honor changed over the years, her attitude to friendship remained ambivalent for most of her life. We have seen that a crucial element in her spiritual evolution was her renunciation of all friends who did not talk of God and the things of God, and her deliberate relegation of any friendship to a position clearly secondary to God. Nevertheless, she had the gift of friendship and she exercised it freely and sometimes in a manner that did not necessarily accord with her own teaching. From childhood onward she developed close, intimate friendships, forming her most significant relationship in 1575, when she was sixty.

How did she resolve this ambivalence? How did she reconcile, for instance, her insistence that phrases such as "don't you love me" and "if you love me" must be used only for "some noble end" with her own correspondence, which reveals her as a demanding friend, easily hurt and almost querulous when she felt neglected? It has been suggested that "moored in the love of God, Teresa could commit herself wholeheartedly to personal relationships that she herself professed would be dangerous for young, inexperienced nuns."[7] While others can safely make that claim for her, ordinary modesty would have inhibited her from making it herself; indeed, she never attempted to justify the inconsistency. That she forbade "special friendships" and yet indulged in them herself is one of the most marked contradictions in her contradictory nature.

There is, though, an acceptable difference between the letter and the spirit. In *The Constitutions* she says starkly: "No sister must embrace another, or touch her face or hands, and there must be no special friendships among them but each must have a general love for all the rest, as Christ often commanded his Apostles."[8] In *The Way of Perfection* this injunction is softened and amplified:

> If our will becomes inclined more to one person than another (this cannot be helped, because it is natural...) we must exercise a firm restraint on ourselves and not allow ourselves to be conquered by our affection.... In checking these preferences we must be strictly on the alert from the moment such a friendship begins.[9]

In this quite explicit warning against intimate friendships she shows a certain lenience, advocating diligence rather than severity in dealing with them and continually saying she would like to see many friendships in the convent, when they have as their object "the service of His Majesty." The nuns must tread the narrow path between loving too little and too much; it is possible to love our friends too much, and this can lead to great harm. She wants her communities to be small and close, with no discord, but where "all must be friends with each other, love each other, be fond of each other and help each other." But she insists that the nuns are not to make individual friendships, for, however holy, they are harmful, even "apt to be poisonous" and do not make for the love of God. In fact, she is "inclined to believe that the devil initiates them so as to create factions within religious Orders."

She is adamant, too, about expressions of affection and endearments. Friendship need not, indeed should not, use expressions like: " 'My life!' 'My love!' 'My darling!' and suchlike things.... They are very effeminate; and I should not like you to be that, or even appear to be that, in any way, my daughters; I want you to be strong men."[10]

In Teresa's teaching friendship ought never be excessive, but should express itself by taking on household tasks, thus sparing others, by the prayerful and speedy settling of differences, by rejoicing in the virtue of others and tolerating their faults. Love of God, love of friends — in that order. That is the goal. "For there is nothing, however annoying, that cannot easily be borne by those who love each other."

In the last four chapters of her *Life,* writing about her years at St. Joseph's, Teresa returns to her inner experiences. Although in many ways by comparison with most of her life her time there was restful, she was constantly receiving visions and being seized by raptures. She was in continual communication with God as with a friend. She did not need a "third party to obtain an audience," and phrases like "while in converse with the Lord today" and "one night, when I was in prayer, the Lord began to talk to me" abound. God was with her, in her, and all around her. Even to one so accustomed to his presence, this must have wearied her with wonder. She never stopped marveling at this relationship, expressing her gratitude for these "favors," yet still they brought their own particular anguish. She ceaselessly questions why these favors should be given to "one as wicked as I," one who has been "an abyss of lies and an ocean of vanities and all through my own fault." She struggles with feelings of awe and terror at her closeness to God, and marvels at his humility and love. Sometimes she is desolate, as when once, for instance, for a "full week" she lost all sense of God. Her life may have become more restful, but it was not easy.

Yet by the mid-1560s her standpoint in one regard had shifted significantly. Now about fifty years old, she recalls how, even just a few years earlier, she was worn out by reconciling God and the world. The soul

> hears itself being told always to occupy its thoughts with God and to be sure to keep them fixed on Him so that it may escape from all kinds of danger. On the other hand, it discovers that it must not fail to observe a single point of worldly etiquette, lest it should give offense to those who think this etiquette essential to their honor.[11]

She need no longer trouble herself with such petty details; she has renounced the world. By choosing God, freely, completely, and unambivalently, she has freed herself from many of the oppositions that used to trouble her. To the outside eye, to her nuns and to her numerous correspondents, she was still both Martha and Mary, both teacher of the way of perfection and the charming, amusing woman who could cope with daily needs and argue with authority. But in her heart the world had become unreal, irrelevant:

> He has given me a life which is a kind of sleep: when I see things, I nearly always seem to be dreaming them. In myself I find no great propensity either to joy or to sorrow. If anything produces either of these conditions in me, it passes so quickly that I marvel, and the feeling it leaves is like the feeling left by a dream.[12]

She may well have thought she would end her days in this comparative peace and tranquility. She could not have known that her life's work had hardly begun.

9

"Restless Gad-about" 1567–1568

Sometime in August 1566 Teresa's calm was shattered by a visit from Alonso Maldonado, a Franciscan friar and an eloquent preacher just returned from the West Indies, where he had been commissary-general. He told the nuns about "the millions of souls perishing there for lack of teaching" and encouraged them to penitence. His words stirred the smoldering fire in Teresa's heart. She was already praying for souls she was convinced were lost to God, mostly European and Protestant. Now she was hearing of more people — in her eyes pagans — living thousands of miles away in distant lands where her brothers had traveled, where her beloved Rodrigo had been killed ten years earlier. She went to one of the hermitages to be alone, weeping and beseeching God to help her convert these people to his service. Once more she agonized. What could she, a woman, do? She envied men who could sail to these faraway places and minister to others while she had nothing to give but prayer.

One night, when she was praying, "Our Lord appeared to me in His usual way, and said to me very lovingly, as if He wished to bring me comfort: 'Wait a little, daughter, and thou shalt see great things.' " She did not know the meaning of these words, but they remained indelibly fixed in her heart while she did what she had been told and waited.

A few months later, in April 1567, the Carmelite general, Juan Bautista Rubeo, came to Avila. In sixteenth-century Spain this was an extraordinary event, as the Carmelite generals always lived in Rome and none had ever visited Spain, let alone Avila. Teresa was in some trepidation. She was doubly afraid, first that Rubeo would be angry with her for placing St. Joseph's under the jurisdiction of the diocesan bishop rather than her own Order, and second she feared he might send her back to the Incarnation, where the Mitigated Rule was still practiced and where she would have been unable to live the austere life to which she had become accustomed at St. Joseph's. She decided complete frankness was both the wisest course and in keeping with religious obedience, so she told him about the founding of the convent and the state of her soul, she showed him the *Constitutions,* and he saw for himself how they lived at St. Joseph's.

The general did not ask her to leave. He was delighted with what he found and was moved to tears. He gave her patents to make more foundations, "as many as she had hairs on her head." He even added censures, lest any provincial try to prevent her.

Undoubtedly Rubeo was impressed by Teresa and by St. Joseph's, but this encouragement was not merely a personal whim. The recently closed Council of Trent had urged the reform of all religious houses, though it was too soon for their promulgations to have percolated through and been put into practice. Pope Pius V, elected in 1566, was a fervent reformer. Rubeo himself, appointed only two years earlier, had come to Spain at the express command of Philip II, who was anxious to reform all the religious orders in his country, where at the time the total number of men and women in religious orders amounted to some one hundred thousand.[1] Teresa reflected the spirit of her age: she had anticipated the decrees of the church, even given them flesh. No wonder Rubeo was impressed.

If the growth of Teresa's Reform reflected the outward climate of religious opinion, so too did it meet a need in her own nature. On one level she was awestruck. True, she had the licenses, but there was no friar to put them into effect, not one secular person to start proceedings; she did not even have a house. "Here was a poor Discalced nun, without help from anywhere, except from the Lord, loaded with patents and good wishes but devoid of all possibility of making them effective."[2] Yet she was not, she admitted, devoid of either courage or hope; everything seemed possible to her. In her mind's eye she already saw more religious houses built and becoming strong centers of prayer; she thanked God for "giving such boldness to a mere ant." After more than four years of a life of quiet enclosure she was ready for action. One of the most remarkable strands in Teresa's mysticism is the extent to which she was, like many true contemplatives, both active and passive. Her mysticism did not divorce her from outward reality, rather it took her deeper into the world. Despite the fact that she says she was living in "a kind of sleep," she could be shrewd and businesslike, full of common sense and practicality. By marrying the contemplative and the active sides of her nature she could bring earth to heaven and heaven to earth. Hers was not a temperament which could have been completely fulfilled by a life of enclosure alone, though she was in no doubt as to its value. The road ahead was to be hard, yet it was not only what she felt called to do for God and his church but also what she personally needed, and at some level she knew it.

Where should Teresa build her second foundation? On this occasion there was no divine intervention to guide her. Her choice of

Medina del Campo, about fifty miles north of Avila, was entirely pragmatic. It was only two days' ride by mule, it was a cosmopolitan commercial center well known in both Europe and the Americas, and, even more importantly, she had friends there. She was an astute judge of people, not ashamed to use them to further her aims. Her charm and tact had already won over many to her cause.

One friend of hers in Medina was her longtime Jesuit confessor, Baltasar Álvarez. He was now rector and novice master of the College of the Society of Jesus, which had been founded in Medina in 1553. She was soon assured of his support, though she had first to calm the inevitable resistance, for Medina was a proud city with arms bearing the legend "No office for the king; no benefice for the pope." Before a word of opposition could be uttered, Teresa mounted a formidable defense. Soon her supporters included a few rich, influential laymen as well as the Carmelite prior Antonio de Heredia, who managed to arrange the purchase of a house without any deposit. Since they still had no money, this was welcome news.

Opposition there was. Her plans received heavy criticism at a meeting of the city authorities and local religious. Once more she was compared to the false nun of Córdoba, Magdalena de la Cruz. It was only thanks to influential friends that her project was sanctioned.

On August 13, 1567, three heavy wagons set out from Avila. The little group had no security, just the precious authorization from Rubeo, but with characteristic optimism they took essential household articles for the future convent. Teresa traveled with six nuns in the wagons. Julián de Avila followed on a mule. This genial, spiritual man was to accompany Teresa on many such journeys and not only proved a stalwart companion but also a lively chronicler of their travels.

That night, tired out from jolting along the rough roads, they arrived at Arévalo, where they were greeted by a friend who had found them lodgings for the night. He had bad news. The house that Heredia had found was near an Augustinian monastery, and the monks were prepared to force the newcomers into a lawsuit rather than let them live there. It was, as she feared, the Avila story all over again: the monks did not want to risk the alms they were accustomed to receiving or share them with a new convent.

Undaunted, Teresa found this problem stimulating. If the devil was at work already, then surely the convent was needed by God. However, knowing that at least two of her companions were easily frightened, she said nothing until they reached their lodgings, where another of her one-time confessors, the Dominican priest Domingo Bañez, awaited her. He was confident that the Augustinians would come round. After a sleepless night discussing the situation, for they had to reach a decision by morning as the nuns could not be kept in ignorance for long, they decided to take possession of the house quickly and quietly, before anyone knew they had arrived. Teresa had experienced opposition before; she was fast learning how to deal with it.

Their arrival at Medina was tinged with melodrama. At midnight they reached the outskirts of the town, where they decided to leave their wagons, whose wheels clattering over the cobbled streets would have alerted the whole town to the presence of strangers. As Julián de Avila recounts:

> There we were in the streets, friars and nuns, laden with the sacred vessels and vestments necessary for saying the first Mass and fitting up the chapel: we looked like gypsies who had been robbing churches: if we had run into a night patrol we should have spent the rest of the night in jail.[3]

They were lucky to meet only a few night prowlers who called out pleasantries and even more fortunate to miss by minutes six fierce bulls let loose through the town as a prelude to the next day's *fiesta*. It was nearly dawn when they arrived at the house, and they immediately began to clean the place. The porch that Heredia had promised could be made into a chapel turned out to be in a tumbledown state; there were holes in the roof and the walls were not even plastered. Teresa observed wryly: "The Lord must have been pleased that the blessed Father should have become blind or he would have seen that it was not fitting to put the Most Holy Sacrament in such a place."[4]

They knew they must work quickly, for once Mass had been celebrated in a chapel it could not easily be dismantled. Racing to beat the dawning light, they cleared the rubbish, fixed a bell in place, and put up hangings. They had no nails, so Teresa scoured the crumbling walls and floors, and retrieved enough to hang the *reposteros*, the large squares of cloth used to cover the loads carried by the mules. These, together with a blue damask bedspread lent by the caretaker, were just sufficient.

One formality remained. To give them legal security and to back up the "taking possession" implicit in the saying of the first Mass, they needed legal confirmation that the convent was being founded with the bishop's authorization. Heredia found a sleeping notary, unceremoniously woke him up and persuaded him to draw up a sworn affidavit.

By daylight on August 15, the feast of the Assumption of the Blessed Virgin, the altar was dressed, the one candle was lit, and they were able to peal the bell for Mass. The inhabitants of Medina, waking to find that a convent had sprung up during the night, were speechless with astonishment.

Five years earlier, after the foundation of St. Joseph's, Teresa's initial elation had been followed by extreme depression. She reacted the same way in Medina. Her joy in seeing one more church where the Blessed Sacrament was reserved was intense. For her, Christ was as present in the Sacrament as if he were in the room:

> The Lord had given this person such a lively faith that, when she heard people say they wished they had lived when Christ walked on this earth, she would smile to herself, for she knew that we have Him as truly with us in the Most Holy Sacrament as people had Him then, and wonder what more they could possibly want.[5]

As soon as the Sacrament was placed in the humble porch-chapel she placed men to guard it, but still she worried that they might fall asleep. So during the night she would get up to check that "Our Lord was still in the porch." By the bright light of the moon she saw that all was well. "His Majesty, never wearying of humbling Himself for our sakes, did not seem to want to leave it."

However, the next day brought her from heaven to earth. Surveying the new house for the first time in the bright Castilian sun, she saw that in places the walls had actually fallen down and needed extensive repairs; they would not even be able to stay in the building. Where, then, could they live? The prosperous town of Medina was full of visitors; there was no accommodation and they had no money. Far worse, the Sacrament was in real danger of being desecrated. "Oh, God help me! What anguish filled my heart when I saw His Majesty turned out into the street, and in times so full of peril as these, on account of those Lutherans!"[6]

She was tormented by doubts, obsessed with her own weakness. Perhaps those who opposed her and compared her to Magdalena de Cruz were right? Was she mistaken in thinking that the Lord would help them? Worst of all, were the revelations she had learned in prayer an illusion? Nothing seemed easy anymore.

Not wishing to distress her companions or shake their faith in the project, she said nothing to them, but kept her troubles to herself. For a week they lived in the appallingly dilapidated house, but then their luck changed. A local merchant offered them the upper part of his house, where they lived for two months while repairs were undertaken. A noble lady, who later took the Carmelite habit herself, gave them enough money to build a proper chapel, and the people began to give alms. Two months later the nuns were able to return to their renovated home. Another Discalced convent had been born.

News that the nun from Avila had founded another convent spread like wildfire. Devout, wealthy benefactors appeared, beseeching her, even pestering her, to found convents in their towns and villages. The rest of her life was to be spent traveling round almost the whole of Spain, setting up new foundations and visiting those already established. As her fame spread, her travels and teaching attracted curiosity and wonder. She became the target of jealousy and ridicule, of adulation and obloquy. She was known as the *andariega*, something between a wanderer and a vagabond.

It is hard for us, cushioned in the relative comfort of railways, air travel, highways, and cars, to imagine what travel was like in sixteenth-century Spain. It is harder still to put ourselves in the shoes of a woman who had, for her first fifty-two years, lived initially the privileged life of an affluent aristocrat and then the protected life of a nun, and who was never in good health and often extremely ill. However, contemporary records and her own lively account, peppered with complaints and anecdotes, help us to breathe with her as she traveled the length and breadth of Spain, from Salamanca to Valencia, from Seville to Burgos.

The roads were never good, often just rocky mountain paths, hazardous and dangerous. The climate varied from scorching heat to bitter cold. Undeterred, Teresa and her companions traveled through snow and rain, icy winds and floods, heat so intense that the wagon coverings were in danger of catching fire and their precious water could not even cool their faces, it had become too warm. Food, even rough food, was scarce and an egg a rare delicacy. The verminous inns must have been particularly unpleasant for someone as fastidious as Teresa; often the beds were so bumpy that they preferred the floor. Nor can she have enjoyed the coarse conviviality of the innkeepers, the rowdy singing and swearing, the quarrels and thieving.

Traveling in covered wagons with solid wooden wheels, unsprung and uncomfortable, they could not even enjoy the scenery. Such wagons remained in use long enough for one of Teresa's nineteenth-century biographers to give a firsthand description of the nuns' blindfolded travels:

> Shut in on every side by sackcloth awning, the interstices carefully covered up with mats of esparto grass, with a wooden crucifix and leather water bottle hung up beside them, the nuns traveled all day long on the monotonous track, seeing nothing of the landscape, hearing nothing but the tinkling of the bells on the mules' collars, or the rough objurations, the guttural *arres!* of a muleteer. . . . No glimpse of fervid sky met the extinguished vision of the nuns, no free wind of Heaven, no blast of sultry sun swept over their faces, pallid from the cloistered life, and recalled them to the earth and sky. To all this they were dead. At appointed times you might have heard, were it not for the clatter of hoofs and the harness and the creaking of the carts, the tinkling of a little bell, followed by a faint murmur from within — the sisters were saying Hours.[7]

These wagons criss-crossing Spain were in reality traveling convents. If they talked, their conversations were of God. As enclosed nuns they were not expected to travel, so they made the best compromise they could and took their enclosure with them. As one of the nuns later recalled, their daily timetable matched convent life as nearly as possible:

> The order of proceedings was this. First of all, each day, they would hear Mass and communicate, and, however hurried they were, this was never omitted. There was always holy water and a little bell, which, at the appointed hours, we rang for silence. And everyone knew that, as soon as it rang, they must all be quiet. There was a clock, to give us the hours for prayer; and when the bell rang at the end of a period of prayer or silence, it was wonderful to see how delighted the men were at being able to speak again; and the Saint was always careful at these times to give them something to eat, as a reward for being so good in keeping silence.[8]

Teresa, the only nun permitted to speak to the muleteers, charmed them as much by her sharp, witty tongue as by her attention to their needs. Accustomed to shouting, swearing and quarrelling as they were, they seemed to adapt cheerfully to the pious conversations. If one of her companions is to be believed, they "would prefer listening to them than to any worldly pleasure: this I actually heard from their own mouths."[9]

When they reached an inn, one of the friars or laymen who always accompanied them would go ahead to arrange the rooms in such a way that the nuns could be together, never seeing anyone, even the innkeeper. They always wore their veils and observed the strictest enclosure possible. If the rooms had no doors, one of the friars would guard the entrance; if there was no private room, they would hang frieze blankets for protection. They became accomplished traveling nuns. As one of her companions remarked, Teresa might "have been going about on mules all her life."[10]

While Teresa admitted she "felt a great dislike to journeys, especially long ones," she took discomforts like "fleas, ghosts, and bad roads" lightly. After all, it was to further the cause nearest her heart and, in any case, there were consolations. The countryside, when they could catch a glimpse of it from their shrouded wagons, was often beautiful; sometimes they would spend the *siesta* hour in shady woods or near a stream; always there was the good humor that emanated from Teresa like smoke from a wood fire. Sometimes, as enthusiastic groups flocked to meet her, all attempts at enclosure broke down. The villagers would crowd around the nuns, delighted by Teresa's practicality as she dispelled their idea of pale pseudo-mystics with her down-to-earth talk of market prices and the progress of crops.

The discomforts, even dangers, that these women endured on their travels are undeniable. More in question are Teresa's real feelings about this life, so extraordinary for any woman of her time, so unsuitable for an enclosed nun. Remembering her childhood wish to "go to the land of the Moors" and considering her wistful admiration of her brothers' adventures in the Americas, it is probable that the hazards, uncertainties, and constant battle for survival stimulated and fulfilled her in a way which enclosed convent life, on its own, could not. The combination of action and contemplation crucial to her spirituality was finding a surprising resolution. By following the voices and intuitions she was convinced came from God, she was also doing justice to both sides of her personality.

At the beginning of 1568, as soon as the house at Medina was in reasonable condition and the nuns settled, the foundress was off on her travels again. Doña Luisa de la Cerda, the noble Toledan widow whom Teresa had consoled after her bereavement six years before, wanted a convent founded in honor of her late husband in the town of which he had been lord — Malagón. Teresa was not enthusiastic. Malagón, lying near Ciudad Real, well to the south of Madrid, was a poor agricultural town so small it would not be possible for a religious community to survive on alms; nor would there be enough people to buy the nuns' work. She would be forced to accept an endowment, something to which she was resolutely opposed.

However, she discussed the matter with "learned men," who told her she was wrong. The Council of Trent allowed endowments, they assured her; she had, in any case, been encouraged to make foundations, Doña Luisa was offering quite enough money, and Teresa had no alternative but to accept. With surprising equanimity, considering her previous determination that her convents should be founded *sin renta,* she agreed. Taking one of the Medina nuns, destined to be the prioress of the new community, they set off to see Doña Luisa in Toledo, stopping at Avila and Alcalá de Henares, just east of Madrid.

The stopover at Avila, where she stayed at St. Joseph's, was short, but happy. This was the first time she had returned to the convent for which she always retained such a special affection; it was a joy for her to see her nuns living the life she had designed for them. Her visit to Alcalá, however, was to stretch her tact and her charm. It was here that María Yepes (who had walked barefoot to Rome to obtain permission to found a reformed Carmelite monastery and whom Teresa had met while she was staying at Toledo) had started her house. Its fanaticism and austerity had attracted bitter criticism, and it fell to Teresa to persuade her to moderate the penitential lifestyle and follow a more humane interpretation of the Rule. It was a curiously ironic situation. The two women had both, independently, decided that reform was needed: both, in their own ways, had brought about a return to a stricter way of life. Now here was one encouraging the other to *less* austerity. That the mission was accomplished successfully was a tribute to both women: Teresa for her tact, María Yepes for her magnanimity.

Teresa stayed three months in Alcalá, before traveling to Toledo, where she stopped long enough to sign documents for the new foundation. Then, accompanied by four nuns from the Incarnation, a Jesuit priest, Doña Luisa, and some of her servants, she went on to Malagón. Both the journey and their arrival there contrasted dramatically with their furtive attempt to beat the daylight at Medina. This time they traveled in style, arriving to open, enthusiastic support from the villagers, and spent the first week, while the house was being made ready, at Doña Luisa's castle. On Palm Sunday 1568 the Blessed Sacrament was taken to the monastery, and the third foundation was established.

Surely everything had gone too smoothly? It was not to last. They soon discovered that the house was too close to the market and they would have to move. This cloud had its silver side, however, for Doña Luisa allowed Teresa to choose a site and to design, build and furnish the house exactly to her own taste. Though it was eleven years before the new convent was ready, it is unique in the precision with which the building expresses Teresa's ideals. It has been carefully preserved, the nuns still carrying out maintenance with the original materials. Requests for the plans come from Carmels all over the world.

An urgent and not wholly welcome invitation to found another convent had been made to Teresa around the same time of Doña

Luisa's request. Her attitude to this suggestion shows just how real her conversations with God were to her.

The offer came from Don Bernardino de Mendoza, a rich bachelor whose brother was bishop of Avila; he wanted to give Teresa a valuable house in Valladolid, with a fine garden and a large vineyard. It would have been hard to refuse such a generous gift, and she accepted, but with reservations, as she always wanted her houses in town. Although Valladolid was one of the principal cities in Spain, the house she was offered was too far from the center to suit her. Two months later Don Bernardino suddenly fell ill and was unable to speak; he could only make his confession with signs asking God's forgiveness. Soon afterward he died.

> The Lord told me that his salvation had been in great jeopardy, but that He had had compassion on him because of that great service which he had done for His Mother by giving her a house for a convent of her Order: but He added that he would not be delivered from purgatory until the first Mass had been said there.[11]

Teresa had been hoping to make a convent at Toledo, but on receiving this locution she responded immediately, gave up all thoughts of Toledo and set off for Valladolid. She had to spend most of June 1568 at St. Joseph's, where she was still prioress, to deal with affairs that had arisen in her absence. Then she made another stop in Medina. While she was there the Lord told her she must hurry, as Don Bernardino's soul was in great suffering. She arrived in Valladolid on August 10, only to find the house was so near the river that it was bound to be unhealthy. Nevertheless, the salvation of a soul was at stake. She engaged workmen to build fences to ensure their seclusion, Julián of Avila obtained the necessary license, and the first Mass was said five days later.

As the priest was bringing her Communion she had a vision. She saw Don Bernardino, "happy and resplendent," standing beside the priest and thanking her for freeing his soul. It was far sooner than she had expected, and she was content; another soul had been saved. If the ease with which she accepted the idea of Don Bernardino's salvation through the foundation of a convent is surprising (even in the sixteenth century, did people really think God's mercy needed to be bought?), it is no stranger than that Masses should be said for the souls of the departed. Both are ways of affirming love and communion. The difference is that Teresa's prayer found, as well as an inner expression, a more obviously concrete form.

Soon, however, her misgivings about the site were justified: one by one the nuns were laid low with malaria, and they realized they would have to move. They stayed with their benefactor's sister until a new house was found and made ready, and, on February 3, 1569, a triumphant procession made its way through streets bedecked with bunting and lit with perfumed candles. This was her fourth foundation and Teresa was beginning to be regarded as a celebrity.

The prioress of the new community at Valladolid was Doña María de Ocampo, Teresa's cousin and one of those present when the idea of reform had first been discussed nine years before. Two other remarkable women also joined the community; the admiration with which Teresa writes about them reveals much about her own character and the qualities that won her heart.

Casilda de Padilla was a young girl from a noble family, who at only eleven years old was promised in marriage. Though it was an arranged marriage, she loved the man "with an intensity rare in a child of her age," but one day she had misgivings. After they had spent some enjoyable hours together she became very sad, suddenly aware that as this day had ended so would all things. She yearned for something that would never end. Casilda's bridegroom could not understand her unhappiness, but Teresa, whose childhood had resonated with similar thoughts of eternity, knew exactly how she felt.

For some time Casilda was painfully torn between human and divine love. A visit to the new Carmelite convent increased her distress, for she was greatly attracted to it, so much that she would have stayed had not her parents, the prioress, and a priest all told her she was too young; later she might enter, but not now. In any case, had she forgotten her bridegroom? She knew he must be told of her indecision, but could not bring herself to speak to him; instead she begged to go into the country for a rest. She persuaded the servants escorting her to take a route past the convent and, when they reached it, told one of them to go and ask for a jug of water. As soon as the door was open Casilda slipped inside and threw her arms around a statue of Our Lady, weeping and begging that she should not be turned away. Soon her grandmother, her uncle, and the unfortunate bridegroom were crowded around the grille, trying to dissuade her. Their arguments simply strengthened her resolution. Eventually they resorted to force, obtaining a royal order to return her to her mother's house.

Still determined, the closely guarded Casilda, now twelve years old, thought up another ruse. At Mass one day, when her mother was in the confessional, she persuaded her governess to speak to one of the priests. As soon as she was done the girl caught up her skirt in her hand and ran across town to the convent. Once inside the outer door she cried out to the nuns, and by the time her governess arrived, she was not only inside but had also somehow been given the habit.

If this story is reminiscent of Teresa's own determination and her dawn arrival at the Incarnation over thirty years before, the passage in *The Foundations* commemorating a distant relative of Casilda's shows how Teresa's concept of perfection differs from contemporary ideals.

Beatriz de la Encarnación was professed at Valladolid in 1570. The nuns and the prioress affirmed that they had never found anything in her that could be considered an imperfection. She was modest, uncomplaining, cheerful, and silent without appearing depressed. She was prompt and obedient, she did her duties willingly, never complained when she was unjustly criticized, and bore a severe illness with good will. These qualities we, too, can admire. But what of other descriptions? "She seemed not to be living or having any interaction with creatures at all, so little store did she set by any of them." "She was so grieved if anyone spoke well of her that she took care not to speak well of anyone in her presence, in order not to distress her." "She used also to say that it would be a cross for her to find pleasure in anything but God."

There is a paradox here. Teresa's admiration of this world-denying attitude to life was certainly genuine. She aspired to it herself, indeed similar things could, in a sense, be said of her. Yet, in practice, though God was firmly at the center of her universe, she also had a healthy enjoyment of her friends and of God's creation. Perhaps for us today her sanctity lies as much or more in her ability to contain these opposites, to live in God and in the world, as in the austerity of her ideals.

It might seem that three foundations in less than two years was fulfilling Rubeo's injunction to found more reformed convents. Yet during this period she had also been pursuing another cause close to her heart.

10

"A Friar and a Half" 1567–1569

Teresa wanted to reform the entire Carmelite Order, and this of course included the men. So, frustrated as she was by the limitations imposed on her by being born a woman, it was not long before she conceived an overwhelming desire to found a male branch of the Discalced Carmelites. She became convinced that the learning and experience of men coupled with knowledge of the austere mitigated lifestyle was needed to complete her reform. While she was at Medina she wrote that she was "continually preoccupied about monasteries for friars, and having no friars, I did not know what to do."

What she did was to consult the most available wise man, Antonio de Heredia, the Carmelite prior at Medina. She was so amazed when he promised to be her first recruit that she thought he must be joking. He was, she admits, "a learned man; he was a good friar, given to recollection, very studious and fond of his cell." But had he sufficient spirituality? Could he bear the privations? Was his health up to the life? He assured her that he had long felt the call to a stricter life, indeed he had resolved to join the Carthusians. Still she was not satisfied. She asked him to wait and, while he did so, to practice the stricter lifestyle to which he appeared to be attracted. Not for the first time she had started by seeking advice and ended by giving it.

Shortly afterward, also at Medina, she met another priest about whom she had no doubts at all. He was considerably younger than Teresa, only twenty-five years old to her fifty-two, yet she recognized his quality immediately, admitting that she could learn more from him than he from her. He came to be known as John of the Cross, Juan de la Cruz.

The youngest of three brothers, he was born in 1542 to an impoverished noble family. One day, when John was at prayer, he had a curious experience. It is said that he heard a voice say, "Thou shalt serve Me in an Order whose former perfection thou shalt help to restore." He had no idea what such a message might mean. He was, in any case, never willing to trust mystical phenomena, but it seemed to be a clear call to the religious life, so he entered the Carmelite monastery at Medina, studied philosophy at Salamanca University, and was ordained a priest in 1567. Like Teresa, he was dissatisfied with the laxity of his Order and was on the brink of joining the silent and strictly contemplative Carthusians when they met.

Teresa used all her charm. She told him of her plans, "pointing out what a great blessing it would be, if he were destined for a higher life, that he should lead it within his own Order, and how much better service he would render to the Lord." He succumbed, only insisting (he knew she had not yet got a house) that there should not be too long a delay.

She had her small quorum, her "friar and a half." John was a man of tiny stature, frail, and worn with the austere life he had already been living. It is generally assumed that it was he whom Teresa dubbed "a half." However, given her reservations about Heredia and her admiration for John, she could equally well have been referring to their spiritual size; perhaps Heredia was the "half"? At all events, she felt she could now make a beginning: "the thing seemed to me settled."

While he was waiting, John went back to Salamanca for a year's theology; Teresa "commended the matter to the Lord." The following summer a citizen of Avila offered them a house in Duruelo, a tiny village with less than twenty families. It was about thirty miles outside Avila, on the way to Valladolid, which she was shortly due to visit, so, on the last day of June 1568, accompanied by another nun and the faithful Julián de Avila, she set out to see it.

They soon lost the road, nobody could direct them to the remote and inaccessible place, and, after a long, exhausting day winding across the hot Castilian plain, they arrived shortly before nightfall, only to find the house in such a poor state that they decided to spend the night in the nearby church.

It was not really a house at all, but a tiny hovel, previously used as a granary. It consisted of a porch, a room divided into two, a loft and a small kitchen, and it was so dirty, full of insects, and small that Teresa's companions declared she could not possibly found a monastery there: "No one, however good and spiritual, could endure this. You must not consider it." However, Teresa was convinced it would suffice. Her reaction to this home for the first reformed Carmelite friars is a cameo of her feelings about poverty:

> O God, how little have buildings and outward comforts to do with the inward life of the soul! For love of Him I beg you, my sisters and fathers, never to be other than very modest in this matter of large and sumptuous houses.... However large the house may be, of what benefit is that to us? We can make use of only a single cell — what do we gain by its being very large and well built? What indeed? We have not to spend all our time looking at the walls. If we remember

> that this house is not to be our home forever, but only for the short period of our life, whatever the length of that may be, everything will become acceptable to us.[1]

It was not a case of praising poverty while living with a full stomach. She positively desired poverty for herself, felt easier with it, needed it: "It is when I possess least that I have the fewest worries and the Lord knows that, as far as I can tell, I am more afflicted when there is excess of anything than when there is lack of it."[2]

Her attitude was shared by Heredia and John of the Cross, who considered themselves extremely fortunate; they would have been prepared to live in a pigsty. General Rubeo had already given permission for the monastery, so nothing stood in their way. John was the first to take up residence, to the annoyance of Heredia, who had an unseemly ambition to be the first Discalced Carmelite friar. However, he compensated for this lapse in virtue by bringing no possessions, nothing to sleep on, just, so the story goes, five clocks to be sure that he could keep the liturgical hours.

The first Mass was said at the end of November 1568, and the following Lent Teresa was able to visit the community, that "little gateway to Bethlehem." She was entranced:

> I arrived in the morning: Fray Antonio de Jesús was sweeping out the church porch with that happy expression which never leaves him. "How is this, Father?" I said to him. "Whatever has become of your dignity?" And he answered in these words, which showed me how very happy he was: "I curse the day when I ever had any." Then I went into the little church and was amazed to see what spirituality the Lord had inspired there. And I was not alone in this, for two merchants, who were friends of mine, and had come as far

> as this with me from Medina, did nothing but weep. There were so many crosses and so many skulls![3]

Though the presence of skulls may not be everyone's proof of spirituality, there was certainly plenty to impress Teresa. She was especially moved by a simple wooden cross above the holy water, on which was stuck a piece of paper with a picture of Christ; the low ceiling of the choir, causing them to stoop very low as they entered to hear Mass; the odd corners turned into hermitages; the hay for beds, the stones for pillows. She must have been delighted, too, that worldly honor had taken what she was sure was its rightful place in Antonio's thinking. The friars spent long hours in prayer, so rapt that they barely noticed the snow which fell through the inadequate roof and covered their habits. Such was their asceticism that, far from spurring them on to greater austerity, Teresa urged them to less severity.

The friars — there were now four of them — had gained a good reputation locally. There was no other monastery nearby, and they would walk four or five miles daily, preaching and hearing confessions, seldom returning till late at night. Until they were ordered to wear *alpargatas,* they traveled barefoot through ice and snow. The people repaid them with enough food to ward off starvation; some of the more affluent even offered them better houses. Eventually, as their life attracted postulants and the community grew too large for the friars to have even the crudest shelter, they accepted one of these offers and moved four miles across the plain to Mancera.

Teresa was impressed, too, by an event considered miraculous. The friars needed water, so — allegedly — Antonio took his staff to a particular place and made the sign of the Cross, saying, "Now dig here." The spade was hardly in the earth before water gushed out. It turned out to be excellent drinking water and inexhaustible.

The other monastery that Teresa founded for men was to the east of Madrid, at Pastrana. The following year, 1569, she was staying in Pastrana when she met two Italians living there as hermits. One was Mariano Azaro, a skilled engineer who had fought for Philip II against the French and who had spent two years in prison after being falsely accused of murder. Teresa was impressed by him, partly because he did not take an opportunity presented to him to avenge this injustice, partly because she found him "a pure and chaste man and dislikes having to do with women"—one of those asides that devalue celibacy into mere preference. The other was Juan de la Miseria, an artist who became famous through the painting he was later to make of Teresa, the only portrait of her known to have been drawn from the living woman. She, incidentally, did not approve. "God forgive you," she exclaimed. "You have made me ugly and bleary-eyed!"

Mariano Azaro and Juan de la Miseria were true hermits, and when Teresa learned how they lived—each in his own cell, meeting only for Mass, receiving no alms, but supporting themselves by their work, eating alone in extreme poverty—she was reminded of the early fathers she strove to emulate. She soon persuaded Azaro that his observances were the same as her Primitive Rule. Why did he not join her Order? The very next day he decided that this was just what he would do; and so, meekly following his example, would Juan de la Miseria. The series of interconnecting caves that had been their hermitage was turned into a monastery, a third recruit joined them, and the second Teresian foundation for men was established.

The change from hermit to friar was to prove hard and to result in some curious practices. There was no shortage of postulants, it is true, but in attempting to rival the desert fathers in their penitential practices, the ardent group verged on madness. One of the new recruits became novice master and

> subjected his charges to the most spectacular mortifications. They were sent to sell firewood at inflated prices so as to ensure the abuse of the townsfolk. He even made them soak their piles of wood with water and continue scourging themselves while praying that God would send down fire from heaven, as he had done in answer to the prayers of Elijah.[4]

This was too much for Teresa, who sent John of the Cross to bring them to their senses. But she had a curious rival in Catalina de Cardona, an eccentric penitent, who for eight years had lived in a cave, surviving on roots, herbs, and the odd crust of bread brought her by some kindly shepherd. One day she declared that she had learned in a vision that she was to found a Carmelite monastery. So, dressed as a Carmelite friar, she appeared at the court of Philip II begging for alms. She was a huge success and soon she not only won the admiration of the king and of his half-brother Don Juan of Austria, the illegitimate son of Charles V, but had collected enough money to found a monastery. The friars of Pastrana were delighted by her, several leaving their monastery to follow her and all regarding the transvestite hermit as their true foundress. Even Teresa, far from feeling rejected, admired Catalina so much that she momentarily doubted her own, gentler, attitude to penance:

> While I was once reflecting on the great penances practiced by Doña Catalina de Cardona, and how I might have done more myself, following the desires sometimes given me by the Lord, had I not been kept from doing so by the obedience due to my confessors, and while I was asking myself whether

> it might be better not to obey them any more in this, he said to me: "No, my daughter. The road which you are following is a good and sure one. I value obedience more than all those penances you see."[5]

Whether this was God or her unconscious speaking, the voice of reason had triumphed.

Despite these temporary aberrations on the part of the Pastrana friars, despite the fact that the first monastery at Duruelo was abandoned in Teresa's lifetime and the Pastrana house is now occupied by Franciscans, Teresa's contribution to the male side of her Order must not be underestimated. She had set her seal on its origins, and from that small acorn the tree of the Discalced Carmelite friars grew.[6] Teresa herself admitted some pride in this achievement. She was all too aware that, in those days, men could do things women could not, for instance in missionary work; in fact, her insistence that they had qualities lacking in women becomes rather tedious. She even wrote, somewhat surprisingly, that the founding of the male branch of the Order "was a much greater grace than He had given me in enabling me to found houses for nuns."

The figure who towers over the early history of the Discalced friars, John of the Cross, also played a major part in Teresa's personal life. Their names are inseparably linked, their union deep and filled with mutual respect. It was not, however, the greatest friendship of Teresa's life — that was to come later; their personalities were so different that they never enjoyed complete intimacy, certainly not the almost romantic relationship sometimes attributed to them.

John was not only a mystic but also a supremely gifted poet. It is significant that, whereas Teresa, constantly lamenting her poor intellect, should be the one to analyze the states of the journeying soul, John, the theologian and intellectual, catches the mystical essence with no need of analytic tools:

> Upon a gloomy night.
> With all my cares to loving ardors flushed,
> (O venture of delight!)
> With nobody in sight
> I went abroad when all my house was hushed.
>
> Lost to myself I stayed
> My face upon my lover having laid
> From all endeavor ceasing:
> And all my cares releasing
> Threw them among the lilies there to fade.[7]

John was a small man, his remains showed him to be about four feet ten inches tall. He was not handsome, but, as one of his penitents recorded, "something shone through him or this witness saw something of God in him, lifting her eyes as it were beyond herself to look at and listen to him. Looking at him she seemed to see in him a majesty beyond that given to men of this world."[8] He was quiet, grave, unworldly, introvert, and reserved. He spoke little, and his laughter was rare and controlled, though he disliked spiritual melancholy and his presence tended to make people feel cheerful and optimistic. He was "unalterably serene as if he had no passions, absolute master of all the impulses of soul and body."[9] How far he was from the impetuous, extrovert Teresa, prone to swings of mood and as at home in the world as in the convent.

Inevitably the two great Spanish mystics have been compared and contrasted, especially in their understanding of spiritual states. Even E. Allison Peers, normally unwilling to make comparisons between two writers of such genius, indulges the temptation:

> Less human than Teresa he [John of the Cross] may be thought, for there is less contact with the world in his writings than in hers, and while he undoubtedly excels her in his portrayal of the highest states of the mystical life, some would say that she surpasses him in her treatment of the life of the beginner and of the slowly progressing soul.[10]

The essential difference between them is subtly captured by a Spanish poet:

> Teresa, alma de Fuego,
> Juan de la Cruz, espíritu de llama.
> (Teresa, soul of fire,
> John of the Cross, spirit of flame.)[11]

While Teresa recognized John's quality immediately, she was not blind to their differences, not least on the most prosaic, practical level. Soon after they met she wrote to her old friend, the *Caballero santo,* introducing the young friar:

> I beg you to have a talk with this Father and help him in his undertaking, for, small in stature though he is, I believe he is great in the sight of God. We shall certainly miss him here, for he is a sensible person and well fitted for our way of life . . . although we have had a few disagreements here over business matters, and I have been the cause of them, and sometimes been vexed with him, we have never seen the least imperfection in him.[12]

Ten years later she wrote of him almost fulsomely. He was "very spiritual and has great experience and learning," indeed she regarded him as "the father of my soul." "He is a divine, heavenly man. I assure you, my daughter, since he left us I have not found another like him in the whole of Castile, nor anyone else who inspires souls with such fervor to journey to Heaven. You would never believe how lonely I feel without him."[13]

There are stories told about the two mystics that may be open to a number of interpretations: for instance, that when talking about the Holy Trinity they both fell into ecstasies and were lifted from the ground still seated in their chairs — an event proudly commemorated in one of the parlors of the Convent of the Incarnation. But there is no doubting the remarkable spiritual affinity between them, nor the beneficial and restraining influence that Teresa's "little Seneca" had on her. Though she would say that mystical graces were not essential to the spiritual life, her constant references to them as "favors" reveal her underlying attitude; she was, understandably, intrigued and obsessed by what was happening to her. Genuine detachment from these manifestations was firmly rooted in John's personality. He really did not see phenomena like visions and locutions as important, and this cool objectivity tempered Teresa's preoccupation. She showed her appreciation both in appointing him confessor to her nuns and, much later, in her response when he was in trouble. For his part, he showed his devotion to her in the loving care with which, for many years, he treasured her letters to him; even more in a moment of supreme abnegation when, in the presence of another friar, he destroyed them — an act of detachment which history can only lament.

11

Toledo and Pastrana
1569

The late 1560s were a busy time for Teresa. In less than twelve months she not only saw the Valladolid nuns into their new house and set up the two houses for friars, but she also started new foundations for nuns in Toledo and Pastrana. She was in her mid-fifties and growing in both confidence and diplomacy. On one hand she knew that "God's ways are not our ways" and trusted that "the Lord would provide." On the other she now accepted her own role as a reformer more fully, more willingly. She wrote to her sister Juana that "I must not be swayed by anybody and everybody" and that "Anyone who is in the public gaze as I am must look carefully into the way she behaves, even as regards things that are virtuous."[1] Another pair of opposites was finding its resolution as Teresa learned the subtle balance between submitting to God's will and using her own gifts and energy, in a special sense between the active and the contemplative ways of being.

She was also confronting, more and more, the tensions produced by a society consumed with the sense of worldly honor she had learned to despise, a value system in which a person's worth is evaluated by other people. In her next two foundations Teresa had to cope with Spanish society at its most petty, ridden with concerns about purity of blood and the whims of a spoiled aristocracy.

She had first heard of the possibility of a house in Toledo when she was in Valladolid, struck down with the fever that had afflicted all the nuns who had moved into Don Bernardino's house in that unhealthy location near the river. One of her Jesuit confessors had persuaded a rich merchant of Toledo, Martín Ramírez, to bequeath money to endow a Carmelite convent and chapel, and Teresa, so ill that she was thought to be dying, began negotiations from her sickbed.

Teresa was not able to leave Valladolid until the end of February 1569 and even then it was to be a long, complicated journey. She called first at Medina, then paid a visit to the friars at Duruelo and went on to Avila, where she stayed for a couple of weeks at her beloved first foundation. Then came the long trek across the Gredos mountains, the party eventually arriving at Toledo, to stay once again with Doña Luisa de la Cerda, on March 24.

There she found negotiations at a standstill. The archbishop, from whom she needed ecclesiastical permission, was imprisoned by the Inquisition on charges of heresy; her benefactor Martín Ramírez had died and his executors were being uncooperative, continually proposing conditions which Teresa could not accept. Even if the money were available, they could not find anywhere to live. After an auspicious beginning she now found herself with no license, no money, and no house.

For two months she struggled. She met opposition from the council that administered the archbishop's affairs and indifference from the ecclesiastical governor of Toledo. Her influential friends either could not or would not help. There were, the argument ran, too many convents in Toledo. With a population of ninety thousand, the city boasted twenty-four convents and some twelve hundred nuns already. New foundations were resisted, and, in any case, they needed the king's permission. But underneath this reasonable resistance ran other currents that were complex and utterly worldly. There was enmity among the church authorities, who seemed unable to agree on anything. Further, and equally perniciously, Toledan society was rife with social conflict. The aristocracy resented a convent being founded by people outside their ranks, especially as Teresa's intention was to found one in the exclusive district of St. Nicholas. The Ramírez family were, in the eyes of society, "only merchants," and Martín's apparently generous offer was thought to be a way to raise their social standing and to ensure that regular Masses were said for his soul. The "Old Christians" were totally opposed to *conversos* (which Ramírez probably was) becoming too influential.

This conflict was rooted deep in Toledan society. In the fifteenth century anti-Semitism in Toledo had led to riots, which in turn resulted in the beginnings of the doctrine of purity of blood (*limpieza de sangre*) and the exclusion of anyone with Jewish ancestry from municipal office. A hundred years later, in 1547, the cathedral itself was the shameful scene of the archbishop's determination to prevent the son of a *converso* from being appointed to the cathedral staff. He persuaded the cathedral chapter to pass a statute making purity of blood an essential condition of preferment in the church; nine years later this received royal ratification. Now there was a legal connection between orthodoxy in the Faith and the accident of birth. Honor, in its worst form, had infiltrated the very heart of the institutional church.

It is hard to imagine what the situation would have become if it had been known that Teresa had Jewish blood, but, if she had fears on her own account, she does not mention them, simply remarking that she did not concern herself with quarrels over honor. "I did not take much notice of that, for, glory be to God, I have always attached more value to virtue than to descent." Nor was she too troubled by the lack of money — it would probably come from somewhere, as it always did. What distressed her was her inability to obtain a license. After two months of confusion, rejection, and disappointment she decided to take the bull by the horns and speak to the governor herself:

> When I saw him, I told him that it was hard that there should be women anxious to live in such austerity and perfection, and strictly enclosed, while those who had never done any such thing themselves but were living a comfortable life should try to hinder work which was of such service to Our Lord. I told him all this and a good deal more, speaking with a resoluteness with which I was inspired by the Lord.[2]

Her forthrightness, no doubt accompanied by charm, was again successful. Before they parted, she had her license — on condition that the convent had no endowment. As she had by then broken off negotiations with her original benefactor, she had no difficulty in agreeing to this; in any case poverty was one of her own original stipulations. In fact, she was delighted, "for, though I had nothing as yet, I felt I had everything." She did have a few ducats with which, in joyful anticipation, she bought two paintings to hang behind the altar, two mattresses, and a blanket.

The tide had turned, and Teresa was happy to be drawn in its wake. A Franciscan friend sent a poor student called Alonso de Andrada to see her, bidding him do whatever Teresa asked. "I was very much amused, and my companions still more so, to see what help the holy man had sent us, for his dress was not that of a person with whom Discalced nuns should have anything to do." But she was not above accepting help from any direction, and she was intrigued by the mysterious dimension to the encounter.

While her companions continued to laugh, she charged the young man to the strictest secrecy and asked him to look for a house. The very next day Andrada returned with a bunch of keys; there was a house quite nearby, and it suited them admirably. Teresa marveled at the ways of God:

> For nearly three months — or at least for more than two: I cannot remember exactly — rich people had been going all over Toledo looking for a house, and they could no more find one than if there had not been a single house in the city. And then there comes along this young man, not in the least rich, but very poor, and the Lord is pleased for him to find a house immediately. On the other hand, when we might have made the foundation without any trouble, if we could have come to an arrangement with Alonso Álvarez (Ramírez), it was not His will that we should, but quite the contrary, for He wanted us to take trouble over the foundation and to have the house founded in poverty.[3]

They lost no time. A rich merchant had lent them enough money for the rent, they had their two mattresses and a blanket, and they borrowed the bare necessities for saying Mass. On May 14, 1569, the fifth Teresian foundation, the *quinta,* was officially opened.

Within a fortnight they had the house at Toledo as they wanted it: the workmen had left and even the curtains were hung. It was the Feast of Pentecost and Teresa was exhausted, though her mood had swung to a happiness so great she could scarcely eat. She was not, however, allowed to rest for long. A messenger came from the princess of Eboli; she was commanded to found a religious house in Pastrana where the princess lived. One of the most curious and distressing episodes in Teresa's life was about to unfold.

The princess of Eboli, Doña Ana de Mendoza y de la Cerda, was, as contemporary portraits bear witness, a beautiful woman; the black patch she always wore over one eye — whether to conceal an injury from a fencing accident or a bad squint has never been ascertained — somehow added a curious piquancy to her fine features. When she and Teresa met, she was twenty-nine and at the height of her considerable, if unpredictable, charms. She was a formidable woman, capricious and imperious: one day she could be overflowing with generosity and piety, the next seething with resentful, even vicious, anger. The king is on record as saying that "she wants everything that comes into her head and sticks at nothing to gain her end; her rages and ill words are unparalleled for one of her rank."[4]

No doubt Teresa could have coped with her temperament alone, but the princess came from the powerful Mendoza family and her husband was Ruy Gómez de Silva, a close friend of King Philip II and one of the most influential figures in the land. The combination of their noble birth, Ruy Gómez's high position, and his wife's determination to have her own way left Teresa with no option but to take them seriously; there were political overtones here she could not ignore. Nevertheless, her first instinct was to refuse, not least because the Toledo convent was so young and after its difficult birth she felt unable to leave it so soon. She told the servant of her decision, but he, with his carriage at the door and the princess waiting at Pastrana solely to meet Teresa, said that this would cause serious offense. No doubt he had learned to be frightened of his mistress's wrath when thwarted.

Teresa invited him to stay for a meal while she wrote to the princess. She was too astute a diplomat not to realize how important it was to have the support of Ruy Gómez, with his influence upon the king. How could she word her refusal without causing annoyance to this powerful couple? She went before the Holy

Sacrament and asked God to guide her pen. To her surprise, and no doubt her disappointment, he told her that she must go without fail and that she must take the Rule and Constitutions with her, adding mysteriously that "there was far more afoot than that foundation."

As so often, these words from the Lord raise the question of her unconscious attitude. At one level there were many reasons not to go to Pastrana, but here was an opportunity to find favor for her Reform in high places; she was by this time far too well versed in the ways of the world not to know this. Might she not have come to the same conclusion without divine intervention? Indeed, *was* it the voice of God or the voice of her unconscious? These are not speculations that can be answered. It could be argued that the source of such communications is ultimately the same, whether understood as superhuman or psychological. The question is, what are the fruits of the experience? Teresa later became quite explicit about the effects which genuine mystical experience brings. At the end of her *Life* she tells how once, when she was struggling with doubts as to the truth of a vision, God told her that if she had surrendered herself completely to him, she should not be troubled:

> He promised me that all I desired should be performed. And in fact what I was then beseeching Him was granted me. He bade me, too, consider the love for Him which was increasing daily within me, and I should then see that this experience of mine was not of the devil. He told me not to suppose that God could allow the devil to have so much to do with His servants' souls as to be able to give them the clearness of mind and the quiet that I was experiencing.[5]

As always it is love that is the test. In any case, Teresa must never be seen as a cypher, simply responding to an unseen voice.

Hers was the far harder task of discerning God's will and working with it, of using her own judgment and common sense in fulfillment of the divine purpose.

She followed her usual custom in such circumstances and consulted her confessor, though she was careful not to tell him of what she had been told in prayer. If she had any remaining doubts, they were resolved, for he too thought she should go.

On the way to Pastrana she stayed for a few days in Madrid. (It was then that she heard of the two Italian hermits who became the first friars of the Pastrana monastery for men.) Here she found herself the center of aristocratic attention; even the king's sister, Princess Juana, came to call. A contemporary chronicler recorded that:

> Many of the leading ladies of Madrid came to see her; some out of devotion, others out of curiosity. Some wanted to witness a miracle, others wanted to know the future. Oh, the natural weakness of women! But Teresa's humility was more than equal to such a situation. She spoke simply and plainly to them, and, after the initial polite exchanges were over, she steered the conversation to such neutral subjects as the beauty of the streets of Madrid.[6]

They were delighted by her. Here was a saint they could imitate. An amazed abbess declared: "She eats, sleeps and speaks like the rest of us, and is completely natural and unassuming."[7]

Teresa and her companions arrived at the small town of Pastrana to a princely welcome and were given rooms in the palace. But these two strong personalities, the dictatorial princess and the determined nun, were as incompatible as fire and water. Doña Ana had already, without a by-your-leave, bought a house and started on the alterations, but it was too small, as, indeed, was the endowment. Far worse, she made intolerable demands, interfering in every aspect of work which Teresa, reasonably enough, considered her business. The capricious princess changed her mind over the revenue and how it should be paid, she tried to dictate the size of the cells, to order the daily routine, to choose which novices were suitable — she even pressed for the acceptance in the community of a friend of hers from another Order. Ruy Gómez, discreet and diplomatic, as always struggled to control his stormy wife, to pacify her and moderate her demands, but to little avail. The arguments became increasingly heated.

The lowest point was reached when the princess found a particularly vicious way to score a point. She had heard that Teresa had written her autobiography and that it crackled with extraordinary mystical experiences. Teresa, loath to share this with anyone but close friends and confessors, was eventually persuaded with fulsome promises of inviolable secrecy to allow the princess and her husband to read it. She should have known better. Not only did the princess entertain Madrid society with her account of the *Life,* but the precious manuscript was allowed into the hands of the servants, and in no time jokes and stories circulated round the palace. Teresa was in an agony of humiliation. This, on top of the princess's endless demands, tried Teresa's patience to the limit, and she was on the brink of leaving Pastrana without making the foundation. It was only thanks to Ruy Gómez's tactful intervention that the princess and the nun eventually compromised, and at the end of June 1569, with great ceremony, the Pastrana convent was founded. Teresa had by then got the measure of her benefactor, and with commendable foresight told the nuns to make a complete inventory of everything in the convent donated by the princess.

Teresa was weary of courts and courtiers, and it was with profound relief that she left Pastrana after just two months. The princess had, however, one more humiliation in store for her: she insisted that her guests should travel back to Toledo in the ducal coach. A priest, seeing Teresa alight from this luxurious carriage, said, "So you're the saint who is deceiving everybody and going about in a carriage?" As he continued to insult her, Teresa said humbly, "You are the only one courageous enough to point out my faults." She never traveled by coach again.

For four years the nuns were "highly favored" by the prince and princess. Then Ruy Gómez died and Doña Ana, overcome with grief, decided to enter the convent as a nun. As soon as she heard the news the prioress exclaimed, "The princess a nun! That will be the end of this house!"

She was right. The princess brought her maids with her, demanding that they be admitted too. One minute she would behave with exaggerated meekness, the next insist on being treated with the honor to which she had been accustomed in the world; she disregarded the Rules, the Constitutions, the hours of Office, the rules of obedience; she came and went as she felt the whim; and she ill-treated everyone who crossed her. "The princess as a nun," wrote Teresa, "was enough to make you weep."

Eventually the scandal was such that the prioress tactfully suggested that her presence in such a humble convent was too great an honor: she should return to the court, the only place worthy of her. The princess, not deceived by this flattering dismissal, appealed to the king. He did not bother to be tactful, but simply said that her rightful place was with her ten children.

Back in her palace once more, the princess continued to find ways to wreak her revenge on the nuns, chiefly by withholding the allowance she had promised them. In an isolated village this left them penniless and starving; Teresa wrote that they were being treated like prisoners. For good measure Doña Ana also denounced Teresa's *Life* to the Inquisition. (How disappointed she must have been at their reaction. Far from condemning it, a Dominican friar appointed as censor gave it so favorable a report that it was allowed to be copied and circulated among the communities of the Reform.) Teresa decided that there was only one thing to do. One night, she sent two trusted friends to collect the nuns. Taking good care to leave behind everything the princess had given them, they stole through the deserted streets. Unfortunately the princess got wind of their plans and sent her major-domo in hot pursuit. Their plans were, however, sufficiently well advanced for them to make their escape to the accompaniment of the major-domo's shouts and complaints in the name of his mistress. They did not stop until they were safely beyond her jurisdiction.

12

Salamanca and Alba
1570–1571

> O my Joy, Lord of all things created and my God! How long must I wait before I shall see Thy Presence? What help canst Thou give to one who has so little on earth wherein she can find repose apart from Thee? O long life! O grievous life! O life which is no life at all! Oh, what utter, what helpless loneliness! When shall it end, then, Lord, when shall it end?[1]

Traveling around Spain with Teresa, witnessing her battles with financial problems, episcopal permissions, and the whims of benefactors, it is easy to forget that under her increasingly competent exterior throbbed a rich inner life; beside the gaiety and good humor ran a passionate longing to be united with God in death. While at this time she was less frequently subject to the public raptures she found so embarrassing, the depositions given at the time of her beatification tell of dramatic experiences that she could not hide. At Malagón, for instance, she was swept off her feet during Mass. Another day, in the refectory, she saw Christ bleeding copiously, not so much from the crown of thorns as from the sins of the world. Isabel de Jesús describes an occasion when she sang this verse:

> Would that my eyes could see You,
> Kind sweet Jesus,
> Would that my eyes could see You
> And then I died.

On hearing this, Teresa was so enraptured that she had to be carried back to her cell in a state of apparent unconsciousness.

However profound the significance of these visible experiences, even if they could be proved to owe as much to her state of mind and body as to the state of her soul, it is to the deep groundswell of her mystical life, beyond phenomena, that we must look to understand the person who had been accused of being "a restless gad-about." Nothing expressed this more movingly than the exquisite *Exclamations of the Soul to God,* written in 1569 on different days after she had made her Communion. These meditations, "white-hot embers from the fire of the Saint's love,"[2] show her, unusually, writing for herself rather than under obedience. It has been suggested that the rhythmical quality in the Spanish is due "to the fact that the author was setting down words which had actually come from her lips, to be repeated by her again and again and not written to be read by others."[3]

> Oh! vida! vida! ¿Cómo puede sustentarte estando ausente de tu Vida? En tanta soledad, ¿en qué te empleas? ¿Qué haces, pues todas tus obras son imperfectas y faltas? ¿Qué te consuela, oh ánima mía, en este tempestuosa mar?[4]

There is a quality of music here which transcends comprehension, and it is vivid in translation:

> O life, life, where canst thou find thy sustenance when thou art absent from thy Life? In such great loneliness, how dost thou occupy thyself? What dost thou do, since all thy actions are faulty and imperfect? Wherein dost thou find comfort, O my soul, in this stormy sea?[5]

Teresa wrote the *Exclamations* at Toledo, during the twelve months from July 1569 that she spent attending to the affairs of her recent foundation. She found Toledo stimulating, partly because she felt better in its more temperate climate. Her health had not been good for forty years, she wrote to her brother Lorenzo, in spite of keeping the Rule dutifully and only eating meat out of real necessity. But she was soon to be on her travels again. A letter came from the Jesuit rector at Salamanca. Would she found a house for Discalced Carmelites there?

She agreed, but she had learned caution. This time she asked the bishop's permission before setting out and she took only one nun and Julián de Avila — she did not want to be caught, as she had been at Medina, with several nuns and no home. Once she reached Salamanca she took care to tell no one that the house was intended as a convent; she knew there would be the familiar resistance to another drain on the city's charity.

It must have been an exceptionally uncomfortable journey, as for once she complained of the "sore trials" they endured. They traveled through snow and heat, they lost their way, on one occasion the mule carrying the money wandered off and disappeared, and they were afflicted with "numerous indispositions and fevers." Bitterly cold and tired, they arrived to find that the house they had leased was still full of students who had been renting the rooms. The young men were hastily evicted and by nightfall the two exhausted nuns gained access to the large, rambling mansion. Teresa's companion was convinced that one of the students, annoyed by having to leave, might still be hiding in one of the attics or cupboards, so they chose a room where there was some straw to serve as bedding and locked the door. Teresa recalls their first night in Salamanca in one of her most vivid passages:

> When my companion found herself shut up in the room, she seemed to be a little calmer about the students, though she did nothing all the time but look around fearfully, first in one direction and then in another. The devil must have helped in this by putting thoughts of danger into her mind in order to upset me, for, with my weak heart, very little is enough for this.
>
> "What are you looking for?" I asked her. "Nobody can possibly get in here." "Mother," she replied. "I am wondering what you would do all alone if I were to die here." If this were to happen, I thought, it would certainly be a dreadful thing; and it made me reflect for a moment, and even frightened me a little; for, though I am not afraid of dead bodies, the sight of them always affects my heart, even when I am not alone. And the tolling of the bells (for, as I have said, it was the Vigil of All Souls) gave the devil an opportunity to make us waste our time upon these childish thoughts; when he finds that he cannot frighten us in one way, he looks for other means of doing so.
>
> So I said to her: "Well, sister, I shall consider what is to be done when the occasion arises: now let me go to sleep."[6]

After two bad nights their fears were soon banished by sleep, and the following day, with the arrival of more nuns, they vanished completely. To clear up the dirt and mess left by the students took longer. Acquiring full legal possession of the house took longer still. The day after the first Mass and the official opening, the owner of the house descended on them in a rage, demanding the house back so he could sell it to provide money for his daughters. Legal wrangles continued for years; the nuns were evicted twice, and the convent was not finally established for forty-four years. "In no monastery have nuns suffered like this one," wrote Teresa.

Nevertheless it was important for her to found in Salamanca, then one of the greatest and most lively university cities in Europe, training thousands of students for service to the church, politics, and the intellectual life of the time. It was here that Luis de León, the Augustinian writer and mystic who edited Teresa's writings within a few years of her death, studied theology. Here, too, that he returned after four years' imprisonment by the Inquisition with the celebrated phrase, "As we were saying yesterday. . . ."

Teresa's own attitude to learning was ambivalent. The controversy between the *letrados* and the *espirituales* (the theologians and the "spirituals") was raging fiercely throughout most of her life, but, while she stood with the spirituals and was adamant that theology should be related to experience, she had a healthy respect for learning and frequently sided with the theologians. Always conscious of her own lack of education as a woman, she looked to men for intellectual support, often saying she never did anything without consulting "learned men." She trusted such people and enjoyed talking to them, frequently commending the habit to others.

This love of learning is most striking in her choice of confessors. One of her favorites, Domingo Bañez, is said to have remarked, "She preferred learned men to those who were merely pious." On the other hand she distrusted the half-educated, feeling that confessors with only a little learning had done her great harm:

> I have discovered by experience that if they are virtuous and lead holy lives it is better they should have none at all

> than only a little; for then they do not trust themselves (nor would I myself trust them) unless they have first consulted those who are really learned; but a truly learned man never led me astray.[7]

She learned first from experience, with its own undeniable truth, but she knew that this must be set in the context of knowledge and tempered with common sense. Her admiration of learning was part of her passion for truth. As she grew older she became more sure of her intellectual abilities, less apologetic for being a "mere woman." She once asked four men to consider a phrase she had heard inwardly and found obscure — "Seek thyself in Me." She was then told by the bishop of Avila to write a *Judgment* on their written commentaries. After the obligatory protest that she was only doing so under obedience, she is remarkably confident. Julián de Avila "begins well, but he finishes badly"; she felt he had missed the point. Of her brother Lorenzo's advice about the prayer of quiet she says memorably, with gentle irony: "God grant that, as he has been so near the honey, some of it may stick to him." And of John of the Cross's contribution she writes:

> This Father in his reply gives some remarkably sound doctrine for those who are thinking of following the Exercises practiced in the Company of Jesus, but it is not to our purpose. It would be a bad business for us if we could not seek God until we were dead to the world. . . . God deliver me from people who are so spiritual that they want to turn everything into perfect contemplation.[8]

The directness of this affectionate reproof to a man she held in such high regard shows the mature Teresa, firm in experience, buttressed by knowledge and free to speak her mind.

Teresa's eighth foundation was at Alba de Tormes, a town near Avila dominated by the castle of the dukes of Alba. The present duke, a soldier, was away at the time suppressing a rebellion in the Netherlands. He was one of the most influential people of his day, but he belonged to a faction of the Spanish court opposed to Ruy Gómez, the prince of Eboli, and his supporters. It is a measure of Teresa's diplomacy that she was able to move so freely between the two families, and a measure of her popularity that both sides were eager to associate themselves with her. Both the duke and his wife were so keen to have one of Teresa's convents in their town that, while she was at Salamanca, only fifteen miles away from Alba, a messenger was sent begging her to make a foundation there. Teresa had no desire to satisfy them. The place was so small that an income would be necessary, and she never willingly gave in to accepting an endowment, though she became fairly pragmatic on the subject, in the end founding seven convents with an income. Alba was one of them, but the foundation might never have been made had not Teresa been moved by the story of the woman who was to become the foundress.

Teresa de Layz was the fifth daughter of a noble family, who were so distressed at producing yet another girl, that, apart from seeing that she was baptized, they neglected the baby completely. The story goes that on the third night after her birth her nanny, upset at such cruel treatment, took the baby in her arms saying, "Why, my poor little child, anyone would think you were not a Christian!" To the astonishment of the woman and others who were with her the child raised its head saying, "But I am." These were the only words she spoke until she reached the normal age of speech, but her mother was sufficiently impressed by the incident to mend her ways and look after her child properly.

The child became a woman, was duly married and lived happily with her husband in Salamanca. There was only one sadness: they had no children. One night, after she had been beseeching God to grant her desire to be a mother, she heard a voice saying, "Do not wish for children or you will send yourself to damnation." She was frightened by this, but the desire did not leave her and she continued praying, particularly to St. Andrew. Then, one night, she had a dream-like vision. She was in a house whose courtyard had a well; outside was a beautiful green meadow carpeted with white flowers. A figure that she knew was St. Andrew was standing by the well, and she heard him say, "These are different children from those thou desirest."

Next morning, with the curious conviction that can come from dream language, she knew that this meant she should found a convent, but what sort of convent and where? Her musings were interrupted by a message from Alba. The duchess wanted her husband to take up a position in the ducal household. Teresa de Layz detested the place, but she had no option. How amazed was she when, waking in her new home on the very first morning, she recognized it, its courtyard and the well, as the place of her vision.

Immediately delighted to be there and confident in the vision, she considered the Order to which her convent was to belong. She knew it must have only a few nuns and that it should be strictly enclosed. She took advice and soon heard of the monasteries of Our Lady of Carmel that were being founded. The two Teresas had some trouble coming to an agreement about the endowment — if it was to be endowed, then it had to be adequate — but eventually the matter was settled to their mutual satisfaction and, on January 25, 1571, the foundation was made.

Writing about the foundress of the convent at Alba, Teresa allows herself a brief outburst on the prevailing attitude to women. Why should the de Layz family be so disappointed at having only daughters?

> It is certainly a matter for deep regret that mortals, not knowing what is best for them, and being wholly ignorant of the judgments of God, do not realize what great blessings can come from having daughters or what great harm can come from having sons, and, unwilling, apparently, to leave the matter to Him Who understands everything and is the Creator of us all, worry themselves to death about what ought to make them glad.[9]

Teresa has been called a feminist, both in accusatory terms and by those who applaud her for it. Whether she truly was can only be decided in the light of what being a feminist really means, and that, given the confusion which surrounds the term today, is not easy to determine.

If to be a feminist is to adopt masculine characteristics and spurn the feminine, then Teresa does not belong to their ranks. If it is to seek to change laws and consciously modify the views of society, then she could not be counted among them. If, however, a feminist is one who takes up the cudgels on behalf of an oppressed group in society and, by her own example, reveals hidden, suppressed potential in her sex; if she is one who becomes fully herself, fully human, by using *all* her qualities; if she is someone who does what she feels has to be done without waiting for permission, then Teresa's light shines across the centuries.

It is true, of course, that she was fighting for God rather than for women, yet simply by being a woman she advanced their position. True also that she was frequently forced by the times she lived in to assert herself deviously, by flattery and humility, and that in doing that she could be accused of colluding with the paternalistic church. Nevertheless, without deliberately setting out to do so, Teresa made her contribution to the cause of women. She might even be considered an example to those Christian women who seek in vain for a role model in the masculine structures of the church.

With certain reservations, she was content to be a woman, though she constantly belittles her sex. Her writings abound with remarks like "since we have no learning," "women have weak constitutions and the love of self that reigns in us is very subtle," "It should be remembered that the weakness of our nature is very great, especially in women," "I should not like your Lordship to pay any heed to what we silly women say," and "women are like that, timorous creatures, most of them." On the other hand she was aware of men's failure to understand women. She wrote firmly to a priest friend telling him not to try to sum women up too easily: "We make our confessions year in, year out, and yet our confessors are amazed at how little they have learned about us. The reason is that even we find ourselves so difficult to understand that we cannot tell our own faults, and our confessors can judge us only by what we tell them."[10]

She regarded herself as of tougher mettle than most women, affirming that she "abhorred what people call 'talking like women' " and that she had "a stout heart." She once wrote to no less a person than the Carmelite general, telling him that, "although we women are not much use as counselors, we are occasionally right." The reprimand behind that apparently humble remark is unmistakable. Her constant deprecations about the inadequacy of her sex were partly tongue-in-cheek, partly a cry of outrage at the discrimination she constantly saw in action and at the position society forced upon them. At heart she admired women, as her spirited defense in *The Way of Perfection* shows. The attitudes she met daily are encapsulated in the fact that this passage was, in the first edition, erased by the censor. Happily it is now restored:

> When you walked on this earth, Lord, you did not despise women; rather you always helped them and showed great compassion toward them. And you found as much love and more faith in them than you did in men. . . . Is it not enough, Lord, that the world has intimidated us, so that we may not do anything worthwhile for you in public or dare to speak some truths that we lament over in secret, without your also failing to hear our just petition? I do not believe, Lord, that this could be true of your goodness and justice, for you are a just judge and not like those of the world. Since the world's judges are sons of Adam and all of them men, there is no virtue in women that they do not hold suspect. . . . when I see what the times are like, I feel it is not right to repel spirits which are virtuous and brave, even though they be the spirits of women.[11]

Her attitude to marriage is also ambivalent. Pragmatic as always, she rejoices when her friends marry, even giving advice — the bridegroom should be mature, the bride of an affectionate disposition. Yet she clearly regards marriage as a hindrance to the spiritual life. She tells her nuns how if her husband is sad, his wife must be sad too; if cheerful, then she must appear cheerful too: "See what slavery you have escaped from, sisters!"

As far as she herself was concerned, beyond her admission that when she was young she was afraid of it, Teresa's thoughts about marriage are veiled in mystery. Nor do her reported denials of sexual feelings accord with the full human being she unquestionably was. What is clear is that she could not see why the "masculine" qualities of courage, determination, daring, effort, and learning should be monopolized by men. Why should not women, as she encouraged her nuns, be "so manly that men themselves will be amazed at you." Her own life, from her childish expedition in search of the Moors, through the maze of normally masculine affairs in which she moved with such determination when reforming her Order, spoke for itself. She did not set out to reform the position of women, but, in living out her own personality, in accepting and using the heady combination of both masculine and feminine elements in her nature, she changed men's perception of women and women's perception of themselves.

Six months after founding the convent at Alba de Tormes, Teresa made a formal renunciation of the Mitigated Rule in favor of the Primitive. Three months later she became prioress of the Convent of the Incarnation in Avila, the very convent she had left in order to live the reformed life. This curious appointment, putting Teresa in a highly embarrassing position, is a dramatic example of her devotion to obedience in practice.

While requests for Discalced Carmelite convents were pouring in from rich and devout benefactors, there were others who saw Teresa's Reform as so threatening that it must be stopped. One of these was the Carmelite provincial, Ángel de Salazar, who had always been ambiguous in his attitude to the Reform. Unwilling though he was to embrace Teresa's ideals, he was worried by the state of affairs at the Incarnation, where numbers were dropping and the novitiate had already been closed, laxity was increased and the finances were in such a bad state that the nuns were approaching starvation. Though the authorities were keen to lay the blame on Teresa, they also realized that she was the one person who might save the convent from total collapse. Even more to the provincial's liking, it would, they hoped, put a stop to the apparently endless succession of reformed monasteries springing up all over Spain. Surely even she had not enough energy and determination to be prioress of one convent, govern eight others, and found yet more? He persuaded the apostolic delegate, the Dominican provincial Pedro Fernández, that Teresa should reform her old convent, though she must not, of course, lure them from the Mitigated to the Unmitigated Rule.

To say that Teresa was unwilling would be an understatement. She would be nearly sixty — a considerable age at that time — when her term of office ended. It was a fearful assignment, to be prioress at the self-indulgent convent she had left in favor of a stricter life, to have to govern the same nuns who had witnessed the turmoil which surrounded the founding of St. Joseph's and who had ridiculed her. She knew that the nuns opposed her appointment, but she could have borne that. Far harder was the knowledge that it would put a stop to her control over the communities she had founded and governed; it could even be the end of the Reform. There was nothing about it that appealed to her, yet she hesitated only briefly. Her instinct, as always, was to obey her superiors, and this instinct was confirmed by her inner voice. While she was at prayer God said to her:

> Oh, daughter, daughter, those nuns of the Incarnation are sisters of mine and thou holdest back from helping them. Take courage, then. See, I will it so, and it is not as difficult as it seems to thee: thou thinkest that by thy going there these other houses will lose, whereas in reality both will gain.[12]

She did not attempt to resist such unequivocal advice. She traveled to Avila and, on October 6, 1571, she walked in formal procession to the convent which had for so long been her home.

The scenes that followed must have surpassed her worst imaginings. The nuns, accustomed to electing their own superiors, were outraged that they should have Teresa forced upon them, were fearful at losing their comfortable way of life, and felt threatened by the austerity they presumed would be imposed on them. The citizens of Avila, though with less personal reasons, resented the return of the nun whom they remembered as the cause of such commotion ten years earlier. As the procession wound its way through the streets, Teresa carrying the statue of St. Joseph which she took for her foundations, the crowds shouted hysterical abuse. They reached the convent only to find their way so firmly blocked by a group of the most vociferous nuns that two friars had to force their way through the doors. At last Teresa was seated in the choir, and Ángel de Salazar read the letters patent. He could have spared himself the trouble, for such was the shrieking, swearing, and jeering that the reading could not be heard. Through the din the provincial shouted, "In short, you do not want to accept Mother Teresa of Jesus!" At this a solitary voice of support made itself heard: "We accept her and we love her." Thus encouraged, a few more showed their timid agreement and began to sing the *Te Deum*, but the pandemonium continued. Only when Teresa stood and faced the angry crowd did the noise subside.

Her first action as prioress showed tactful diplomacy amounting to genius. In the afternoon the nuns went to the chapel for their first chapter meeting with their new leader. To their amazement they saw in the prioress's stall, not Teresa, but a lifesize statue of Our Lady, the keys to the convent hanging from her hand; Teresa sat at her feet. It was Our Lady, not Teresa, who would be the new prioress. The words which accompanied this dramatic symbolic act were recorded by some of the nuns present. They are a model of discretion and leadership:

> My ladies, mothers and sisters: Our Lord has sent me to this house, by virtue of obedience, to hold this office, which I had never thought of and which I am far from deserving.
>
> This election has greatly distressed me, both because it has laid upon me a task which I shall be unable to perform, and also because it has deprived you of the freedom of election which you used to enjoy and given you a prioress whom you would not have chosen at your will and pleasure, and a prioress who would be accomplishing a great deal if she could succeed in learning from the least of you here all the good that is in her.[13]

They need not fear, she went on. Though she would continue to follow the rule of the Discalced, they need only follow their own rule. Her one desire was that they should all "serve the Lord in quietness." God would see that their deeds became commensurate with their desires and intentions.

13

Reluctant Prioress
1571–1574

Teresa once said that she feared a discontented nun more than she feared many devils. Now she was in charge of close to two hundred nuns not only generally discontented but also many of them quite specifically discontented with her and her appointment. Teresa, for her part, would have preferred to found any number of convents with small numbers of eager applicants longing to follow her ideals than to reform this huge, undisciplined house filled with nuns who were quite happy as they were. But *determinación, determinación.* She had committed herself to the task, and she would do it.

The way she had dealt with her turbulent induction had given her an auspicious start, but she found little comfort in it. Nor did she find the climate of her hometown suited to her health. She was rarely well, suffering from quinsy, quartan ague, and pains in both her side and her face. After just a month she was writing wistfully to Doña Luisa. "Oh, my lady, to have experienced the tranquillity of our (Discalced) houses, and then to find oneself in this hurly-burly! I don't know how anyone can live here at all." Yet, even as she wrote, she was able to add: "Glory be to God, there is peace here now — that is something."

The irony was that she had achieved peace by imposing some of the restrictions the nuns had dreaded: for instance, she admits she cut down on the nuns' entertainments and curtailed their freedom. But, true pragmatist that she was, she had lost no time in improving their material circumstances and at least they had full stomachs. Much against her will — she never quite gave up her preference for her convents to pay their own way — she appealed for money to feed the hungry nuns; more cheerfully she wrote to her sister Juana, "Send me the turkeys, since you have so many." Once the debts were paid, she showed tact and sensitivity in giving a tiny weekly allowance to the poorest of the nuns, thus giving them an equality and dignity worth far more to them than their poverty-stricken laxity and freedom.

Her first Lent was marked by the imposition of further constraints, as she forbade all visitors, even parents. One gentleman visitor was so persistent and abusive that she eventually showed her mettle in a way unusual for her: If he did not desist, she informed him, she would appeal to the king. The story soon spread round Avila and the citizens approved. So did the clergy, one of whom remarked to a friend who had told him Teresa was a woman: "You informed me wrongly. I' faith she's a man and one of those most worthy to wear a beard." Strength and determination were not considered possible attributes in a woman.

Peace was sustained. Five months into her unwilling tenure of office she wrote of the nuns: "Our Lord be praised for the change which He has wrought in them. Those who were the most obstinate before are now the most contented, and I get on better with them. . . . Really some of them are great servants of God, and nearly all of them are better than they were."[1]

What was the secret of her success as a leader? She was decisive, humorous, tactful, pragmatic, efficient, and strict. Yet it was, above all, the mixture of characteristics responsible for many of the tensions in her life which combined to make her one of the outstanding Christian leaders of the past 450 years: her charisma, matched by what has been called her "extraordinary ordinariness,"[2] her ability to lead from the front and to inspire confidence, curiously balanced by a deep and genuine humility, her willingness to change traditional structures while remaining firmly in the arms of the church, and her sense of outer purpose finding its strength in the ready ear she gave to her inner voices. Her own writings, in particular her letters, supply ample proof of these qualities. Who, reading these instructions on the wearing of veils, could be in any doubt as to her intentions?

> There is no reason why they should ever be seen without their veils by their confessors or by friars of any Order — least of all by our Discalced friars. It might be explained to them that they need not wear their veils when they are with very close relatives, or with an uncle who has brought them up because she has no father — that is quite reasonable — or in the presence of a duchess, a countess, or any other person of importance. Anywhere, in fact, where there is anything to be gained, and no risk run. Except in such cases, the veil may not be raised. If any other doubtful case presents itself, the provincial had better be communicated with and his permission asked. If it is not granted, the veil must be worn.[3]

This decisiveness could lead to an almost peremptory tone. Teresa was never frightened of saying precisely what she meant: "She cannot be given the habit till she is twelve, nor be professed till she is sixteen, so there is no point in discussing the matter yet."[4]

Like many strong leaders, she had problems with giving up control, even of delegating. Though she found the trappings and responsibilities of leadership wearisome, she enjoyed power and was in no hurry to relinquish it. Her attention to detail — another characteristic of many pioneers and reformers — meant that she found it hard to leave decisions, even tiny ones, to others. Up to the end of her life she was issuing instructions on even the most minor matters — the purchase of a stove so that its metal could be wrought into a chalice or the material used for the stockings and coifs worn by the nuns. One of the prioresses of St. Joseph's at Avila admitted that Teresa's concern for her beloved first convent (and, she might have added, her difficulty in delegating) led to her always being, in effect, the prioress and "the nun whom she left in charge had very little to do in the governing of it."

If her constantly controlling hand or her assertiveness caused offense, it must have been healed by the pragmatic pliancy of which she was capable when occasion demanded. Again this sometimes concerned the most minute details: "It would matter very little if it were necessary for her to eat meat all the time, even during Lent. In cases of real need this is not contrary to the Rule, so you must not be too inflexible about it."[5]

To be flexible requires great inner confidence — it is the weak who need to keep to the letter rather than the spirit. Teresa could be almost harsh in her dismissal of a rigid adherence to some unrealistic ideal and she had no hesitation in saying so: "I am annoyed at the way the prioress is fasting. Tell her so: I don't want to write to her myself, or to have anything to do with her, for that very reason. God preserve me from people who would rather have their own way than do as they are told."[6]

The recipient of her rough pragmatism could have been stimulated, disturbed, or enraged. It might have shaken the fearful who preferred to cling to the rules; it could have offered a welcome relief from conventional attitudes. From the safe distance of the twenty-first century it is, above all, refreshing. For instance, she gave a bracing reprimand to an unknown benefactor who feared he was wasting Teresa's time by coming to see her and felt such self-indulgence should be regarded as a sin. "As for your saying that there is anything in this to go to confession about, or that you ought not to come here, there seems more scrupulousness in that than virtue. I am very much displeased with you about it, but I suppose you cannot be faultless — after all, you are a son of Adam."[7]

In advising her prioresses Teresa took the same approach — good sense blended with a firm grasp of reality. It is not possible, she asserts, to guide all souls by the same yardstick: "You must treat that sister to whom our Father gave the habit as though she were ill; do not trouble in the least about how perfect she is. It will be sufficient if she does what she can as well as she can."[8] Often this cocktail of common sense was laced with humor. She could not, for instance, bring herself to share the distress which many priests working with her felt at the inaccurate and hurtful things often said about them: "I was extremely distressed that our Father should have brought evidence in disproof of those particularly scandalous things that have been said against us. They are so ridiculous that the best thing to do is to laugh at them. For my own part, I almost like hearing them."[9]

The business side of leadership occupied much of her time and energy, which she resented; she would have preferred to spend the time in prayer. She herself often recorded the daily income and expenditure of her convents, as shown by her signature in the account books. She continually faced lawsuits and was rarely free from financial worries. If, in truth, this provided a necessary balance in her life, the bread and butter to the honey of her mystical experiences, she would have preferred it otherwise:

> Once, when I was thinking how much purer are the lives of those who have not to engage in business, and how badly I always get on and how many mistakes I always make in business matters, I heard these words: "There is no help for that, daughter. Strive thou always to have a right intention and to be detached in everything, and look to Me, so that all thine actions may be in accordance with Mine."[10]

There is as much comfort in this reconciliation of the mundane with the spiritual as in the higher flights of Teresa's mystical prose. Her life shows that involvement with prosaic details need not be incompatible with a life whose real purpose is seeking God.

Of her characteristics as a leader the most profound and ail-embracing were her humility and her love. One of her prioresses testified that she was the first to use the dustpan and brush, and that she would frequently prostrate herself at the feet of the nuns, entreating pardon for her faults. If she realized that a nun was cherishing a grievance about a reproof, she would throw herself at her feet, begging forgiveness.

Her mature thoughts on leadership have the simplicity of authority and experience. Whatever the virtues of directness, decisiveness, or efficiency, she was in no doubt where real leadership lay. In her mid-sixties she wrote to one of her prioresses encapsulating her attitude: "You know, I no longer govern the way I used to. Love does everything. I am not sure if that is because no one gives me cause to reprove her, or because I have discovered that things go better that way."[11]

A good leader knows her priorities. A woman as practical, down-to-earth, and motherly as Teresa knew that hungry nuns would not be open either to reform or to spiritual guidance. But once the convent was running smoothly and material needs were assured, she lost no time in caring for their souls. In the summer of 1572 she requested that John of the Cross, her "Father in God," be appointed as confessor to the nuns. He remained with them for nearly five years.

It was an inspired choice, and she herself was delighted. "I am bringing you a saint for your confessor!" she announced triumphantly. His suitability rested not only in his sanctity and his skill as a director, but in the complementary natures of the two mystics. Where she was subjective and personal, he was objective, detached; where she was a pragmatist, he moved easily in theories and absolutes; ironically, where she was almost masculine in her determination and forthrightness, he was almost feminine in his sensitivity. With one as prioress and the other as confessor, the nuns could call on the full range of spiritual qualities.

Any personal problems between John and Teresa were slight and usually amiable enough. His feelings for her were such that he was able to tease her, for instance saying, "When you make your confession, Mother, you have a way of finding the prettiest of excuses!" But his respect ran so deep that he excused himself from describing the states of rapture and ecstasy on the grounds that "the blessed Teresa of Jesus, our mother" had already done it so well there was no need.

Though by now, partly as a result of John's influence, she placed less emphasis on mystical phenomena, through her entire period as prioress at the Incarnation, her health bad and her task daunting, she found constant sustenance in her inner voices; her intimate friendship with God continued to manifest itself in visions, locutions, and raptures. Her diplomatic coup in placing a statue of Our Lady in the prioress's stall was affirmed when, during the singing of the *Salve Regina,* she saw the Mother of God herself seated in that very place, surrounded by angels. One Palm Sunday, such was her identification with Christ's suffering that she felt her mouth fill with blood as she took the communion host. Toward the end of her first year as prioress she had one of her most remarkable intellectual visions of the Holy Trinity. In this revelation she perceived three distinct persons. The Son alone took human flesh, but:

> In all Three persons there is not more than one will and one power and one dominion, so that none of them can do anything without Another. . . . Could the Son create an Ant without the Father? . . . Could we love the Father without loving the Son and the Holy Spirit? No, for whoever pleases One of these Three Divine Persons pleases all Three: and equally so with whoever offends them.[12]

Now, she wrote, she knew exactly what she had been taught by "learned men"; she had, through direct experience, understood the mystery that has taxed the greatest theologians for two thousand years. But she had grasped it with her intuition and her heart, rather than with her mind. So, for instance, she knew that all three persons of the Trinity were involved in the Incarnation, but "I do not busy myself in thinking a great deal about it." Though she knew, resoundingly, that God is all powerful, "the less I understand this, the more I believe it and the greater is the devotion it arouses in me. Blessed be He forever! Amen."

One of the highest mystical graces of her life was a direct result of John's gentle chiding. It occurred on November 18, 1572. Teresa was making her communion when John deliberately divided the host between her and another sister. Though Teresa's intellect told her she was receiving the Lord "whole and entire" in the smallest particle, she preferred a large host, and John knew it. He was, Teresa was convinced, wanting to mortify her. The Lord assured her that she need not fear, nothing would be able to separate her from him. Then he appeared to her in an imaginary vision, giving her his right hand and saying:

> "Behold this nail. It is a sign that from today onward thou shalt be My bride. Until now, thou hadst not merited this; but from henceforward thou shalt regard My honor not only as that of thy Creator and king and God but as that of My very bride. My honor is thine, and thine Mine."
>
> This favor produced such an effect upon me that I could not restrain myself but became like a person who is foolish, and begged the Lord either to exalt my lowliness or to show me fewer favors, for I really did not think my nature could endure them. For the whole of that day I remained completely absorbed.[13]

This was the mystical marriage of Teresa of Jesus and her God. One by one the threads that bound Teresa to her own will were being severed. Now she was completely detached from the things of the world, free of desires for herself; she was joined forever with God. To this day the sisters approach with awe the communion rails where this miraculous espousal took place.

For well over a year Teresa was confined to the Convent of the Incarnation, not only by the pressure of her duties, but by those in authority over her. By now she was responsible for eight convents; she needed to visit them, to support the nuns and settle business affairs. But her superiors, backed by Rome, would not let her leave Avila. She was virtually imprisoned.

Even an appeal from the duchess of Alba failed, so Teresa overrode ecclesiastical authority and wrote to King Philip II, who immediately granted her request. In February 1573 she left for

Alba, where she had one of her numerous practical affairs to deal with, this time settling a quarrel between her brother-in-law, Juan de Ovalle, and the nuns about who should be responsible for surfacing a lane. Her immediate return to Avila must have given her superiors confidence that she would not stray too far or for too long, for thereafter she was free to travel. In August she set out for Salamanca.

It was a terrible journey. To avoid the heat, they set out late at night. Two of the company fell from their mounts, they lost the donkey carrying the money, and for a while they even lost Teresa herself. Then, as Julián of Avila recounts:

> We stumbled upon an inn so overcrowded with muleteers that they were even sleeping on the ground, and it was impossible to take one step without treading on harness or on sleeping men. At last we found a small space for our Holy Mother and the sisters we were bringing with us, although there were not six feet of empty space; to fit in at all they were obliged to stand up. Such inns had one good point about them, that we impatiently awaited the hour of our departure.[14]

The main purpose of Teresa's visit to Salamanca was to arrange the transfer of the nuns to their new house, but it was while she was there that, once again under religious obedience, she somehow found time to write the first nine chapters of the charming account of her Reform known simply as *The Foundations* (*Fundaciones*). She also received instructions to found yet another convent: "One day when I was in prayer there, I was told by Our Lord to go and make a foundation at Segovia."

One reason why Teresa was keen to found a house in Segovia was that she needed a refuge for the Pastrana nuns, harassed as they were by the autocratic princess of Eboli. But how could she? She had received no invitation; Pedro Fernández, the apostolic delegate for Castile, did not want her to make any further foundations; she had not yet finished her term at the Incarnation — and she was more than fully occupied. But the Lord insisted, telling her to write to the delegate and that all would be well.

At her most diplomatic, she penned a careful letter, assuring Fernández that she was only writing to relieve her conscience and that she would do just as he wished, but slipping in a reminder that the Carmelite general had ordered her to make foundations wherever she saw the opportunity and that she was sure such a convent would be of service to God. As so often, her tact paid off. To her astonishment, Fernández replied at once, giving her permission and sending the license.

She had neither money nor benefactor, so she arranged to take a house on lease, confident that God would provide. He did. A rich and devout widow, Doña Ana de Jimena, promised to cover all their material needs, and the founding party set out from Avila. It was larger than usual. There were four nuns, John of the Cross, Julián of Avila, a devout layman from Alba called Antonio Gaytán, and Teresa herself. They arrived after dark, but everything had been so well prepared for them that all they had to do was decorate the altar. The next morning, March 19, 1574, Julián said Mass and reserved the Blessed Sacrament. Segovia could now boast Teresa's ninth foundation.

Teresa was ill, for she had arrived with a fever, and she was also suffering from "a distaste for everything and much aridity and great darkness of soul." Even so, she was so accustomed to practical problems that she was puzzled by their apparent absence.

Her apprehensions were soon justified. The scenes that were to take place savor of theatrical farce.

The people of Segovia, seeing a convent spring up in their town, complained to the vicar general, who arrived in a tearing rage. He refused to allow the Mass to be said, ordered the altar to be dismantled and the Blessed Sacrament removed. He even tried to imprison the priest, John of the Cross himself. Julián de Avila hid under the stairs, while the nuns retreated behind the grille. Only Teresa, never particularly troubled once they had taken possession of a house, was calm. Eventually the irate cleric left, but not before stationing a policeman at the door.

The vicar general had met his match. Teresa "sent for some people...who were important people in the town." They explained that Teresa had a license from the bishop, albeit only a verbal one. The vicar general had known that all along, he later admitted, but his dignity was affronted — why had he not been informed beforehand? Teresa's friends mollified him, eventually persuading him to allow the nuns to remain, but, as if anxious to prove he had some authority, he insisted on removing the Blessed Sacrament.

In less than three weeks Teresa had installed the unhappy nuns from Pastrana,[15] but she stayed in Segovia for a few months, as so often dealing with the seemingly inevitable lawsuits. This time they concerned two religious Orders, the Franciscans and the Mercedarians (a religious Order for men founded in the thirteenth century).

> O Jesus, what a trouble it is to have to strive against the opinions of so many people! When I thought it was all settled, it all began again, for it was not enough to give them what they asked: they at once found some fresh obstacle.

> When I write of it like this it seems nothing, but it was very hard to endure.[16]

Teresa was back in Avila by the end of September 1574, where a week later, her term as prioress over, she returned to her beloved St. Joseph's. Now she had to prepare for the longest journey she had yet undertaken.

14

Gracián
1575

By 1575 proposals to make foundations were flooding in, and to some extent Teresa could pick and choose. Some offers were considered and rejected, some fell through, some were postponed and some accepted. But always Teresa gave the invitations serious consideration and often she was surprisingly rewarded, never more so than when she agreed to found a house in Beas de Segura.

The invitation had come from a group of people living in this town on the border of Castile and Andalusia, including the parish priest. In some ways it was a tempting offer. Beas was a delightful place with a pleasant climate, a house was ready for their use, and a warm welcome was assured. But there were serious objections. It was a long journey, well over 350 miles from Salamanca, where Teresa was staying when she received the invitation; she was at the time still fully occupied with her duties as prioress at the Incarnation and, most seriously of all, she knew that many of her superiors were opposed to her making further foundations. But she could never forget Rubeo's instructions to found as many convents "as she had hairs on her head," so she did not feel able to refuse without first referring the matter to the apostolic commissary.

He, too, played safe. He was not overkeen on Teresa traveling around Castile looking after the convents she had already founded, still less did he want her founding yet more and in such distant parts. But he did not want to be the one to stand in her way, so, as Beas belonged to the Knights of Santiago, he told her to ask their permission, confident that the request would be refused, as so many before had been — indeed there was at the time no convent of any sort in Beas. However, the commissary's confidence was misplaced. To his chagrin and to everyone's surprise a license was obtained without any difficulty, and as soon as Teresa's term as prioress at the Incarnation had ended, preparations for the journey were begun.

The large party — ten nuns, including Ana de Jesús, so beautiful that she was known as "Queen of the World," Antonio Gaytán, Julián de Avila, and another priest — arrived at Beas on February 16, 1575. In the midst of winter they had crossed the plains of La Mancha, the Guadarrama mountains and the notorious Despeñaperros pass, yet the journey seems to have been, for the most part, surprisingly uneventful. But by now legends were gathering round these traveling religious, and in some parts of Spain to this day, over four centuries later, stories are told about them and their redoubtable foundress. Two of these, said to originate from this journey, have a distinctly Teresian ring.

Tradition has it that Teresa and her party stopped at the house of a nobleman, who prepared a banquet in their honor, at which such luxuries as partridge were to be served. How would Teresa react to such a delicacy? Would she refuse it? Typically, she simply enjoyed the meal, saying, "If it's partridge, then let it be partridge; if penance, let it be penance."

The other incident savors of the supernatural. Near Despeñaperros the party took a wrong turn, realized they were lost, and, at Teresa's injunction, began to pray to St. Joseph. At once they heard a distant voice calling out that they must stop immediately, otherwise they would fall over a precipice. They obeyed the invisible command and discovered they were indeed in a perilous position, a chasm yawning beneath the wagon wheels, but what could they do? How could they turn round in the narrow path? The voice told them to go gently backward for a hundred turns of the wheels; they would come to no harm and would find the track again. It was just as the voice said. The grateful muleteers searched for their benefactor, thinking to find a friendly shepherd, but could find no one. Teresa knew they would not. She knew it was the voice of St. Joseph, answering their prayers.

They arrived in Beas in sunlight and triumph. Julián de Avila recorded the warm welcome they received:

> The whole town, young and old alike, turned out to greet them with great rejoicing. Outriders on horseback escorted their wagon to the church grounds, where everyone had gathered to meet them. The clergy, dressed in surplices and led by a cross-bearer, formed a procession, and thus conducted them to the church with all due solemnity.[1]

If the founding of this convent had been the smoothest of the ten Teresa had so far established, the joy ahead of her was even greater. It was in Beas that she met the man who was to be, for the rest of her life, her closest friend. Though she was sixty at the time, ill and tired, and he was only half her age, it was in this relationship that Teresa was most herself—foundress and woman, mystic and mother, lover and beloved.

Jerónimo Gracián was born in 1545, one of a family of twenty-one children. His father was secretary to Emperor Charles V, his mother a daughter of the Polish ambassador to Madrid. Jerónimo was educated by the Jesuits and took a brilliant degree at the University of Alcalá. He was ordained a priest in 1570 and joined the Discalced Carmelites at Pastrana two years later. He was clearly the most exceptional young man: gifted, eloquent, learned, courteous, modest, zealous, and courageous. He is said to have deputized for his teachers while still a student at university and, at Pastrana, was made novice master while still himself a novice. Just over a year after joining the Carmelites he was made apostolic visitor to the Calced Carmelites in Andalusia, and two years later (just after he met Teresa) he was also given authority over the Discalced friars and nuns in Castile. This uncomfortable dual appointment, together with his personal success, inevitably made him the object of jealousy and criticism.

Teresa and Gracián had, of course, known of each other for some time and had already exchanged letters. Having heard such good reports of him, Teresa was anxious to meet him, but when they began to talk "he pleased me so much that it seemed to me as if those who had praised him to me hardly knew him at all." The rapport between them was immediate. Gracián has recorded how they had spoken to each other without any reservation and agreed about everything. For her part, Teresa was not only charmed by him but also saw how useful he could be to the reform. She wrote to one of her prioresses with almost girlish enthusiasm:

> Oh, Mother, how much I have wished you were with me during these last few days! I must tell you that, without exaggeration, I think they have been the best days in my life. For over three weeks we have had Father-Master Gracián here; and, much as I have had to do with him, I assure you I have not yet fully realized his worth. To me, he is perfect, and better for our needs than anyone else we could have asked God to send us. What your Reverence and all the

> nuns must do now is to beg His Majesty to give him to us as a superior. If that happens, I can take a rest from governing these houses, for anyone so perfect, and yet so gentle, I have never seen. May God have him in His keeping, and preserve him; I would not have missed seeing him and having to do with him for anything in the world.[2]

Soon, as her priestly friends so often did, Gracián became her confessor, though she stresses that she did not allow herself to be directed by him entirely. (Apart from any other considerations, she did not want to offend the priest who was already her confessor.) After she had made her confession to Gracián several times, she had a vision. It only lasted for as long as a flash of lightning, but it was to have lasting consequences. She thought she saw Christ "in the form in which His Majesty is wont to reveal Himself to me." Gracián was on his right side, while she was on his left. Christ took their right hands, joined them and told Teresa that, for the rest of her life, Gracián was to take his place and that they were to agree in everything.

Twice this vision was repeated, until she was convinced of what she had to do: she would make a solemn vow of lifelong obedience to Gracián. It was not an easy decision. "I realized that, if I made this promise, I should have no freedom, interior or exterior, for all the rest of my life.... I feel I have never in my life done anything, or made any profession, that caused me more repugnance, save when I left my father's house to become a nun."[3] And then, remember, she felt that every bone in her body seemed to be "wrenched asunder." But she did not find the promise as oppressive as she feared, for she adds: "Blessed be He Who has raised up someone to satisfy my needs and thus to give me strength to do this." She must also have been fortified by Gracián's similar, though less formal, promise. He wrote that from the moment of their meeting he did nothing of importance without first consulting her.

The importance of Gracián in Teresa's life owes much to the fact that he complemented and fulfilled her at so many levels. With him she could be totally open about all things, whether her spiritual life, the problems concerning the convents, her health, or her hopes for the Reform. He was her father in God, her superior, her son, her brother, her friend and confidant: she cherished him and treated him with the teasing familiarity of a lover.

All these aspects of their friendship can be seen in her letters, both to Gracián himself and when she writes of him to others. Unfortunately none of his letters to her survive, but of the numerous letters she wrote to him over a hundred remain to vouch for this intimate and rewarding relationship. Though he wrote less frequently than she — something that worried and saddened her — he valued her letters so highly that he bound them lovingly into a book said to measure four inches thick.

Writing to Gracián Teresa is at her most lively, impulsive, and loving. Their intimacy is enhanced by her use of code-names, partly for fear of prying eyes (much of their correspondence took place during the strife that was to disrupt the Order for several years), partly because of her clear delight in this conspiratorial dimension of their relationship. She refers to herself as "Angela" or "Laurencia," to him as "Paul" (because, like the apostle, he was either in an abyss of despair or on a mountain peak of joy) or "Eliseus" (a tribute to his large bald head). She refers to God as "Joseph" and the devil as "Hoofy." She even has pseudonyms for the different branches of her Order and for various dignitaries of the church, but that is to anticipate the story which follows.

Many years before, Teresa had found she was only able to form a deep friendship with people who she deemed "to love God and to be striving to serve him." Thus their all-consuming love of

God, always assumed, often discussed, was at the center of their friendship. The equality of their relationship is seen in the way she writes sometimes as penitent: "So Angela is very happy, my Father, now that she has made her confession to him; and she is happiest of all because, since she first saw Paul, her soul had found relief and happiness with no one else."[4] Sometimes the roles are reversed and she becomes his spiritual director:

> Your Paternity should tell Paul to be perfectly content now with his prayer and not to trouble about performing acts with the understanding when God grants him favors of another kind. . . . The fact is that, in these interior, spiritual things, the most potent and acceptable prayer is the prayer that leaves the best effects.[5]

So interwoven is their relationship that these two aspects of their spiritual relationship can run together, one thought tumbling after the other:

> I cannot think how Paul can say he knows nothing about Union, for [what he says about] that bright darkness and impetus shows that that is not so, though, as it is not a common experience, it is impossible to recall it clearly once it is past and gone. I am extremely envious of the souls whom it is his duty to help. . . . How well I remember the sermons that your Paternity used to preach us![6]

Though her letters abound with details about business affairs concerning the convents and the endless problems of the reform, their poignancy lies in the way they reveal the very human side of Teresa—loving, infinitely caring and motherly, demanding, even jealous.

Her maternal instinct finds expression with Gracián as with no one else. Her solicitude for his physical and material needs is both touching and reassuring; saints can concern themselves with such things, can be Martha as well as Mary. For Teresa man is body as well as soul. So she chides him if he does not get enough sleep, questions whether in cold weather he has enough clothes, in heat whether he must travel so far. She cannot bear him worrying, asks after his chilblains, tells one of the nuns to see that he wraps up his feet and, in a moment of glorious incongruity, urges him not to "preach so many sermons during Lent or eat such bad fish." Indeed, whether he is eating properly is her constant refrain. Her wish to care for him was as primitive as that of any mother for her son, any wife for her husband. "How Angela would have loved to get Paul a meal when he was hungry like that." And, oh, her delight when he signs himself "Your dear son."

If Gracián found her a demanding friend, he left no record of the fact, but it is clear that she was. Soon after they met, she wrote: "When I reflect that I shall have news of you only occasionally, I do not know how I shall bear it." Nor did she hesitate to reprimand him if, as was often the case, he was dilatory in writing: "I can see that there have been causes for your silence, but, as it has been a cause of such suffering to me, nothing should have kept you from writing." She was not beyond envying the other sisters when they had Gracián staying with them, even of outright jealousy:

> Angela's mind is still not entirely at rest about the suspicion she was entertaining. That is not to be wondered at, for she has nothing else to console her but your friendship and she wants no other consolation than that. And, as she herself says, she has a great many trials and is weak by nature, so that she becomes distressed when she thinks [her affection] is not repaid.[7]

She once went to the extreme of putting his love for her to the test, writing: "I have been wondering which of the two your Paternity loves better — Senora Doña Juana [his mother], who, I reflected, has a husband and her other children to love her, or poor Laurencia, who has no one else in the world but you, her Father." She need not have worried. Gracián wrote that "she loved me, and I her, more tenderly than any other creature on earth." For him, too, their relationship was inextricably bound up with the love of God: "This love that I had for Mother Teresa and she for me produced in me purity, ardor and love of God, and in her, comfort and relief in her work as she often told me, and so I loved no one, not even my mother, more than her."[8]

Well versed in the ways of the world, Teresa knew, as the ingenuous Gracián apparently did not, that their friendship could be open to misunderstanding. She admitted that there was a substantial difference between her treatment of him in private and the way she talked of him to others. She urged him not to read her letters in public and sought to justify their friendship: "For many reasons it is permissible for me to feel great affection for you and to show it in the dealings we have together. But it is not permissible for all the other nuns to do so."[9] One law for the general, another for the troops? Teresa does not explain her reasons, though she suggests that her age gives her license. More explicitly, she clearly believes that their friendship and her vow of obedience to Gracián has God's blessings; the knot is so firmly tied that only death would break it, "Nay, after death it will be firmer than before." Once again, speaking of herself in the third person, she writes: "The very thought of it helps her to praise the Lord. That freedom which she used to have has been nothing but a hindrance to her. Now she thinks her present bondage better and more pleasing to God, for she has found someone to help her bring souls to Him and who will praise Him."[10]

There is no doubt that Gracián was the closest friend of Teresa's heart and the one with whom she could be most fully herself. But Teresa was, it can hardly be too much stressed, blessed with the gift of friendship, and there were many relationships in which her need to give and receive love was revealed. Many years earlier she had written of Doña Guiomar that they were "closer than if we were sisters." Later there was María de San José, once Luisa de la Cerda's maid, whom Teresa sometimes got such longings to see that she could think of nothing else and to whom she wrote: "Provided you love me as much as I love you, I forgive you everything, whether in the past or in the future." And by whom she could be wounded: "I was treating you as one of my dearest daughters, it hurt me terribly not to find the same frankness and love in you." As in her correspondence with Gracián, she is not too proud to admit that she has been hurt. "I am surprised at your neglect of me, when you know how many trials I have," she wrote to her sister Juana, and to María Bautista: "It is wrong of you to let such a long time pass without writing to me, for you know how I like your letters." The more Teresa loved people, the more she expected from them and the less she could bear their faults; to neglect her was a serious failing, reducing her occasionally almost to petulance: "If your head ached as much as mine, your Charity might be excused for not having written to me for so long, but, as that is not the case, I cannot help complaining of you."

Teresa's capacity for friendship begs many questions. Should one claiming to be dedicated solely to God admit to these all too human emotions? Are they compatible with sanctity? What is one to make of it? Friendship is a matter over which Teresa struggled all her life and on which she is inconsistent. She recognizes her own need for it and somehow convinces herself that she need not follow the advice she gives her nuns.

Ironically, her strictest advice is given in her notes on the visitation of convents, written at Gracián's request. Here she warns against special friendships of any kind and insists that the visitor should check excessive friendship. In both *The Constitutions* and *The Way of Perfection* she warns against special friendships, saying they are "seldom calculated to make for the love of God." On the other hand, when writing on her own account, in her *Life*, she shows an ordinary human attitude much nearer to her own behavior:

> I would advise those who practice prayer, especially at first, to cultivate friendship and intercourse with others of similar interests. This is a most important thing, if only because we can help each other by our prayers, and it is all the more so because it may bring us many other benefits. Since people can find comfort in the conversation and human sympathy of ordinary friendships, even when these are not altogether good, I do not know why anyone who is beginning to love and serve God in earnest should not be allowed to discuss his joys and trials with others — and people who practice prayer have plenty of both.[11]

From the conflicting advice Teresa gives to her nuns over the years a pattern begins to emerge. Special friendships should be avoided; they must aspire to loving each other equally; God should be (and is, if they did but know it) their greatest friend. "I cannot conceive, my Creator, why the whole world does not strive to draw near to Thee in this intimate friendship."

Those who read only her formal advice in, for instance, *The Constitutions* may be forgiven for finding her injunctions harsh and inconsistent with her behavior. Indeed, they presented a challenge which, in view of Teresa's own unabashed favoritism and occasional dislikes, the nuns may have viewed somewhat wistfully. But once it is accepted that the constant factor in her attitude to friendship is that love of God should be first and all consuming, that, far from detracting from God, the friendship of others can help us to love God more, her apparent failure to follow her own advice becomes an acceptable license which she herself has endorsed and which she has learned painfully to live.

Painful it certainly was. When Teresa was young, her affections overwhelmed her at the expense of her love for God. In old age her love flowed toward both the human and the divine, one enhancing the other. Whether or not she is judged for her demands on her friends, whether or not her inconsistency shows her fallible in this, it is because she was utterly confident of her relationship with God that she could feel such love for her friends and express it so freely. If we wonder at a saint having such ordinary, human reactions, it is because our conception of sanctity is at fault. Teresa's sanctity lay, at least partly, in her ability to combine her mystical life and her relationship with God with a complete immersion in the trials and delights of being human. Her love for her friends was not replacing or diminishing her love for God, but was an expression of it.

In *The Way of Perfection* Teresa asks rhetorically whether spiritually minded people should love anyone but God. Yes, she affirms, "they will love others much more than they did, and with a more genuine love, with greater passion and a love which brings more profit; that, in a word, is what love really is." Holiness is wholeness.

If ever Teresa needed a good friend it was at this point in her life. Soon after she met Gracián she discovered that, though she had agreed to make her most recent foundation in good faith and though she was right in thinking that politically the town of Beas was indeed in Castile, as far as ecclesiastical boundaries were concerned it was, in fact, in Andalusia and she was well aware that her mandate to make foundations did not extend beyond Castile. From the casual way she tells one of her correspondents of her mistake, she does not foresee any serious trouble. However, her latest convent was, as far as the church authorities were concerned, illegal. To make matters worse, Gracián, by then the apostolic visitor for Andalusia, thought he could authorize her to found in Seville, where the archbishop had promised his support and rich novices were already waiting to take the habit. She had no wish to go to one of the hottest places in Spain at the height of the summer. She knew, too, that it was only five years since the last Moorish insurrection had been crushed, that the Lutherans there were strong and vocal, and the Inquisition more suspicious, repressive, and cruel than in Castile. However, she had made a vow of obedience to Gracián. Given her devotion to obedience and her love for him, she had no option. On May 18, 1575, she began the journey to Seville, quite unaware of the storm clouds that were gathering.

15

Andalusia
1575–1576

"The older she gets, the more she travels," moaned Julián of Avila. It was true. Whereas Teresa's first foundations were all made near Avila, in her old age, despite persistent bad health, her journeys took her further and further afield. Her next foundation, in Seville, was the most adventurous and the most vividly chronicled of all her travels.

Wednesday, May 18

Teresa gave her mantle to the prioress at Beas, saying that it was new, befitting a young person like her. She would take the prioress's mantle, old and worn as it was, and suitable for the sixty-year-old foundress. The party set out, the six nuns so carefully chosen that Teresa felt "they were such that I would have dared to go even to the land of the Turks with them." They traveled in four covered wagons with plenty of water, some food (which soon rotted in the sweltering heat) and little else. They had received glowing reports of their new house and its furnishings — why should they burden themselves with more? They started early and made their first stop in a forest, on the banks of a stream. Teresa wandered off in delight and María de San José recounts how: "We could hardly drag our holy Mother away from it, for all the various flowers and the thousands of singing-birds seemed to be losing themselves in giving praise to God."

Soon the heat became more intense. Teresa herself describes how they coped with the long journey:

> Though we did not travel during the siesta hours, I can assure you, sisters, that when the sun beat down on the carriages with all its might, going into them was like entering purgatory. Sometimes by thinking of hell, and sometimes by remembering that we were doing and suffering something for God, the sisters bore the journey with great contentment and joy.[1]

The first night was spent at a hermitage near Santisteban, praying and trying to sleep on the stone floor. They rejoiced in this mortification, just as they praised God for the fleas and the bad roads. The greater the suffering, the more confident they were that they were doing his will.

Thursday, May 19

At first light they forded two rivers on the way to Linares, later famous for being the place to boast the birth of the guitarist Andrés Segovia and to witness the bull-ring death of the matador Manolete. By mid-day the heat was unbearable, a cup of water — more thirst-quenching than wine and more expensive — cost two maravedis; for food they had beans, bread, cherries, and a rare treat, an egg. At mid-day they stopped at a roadside inn. Julián de Avila takes up the story:

> There were some men there, and I have never seen such a depraved lot in my life.... They shouted all sorts of vile things at Fr. Gregorio Nacianzeno [a Discalced Carmelite

> from Beas] and there was no way we could prevail on them to stop it. . . . In the end they drew knives and began fighting among themselves. . . . While all this was going on the Mother and sisters remained in their covered wagons and were not seen. Had the men seen them, they would have treated them as they had treated Father Gregorio.[2]

When they reached the ferry to cross the Guadalquivir, another adventure awaited them. The boatman tried to cheat them, claiming he could take them all across in one trip. It proved, as he must have known, to be too heavy a load and one of the wagons, with several nuns aboard, broke loose and drifted downstream. The remaining nuns called on God or hauled on ropes as their temperaments determined until, fortunately, the wagon was grounded on a sandbank. Teresa dismissed such incidents as being of no great importance; her most vivid memory was the boatman's little son, anxiously watching and fearful for his father's safety.

Friday, May 20
An uneventful day as they followed the course of the Guadalquivir, passing through the villages of Villanueva, Argonilla, Pedro Abad, and El Carpio.

Saturday, May 21
Teresa was ill with a high fever. Though never well, she usually managed to keep traveling, but on this day, "I seemed to have fallen into a lethargy, so completely helpless was I." They splashed water over her face, but it was so warm from the sun that it hardly refreshed her. They realized they must stop at the first inn they reached. It was, according to Father Julián, "a little room in which pigs used to be kept," the ceiling so low that they could hardly stand upright. Teresa does not mention the shouting and swearing

of the other guests, the noise of the dancing and tambourines, the vermin crawling round. She simply recounts that:

> They gave us a little room roofed like a shed and without a window, into which the sun streamed whenever the door was opened. You must remember that the heat there is not like our Castilian heat but is much more trying. They made me lie down on a bed, but it was so full of ups and downs that I would rather have lain on the floor: I cannot think how I endured it — it seemed to be full of sharp stones.[3]

In the end she decided even the blazing Andalusian sun was preferable, so they shook the dust of the dirty hovel off their feet and went on their way.

Pentecost Sunday, May 22

Frightening and unpleasant though these experiences were, for Teresa the worst was to come. They arrived early in Córdoba, hoping to find somewhere they could hear Mass without being seen. They were directed to a church over the river, assured that it would be quiet, but found that they needed a license from the governor in order to cross the gated bridge. As they waited — it was so early that bureaucracy was not yet in action and someone had gone to wake the governor — curious crowds began to gather round the wagons. When at last the license arrived, the carriages proved too large to pass through the gate and the projecting ends of the axles had to be sawn off. All this was attracting the attention such things always do, but perhaps they had been identified and word had spread? Their wagons had chosen an unfortunate site to become immobilized — just outside the walls of the Alcazar, the headquarters of the Inquisition. Teresa knew, though the other nuns did not, that at that very time the Inquisition were looking for her autobiography in order to examine it on suspicion of heresy.

Whether or not the officials knew who they were, no action was taken against them and eventually they reached the church, only to find it was not quiet at all, but full of people preparing for the festival of Pentecost. Teresa would almost have preferred to miss Mass altogether than endure staring eyes but, as always in such matters, she deferred to Julián, "as he was a theologian." They would, he insisted, go to Mass.

> We alighted near the church: nobody could see our faces, for we always covered them with large veils; but their seeing us in the white frieze mantles which we wear, and our hemp-soled shoes, was enough to cause a commotion, and a commotion there was. This was a great shock to me, and for all of us, and it must have taken away my fever altogether.... I assure you, daughters, that, though you may perhaps think all this were nothing, it was one of the worst experiences I have ever been through in my life: there was such an uproar among the people that you would have thought the church had been invaded by bulls.[4]

She could bear heat, hunger, illness, and danger, but the invasion of their enclosure was too much. Under the eyes of the Inquisitors as they were, she must also have been afraid, though she does not admit to it.

Monday, May 23

By the sixth day they reached Ecija, so hot that it is known as "the frying-pan of Andalusia." They attended Mass in peace and Teresa spent the day in prayer. It is thought that it was on this day she made her vow of obedience to Gracián. The afternoon was to bring another frightening incident, recorded by one of the nuns in the party: "Near an inn they call the Andino Inn, we came on a group of soldiers and muleteers fighting with knives. There was complete disorder and nobody could make them stop. Mother [Teresa] stuck her head out of the wagon and with one word calmed them all down."

They arrived in Seville expecting to make the foundation, rest for a few days, and return to Castile. The truth was very different. There was a house, that much was true, but it was only rented; it was too small, and it was damp. It was, as promised, furnished, but the furniture had only been lent for their arrival and most of it had to be returned almost immediately. The house lacked such basic necessities as a table, a candlestick, and a frying pan. Nor was it true that the women of Seville were, as she had been promised, pressing for admission to the convent. Most serious of all, the archbishop of Seville, while welcoming the party, was doing so under a complete misapprehension. He had thought that Teresa was coming to help him reform the existing convents of Seville, not to found a new one and in poverty at that. Seville already had twenty-four convents and eighteen monasteries; even in such an ostentatiously devout city this was enough.

They seemed to have reached an impasse. Teresa would not agree to found a convent with endowment in a large, rich city like Seville. They had no money, they had brought nothing except the clothes they stood up in, and they were four hundred miles from home. "The Lord was pleased that none of my foundations should be made without my enduring great suffering, sometimes in one way and sometimes in another."

Gradually, with Teresa's winning mixture of determination, willfulness, and charm, the house became a reality. First they were given permission to say Mass on condition no bell was rung or installed, "though actually," she admits casually, "we had installed one already." Then the archbishop began sending them visitors. Finally, he came himself. Once again Teresa's charm had won the day. She spoke to him bluntly of the trouble he was causing. "Eventually he told me I could do just what I liked, as I liked, and from that time forward he was helpful and kind to us on every possible occasion." That was all very well, but they still had no money and no permanent place to live.

One day Teresa was begging God for his help when she heard him say: "I have heard you; let Me alone." (Teresa's God was capable of gentle irritation.) His instruments were to be various local benefactors and Teresa's brother Lorenzo, who had just returned with his three children from thirty-four years in the West Indies. He was horrified that the Seville nuns should be living so precariously in rented rooms and gave Teresa enough money to enable her to buy a house.

Teresa was, of course, grateful, but the ambivalence of her reaction reflects her contradictory feelings toward her family. On the one hand she was devoted to them — as a child she had been so distressed at the death of her mother that she had begged Our Lady to take Doña Beatriz's place, and after the death of her father, she felt as if "her heart was torn from her." So, too, did she love her siblings, for whom she felt both compassion and a sense of responsibility. When they were children, it was Rodrigo who won her especial affection; despite her distress at the moral lapse, she arranged a dowry for her brother Jerónimo's illegitimate daughter; she took tender, motherly care of her young sister, Juana, only a baby when their mother died; and she was particularly devoted to Lorenzo and his young daughter Teresita. She was, however, well aware of the problems relations can bring and knew that they could be a distraction to those trying to devote themselves wholly to God. She distinguishes between parents and siblings on the one hand, and the "extended family" on the other, and it is probably of the second group that she is thinking when she gives some of her more abrasive advice on the subject. For instance, in the *Constitutions*, she tells the nuns to avoid talking to their relatives; in *The Way of Perfection*, she writes that, if a nun does not tire of her relatives after the second visit, she must consider herself imperfect. She once admitted to María de San José how she was suffering from her relatives: "I spend my whole time trying to avoid getting mixed up with them."

Writing about the situation in Seville, when she once again became indebted to Lorenzo, it seems as if, after some inner debate, her reaction was in accord with the rules she had herself devised, even though, in this instance, it concerned her beloved brother and his generous offer:

> I remembered that in our *Constitutions* we are told to turn from our kinsfolk. I then began to wonder if I had any such obligation, when the Lord said to me: "No, daughter, your institutions must never fail to be in conformity with My law." The truth is that the *Constitutions* mean us not to be attached to our kinsfolk; it rather wearies me, I think, to be so and it wears me out when I have much to do with them.[5]

Nonetheless it was thanks to Lorenzo's help that a house was purchased, and on May 27, 1576, just over a year after she had arrived in Seville, the prioress and Teresa, with two other nuns, moved in. They went at night, for fear of their Franciscan neighbors, who did not welcome their presence; so great were their apprehensions that they thought every shadow was a friar. The next morning the first Mass was said and, with decorated streets, music and minstrels, the archbishop himself reserved the Blessed

Sacrament. By now his admiration for Teresa was such that, to her great embarrassment, he insisted on her blessing him in public.

Always eager to share anything that could be construed as showing God's intervention, Teresa ends her account of this foundation with a curious anecdote:

> After a great many salvos of artillery had been fired and rockets had been let off, and when the procession was over and it was nearly night, the people got the idea of letting off more guns, and a little powder caught fire, I do not know how, so that it was a great wonder the person it belonged to was not killed. A huge flame leapt up to the top of the cloister, the arches of which were covered with silk hangings which they thought would have been set on fire. But they did not take the least harm: they were crimson and yellow hangings. What I consider most astonishing is that the stonework of the arches below the hangings was blackened with smoke, and yet the hangings above them were not touched: it was just as if the fire had not reached them.[6]

During her year in Seville Teresa founded another convent, the only one inaugurated in her absence — in fact she never saw it — and the one which caused her the fewest problems. The site was in the old town of Caravaca, which in Teresa's time belonged, like Beas, to the Knights of Santiago.

The initiative had come from a lady called Doña Catalina de Otalora and a group of her friends and relations. Doña Catalina had recently been widowed and she, together with three girls (all, curiously, called Francesca) decided they would leave the world and enter a convent. Since there was no convent in Caravaca, they decided to found one themselves and, on advice from the

Jesuits who had recently established themselves in the town, they sent a special messenger to Teresa, just when she was about to leave Avila on her way to Beas in early 1575.

Teresa was impressed by their ardor and determination, and could not foresee any problems so, learning that Caravaca was not too far from Beas, she took more nuns with her than usual, intending to go there after completing the foundation at Beas. On arriving at Beas, however, she discovered that the roads to Caravaca were virtually impassable, and her enthusiasm waned. Even if the nuns could make the journey once, when the weather was temperate, how would confessors be able to make regular visits? But she had given her word. She sent Julián de Avila and Antonio Gaytán to reconnoiter. They were so impressed by the women that, in spite of the roads, which were indeed terrible, they were happy to draw up an agreement.

There was only one hurdle. The Knights of Santiago were only willing to authorize the foundation if the nuns would become subject to them, and Teresa, not surprisingly, refused to tolerate that. The Carmelite general had told her to make foundations within the Carmelite Order, and she had no intention of disobeying him. She appealed, as she often did in such cases, directly to the king. He was prepared to make an exception for her, so long as the nuns agreed to pay tithes to the Knights of Santiago.

By the time these arrangements had been made, Teresa was in Seville, so the convent was inaugurated without her on January 1, 1576. Even though she never saw it, the convent at Caravaca had a special place in her heart. For the rest of her life she carried a reproduction of the Caravaca Cross, said to contain a relic of the true Cross.

Her love for this cross was not blind fetishism or undiscriminating faith in relics. Teresa had an intuitive love of symbols and allegory. The soul might be a garden, where God is the gardener and the various methods of irrigation correspond to the different stages of prayer; or a castle, the door representing the practice of prayer and the central room the soul's spiritual destination. She sees the life of the spirit as the silkworm destined to be transformed into a butterfly, the nourishment of Christ as water, the passions within the human soul as fire. For such a thinker the Caravaca Cross was a tangible reminder of the mystery of the Crucifixion.

On May 28, 1576, as soon as the nuns had moved into their new house in Seville, Teresa left to return to Castile. She was not sorry to go: she did not like Andalusia or the Andalusians and made no secret of the fact. So many rich people, so little help. Was it the climate? She had heard it said that the devils were powerful in those parts: "They certainly harassed me, and I have never found myself as cowardly in my whole life as I did here. I really did not know myself." She wrote to her prioress at Valladolid: "It is amazing what injustices are committed in this part of the world — what untruthfulness there is and what double dealing! I can assure you, the place fully deserves its reputation." And to a priest friend: "Oh, what falsehoods go round here! They make me quite dizzy." She did, however, feel better in health in Seville than in Avila. And, with typical humility, she was delighted "that there is no suggestion of my supposed sanctity which people talked of in Castile" and glad "not to be reminded of the flattering things they say about me in Castile."

Even if she had enjoyed both the place and its people, there were other reasons why her stay in Andalusia was a difficult time. The tensions within the Carmelite Order had reached such an explosive point that Teresa's work almost came to a complete end. Her departure from Seville was part of the bitter persecution that was mounting against the Reform.

16

Persecution
1576–1579

Now in her early sixties and the foundress of twelve convents, Teresa was accustomed to the delays of bureaucracy, the rivalries and complex interaction of personalities, and her struggle to be obedient to the church while remaining true to the instructions and advice she received from her inner voice, from God. But worse, far worse, was to come. Such trouble lay ahead that, for more than four years, there were to be no more foundations:

> The reason for this was the very sudden beginning of the great persecutions which both friars and nuns of the Discalced Reform had to endure: though they had had many such already, none of them were so severe as these last, which almost brought the Reform to an end. It became clear how angry the devil was at this excellent beginning which Our Lord had made, and which, as it prospered so greatly, was clearly His work. The Discalced friars, and more especially their leaders, suffered greatly from the gross calumnies and opposition which came from nearly all the Fathers of the Mitigation.[1]

There was civil war within the Carmelite Order. But why? No Calced friars or nuns were forced or even encouraged to join the Discalced — those who joined did so freely; there was no attempt to stop the Calced continuing to lead the religious life in their own way. The reason for the tensions between the two branches lay partly in the differences between King Philip II, consistently zealous for monastic austerity, and the Carmelite general, whose attitude was more ambivalent; partly in misunderstandings, exaggerated by letters going astray; and partly in the all too human emotions of jealousy and guilt. The Calced could not tolerate the success of the Reform or the veneration given to its foundress; nor did they enjoy the contrast between the austerity of the Discalced and themselves, well clothed, comfortably housed, abundantly fed. Might they be forced to lead a life of greater mortification and penance? Or, more subtly, were their consciences pricked by being presented with an ideal which they felt they *ought* to follow?

These personal fears and rivalries were inflamed by two appointments. At the end of 1574 the king had persuaded the pope to appoint Gracián and two Dominicans as joint Reformers of Castile and Andalusia. The very title of their posts was provocative enough, but to the consternation of the Calced (and without Rubeo's authorization) they began to found monasteries of Discalced friars to provide an example of strict observance, the very moral posturing the Calced were dreading. Their fears were exacerbated when, a few months later, Gracián was given the additional post of apostolic visitor to the Calced in Andalusia. How could he, who also held the position of provincial to the Discalced, understand their way of life? As a close friend of Teresa's, surely he would at the very least encourage them to more austerity? As for Gracián, he was in an impossible position, torn between obedience on the one hand to the pope and the king, who were responsible for his recent appointments, and on the other to Rubeo, the superior of his Order, who had not given these appointments his blessing.

This was the situation in April 1575, when Gracián and Teresa met. And the next month, while she was inaugurating the foundation in Seville, a general chapter of the Order was meeting at Piacenza, in Italy, under the presidency of Rubeo to decide how to deal with the Discalced Carmelites, who, incidentally, were not present to defend themselves.

Their measures were severe; the general who had so warmly encouraged Teresa in her reform now seemed to have no wish but to destroy it. A resolution was passed suppressing all monasteries founded without Rubeo's permission, and Teresa was forbidden to make any more. She was ordered to return to Castile and never again leave the convent of her choice; she was to be, in effect, a prisoner. Further she was declared apostate and excommunicated, and her Discalced sons and daughters branded rebellious and disobedient.

Perhaps hardest of all to endure, because most elusive to pin down and refute, the Calced started a slanderous campaign about the friendship between Teresa and Gracián. We have Gracián's own reaction to this:

> Malicious people judged from the great communication and familiarity that we two had that it was not a holy love, and even if she had not been as holy as she was, and if I had been the most evil man in the world, wickedness should not have been suspected of a woman sixty years old, and so cloistered and modest. With all that, we had to conceal this very intimate friendship, so that we should not be maligned.[2]

Though the Piacenza resolutions were not confirmed until the following year, Teresa must have heard of them, for she lost no time in picking up her pen in response. In June of 1575 she wrote a long, flattering letter to Rubeo, defending the exemplary lives of the Discalced, especially Gracián. The following month she wrote to the king, begging for his help for the Reform and pleading that the Discalced should be made into a separate province and put under the charge of Gracián. Unless that were done quickly, "much harm will be done, and further progress will, I think, be impossible." She was now so confident in her cause and in her right to communicate directly with both secular and ecclesiastical authorities that, untypically, she writes in another letter to Rubeo: "When we both stand before His judgment seat, your Reverence will see what you owe to your loyal daughter, Teresa of Jesus."

She did not, however, leave Seville immediately, as Gracián authorized her to stay until the following spring to oversee the affairs of the new convent. Teresa, too, was in an unenviable position, divided by obedience to the general of her Order and to Gracián, the Visitor appointed by the highest authority, the pope himself. (She was not constrained by the vow of obedience she had made to Gracián, as that contained a clause protecting her from having to disobey her superiors.) When she left Seville eventually she went to Toledo, where, as instructed, she shut herself up in her own convent. It seemed as if everyone was against her: Rubeo, the Calced, the nuncio, and the pope — even the king seemed to be having doubts. But she did not appear to resent the curtailment of her foundations or even to be distressed at being the subject of so much slander and oppression. Far from feeling unhappy at this harsh treatment, Teresa rejoiced. If she was being treated like this by her fellow human beings, she must, she argued, be pleasing her Creator:

> Not only did this not distress me, but it made me so unexpectedly happy that I could not control myself; I am not at

all surprised now at what King David did when he danced before the Ark of the Lord. I had no desire that they should do anything else than what they were doing, and my joy was so great that I did not know how to conceal it.[3]

So, in ecstatic confinement, content in her secluded cell overlooking the garden, Teresa witnessed subsequent events from the Toledo convent, waging war only with her pen. From her cell she governed the affairs of her houses by letter, as usual mindful of the spiritual well-being of her correspondents, attentive to the minutest details of their lives, such as the style and material of the nuns' habits, ready to give advice on any subject from prayer to the admission of novices, beseeching everyone who knew him to look after her beloved Gracián.

Nor does she let the ecclesiastical storm raging about her blind her to ordinary life. She sends and receives sweets, scented orange-water, petals preserved in syrup, quinces and sardines; meticulously apologizes for "marking the porterage so high"; laments that she has been having raptures in public again; writes Lorenzo a memorandum on the education of his sons; and advises him on prayer and sends him a hair shirt, though he must not wear it more than twice a week. "It can be worn on any part of the body, and put on in any way so long as it feels uncomfortable. . . . it makes me laugh to think how you send me sweets and presents and money and I send you hair shirts."

Lest her letters to Gracián fall into the wrong hands she adopted a series of pseudonyms for the *dramatis personae* involved in the Carmelite struggle. In addition to her pet names for herself and Gracián she termed Ormaneto, the papal nuncio, "Matusalem"; Tostado, the vicar general, "Peralta"; the Jesuits "ravens," and John of the Cross "Seneca." The Inquisitors are "angels" and the Grand Inquisitor "the archangel." The Discalced nuns and friars are variously "eagles," "doves," "grasshoppers," and "butterflies"; the Calced become "owls," "night-birds," "cats," and "Egyptians." It probably worked. Prying eyes would make little of this: "He has a brother who has been turned out by the owls: a great saint, a fine preacher in fact, absolutely perfect. He was originally a Dominican and he wants him to join the eagles."

The next act in the drama between the two branches of the Carmelites had its origins in the arrival in Spain, early in 1576, of a Calced Carmelite named Jerónimo de Tostado, who was sent as Rubeo's personal representative to enforce the Piacenza decrees. Again the conflict was complicated by the power structures: Tostado represented the general of the Order, while Gracián had the blessing of the king and owed his position, through Francisco de Vargas, to the pope.

As Teresa was leaving Seville and on her way to incarceration at Toledo, the conflict sharpened. Tostado convened another provincial chapter, held at La Moraleja. It declared that the two branches of the Carmelites should be fused, which meant, in effect, the suppression of the Reform. Within two months Gracián responded by calling a meeting of the Discalced at Almodóvar. Slightly exceeding their powers (such decisions should normally have included the Calced), they declared the Discalced a separate province and sent two friars to Rome to present to the pope this idea so warmly favored by Teresa. When the chapter was over, several members visited Toledo in high good humor to give the exiled foundress an account of the proceedings.

As if being pursued by Tostado were not enough, fate dealt the Discalced another blow when, in June 1577, Ormaneto, the papal nuncio who had been such a doughty supporter of the Reform, died and was succeeded by Filippo Sega. "God seemed to have sent him to try us by suffering," writes Teresa. The best she could say about him was that "he was related in some way to the pope and must have been a servant of God." Sega was already prejudiced against the Reform; indeed it was he who dubbed Teresa

> a restless, gad-about, disobedient and contumacious woman, who invented wicked doctrines and called them devotion, transgressed the rules of enclosure, in opposition to the Council of Trent and to her superiors, and taught others, against the commands of St. Paul, who had forbidden women to teach.

Her reaction to this diatribe is not on record, though it is likely she heard of it. Perhaps, as when she was denounced from a pulpit in Avila, she laughed?

Sega was as harsh on the Reform as he was on its foundress. He embarked on a ruthless policy of annulling all patents and faculties granted by Ormaneto, and condemning, imprisoning, and exiling those he thought might resist him.

After she had spent a year in Toledo, Teresa was sent to Avila to arrange for the transfer of St. Joseph's from the jurisdiction of the bishop of Avila, where it had remained since its foundation fifteen years earlier, to that of the Carmelite Order. So she was there in October 1577 when the most amazing scenes accompanied the election of a new prioress at the Convent of the Incarnation. The same nuns who, six years earlier, had so resented Teresa's appointment now wanted her back as prioress. Fifty-five intended to vote for her, forty-four against. Furious at hearing this news, Tostado sent the provincial of the Calced, armed with severe censures and excommunications, to preside over the election. Teresa wrote to

María de San José about this event, "the like of which, I should think, has never been seen before":

> In spite of all that [the provincial's threats], they took no notice, and fifty-five of the nuns voted for me just as though he had said no such thing. And as each of them handed the provincial her vote he excommunicated her, and abused her, and pounded the voting papers with his fist and struck them and burned them. And for exactly a fortnight he has left these nuns without Communion and forbidden them to hear Mass or enter the choir even when the Divine Office is not being said. And nobody is allowed to speak to them, not even their confessor or their own parents. And the most amusing thing is that, on the day after this election by poundings, the provincial summoned these nuns to a fresh election; to which they replied that there was no need to hold another as they had held one already. On hearing this, he excommunicated them again, and summoned the rest of the nuns, forty-four of them, and declared another prioress elected, and sent to Tostado for confirmation.[4]

It was only through the intervention of the king that Tostado was reluctantly forced to release the fifty-five nuns from all censures. As for Teresa, while she would have been allowed to live quietly at the Incarnation so long as there was no question of her being prioress, she admitted she had "no desire to find myself in that Babylon again, especially with my poor health."

The next victim of the persecution was John of the Cross. On the night of December 3, 1577, he was kidnapped by the Calced and taken as a prisoner to Toledo. There, for nine months, he was enclosed in a cell ten feet long and six feet wide. The only light came from a tiny hole in the wall of a corridor; he was allowed no change of clothing, little to eat apart from bread and water; and he was beaten — sometimes publicly — until the blood caused his tunic to stick to his back. And there he wrote some of his most famous poems.

As soon as Teresa heard of John's imprisonment she appealed to the king. She claimed she would rather see the friars among the Moors, who might show them more pity. John was so weak from suffering that she feared for his life:

> For love of Our Lord, I beseech your Majesty to command that he be set free immediately, and to issue an order, so that all these poor Discalced friars may not have to suffer so much from those of the Cloth. They do nothing but keep silence and suffer, and they gain a great deal by doing so, but the matter is a cause of public scandal.... They go about saying the Reform is to be suppressed, because Tostado has ordered it. Blessed be God, but the very people who should be the means of preventing offenses committed against Him are being the cause of all these sins and are committing worse sins every day. Unless your Majesty orders all this to be remedied, I do not know what will be the end of it all, for we have no other remedy upon earth.[5]

The king sent for Teresa, who, untypically, was too confused to be able to speak, "for his penetrating gaze — one of those that probes the soul itself — was fixed on me and seemed to pierce me through and through." Though she left the royal presence in jubilation, Philip II clearly did not help John, for it was not until the following August that he was free and then, tradition has it, it was thanks to a vision of Our Lady, who showed him how to escape. He made a rope out of bedcovers, let himself out of a window in his prison and hid with the Discalced Carmelite nuns in Toledo until signs of the search had abated.

Soon after her meeting with the king, Teresa's poor physique was subjected to another trial. She became giddy at the top of the stairs leading to the chapel at the Incarnation, fell and broke her left arm. (The nuns preferred to believe it was the devil who threw her down, a view commemorated by the fact that the staircase is, to this day, known as the Devil's Staircase.) Eventually a *curandera* arrived. The arm had to be broken again and reset, but it never healed properly, and for the rest of her life Teresa needed help dressing and undressing.

She was ordered to remain in Avila; thus, as the persecution of the Reform reached its height, she was again watching from the wings. She learned of the death of Rubeo, an event which distressed her deeply. This was the man who had given her support when she most needed it, and she easily forgave the difficulties he later caused. "I feel deeply moved by it. On the day I heard about it I wept and wept — I could do nothing else — and I felt very much distressed at all the trouble we have caused him, which he certainly did not deserve." She heard how John had escaped from prison just in time to attend Gracián's second meeting at Almodóvar, an event about which she and Gracián had serious disagreements. She had warned him not to proceed without permission from the pope and the general; he had insisted on going ahead. Her premonitions were justified when Sega annulled the decisions made by the chapter, excommunicated and imprisoned its members, and fulfilling Teresa's worst fears, put the Discalced under the jurisdiction of the Calced. Gracián was tried and confined for over a year. The situation could hardly have been blacker.

While Teresa reacted to these events by giving shrewd practical advice, staunchly defending her own and fearlessly writing to secular and ecclesiastical authorities, the true depths from which she operated are seen most movingly in a letter she wrote to the nuns of Seville in January 1579:

> I assure you I have never loved you as much as I do now and you have never been bound to serve Our Lord as much as you are now, when He is granting you the great blessing of being able to taste something of the meaning of His Cross. . . . If you help yourselves, the good Jesus will help you; for, though He is asleep on the sea, when the storm rises He will still the winds. . . . Let your Spouse do His will, and you will see how, before long, the sea will swallow up those who are making war upon us, as it did King Pharaoh, and God will free His people. . . .[6]

As she wrote, freedom was indeed in sight. In March 1579 the king appointed four assessors to examine the issue between the Calced and the Discalced. The next month the Discalced were removed from the jurisdiction of the Calced, and three weeks later the king's assessors declared for the foundation of a separate Discalced province. In May Teresa was authorized to resume visiting her convents. Though the Discalced were not to be formally recognized as a separate province until June 1580, the storm was subsiding and calmer seas lay ahead.

It is easy to see the Calced as the sole troublemakers, the persecutors and villains of the piece. However, as the great twentieth-century Carmelite historian Father Silverio de Santa Teresa (himself a member of the Discalced) pointed out, with admirable detachment, the Calced were not, at the time, in a position to appreciate the fruit which Teresa's reform would bear:

> It is not surprising, therefore, that the Calced Fathers should have had some misgivings about it and even opposed it. Apart from some excesses, which are inevitable whenever feelings run high, Calced and Discalced proceeded with the best of intentions, and God availed of the struggle between them to purify the virtue of their holy Foundress and make the Reform more vigorous. When the long and exhausting storm was over, the Reform came out of it strong and buoyant. Calmly evaluating those events today, it is easy to excuse both sides for what they did.[7]

Seen from Teresa's point of view, indeed in the light of the bare facts, it is less easy to excuse the excesses of the Calced. Teresa wistfully recognized that she was the cause of all the troubles ("if they had thrown me into the sea, as happened to Jonah, the storm would have ceased"), but affirmed that "it was quite evident that all this came from God, and that His Majesty was allowing it for the sake of some greater good."

Her attitude to her own sufferings was joy: She constantly affirms her pleasure in all the trials of the last four years. One of the most extraordinary aspects of this period of strife is that, surrounded as she was by people determined to silence her, in the midst of tension, argument, uncertainty, and danger, acutely aware of the suffering of her friends and the very real threat to her Reform, her inner life was at its most sublime. While the persecution was at its height, she was writing the book that has been described as one of the most celebrated books on mystical theology in existence.

17

"In My Father's House"

In 1577, between June 2 and November 29, Teresa wrote *The Interior Castle,* known in Spanish as *Las Moradas* (*The Mansions*). Anyone seeking proof that she had by this time attained a perfect balance between the inner and the outer can find it here, for she wrote this, the most profound of her works and one of the great classics of mystical life, in a period of extreme activity and stress. During these six months, while Tostado was bent on curbing the influence of the Reform and Teresa was pleading with Philip II on its behalf, while she was dealing with business affairs at St. Joseph's and while storms raged around the election of a new prioress at the Incarnation, she took every opportunity to move into her inner world, writing with an intensity and concentration which was noted by her sisters. "I often saw her as she wrote," affirms one witness, "which was generally after Communion. She was very radiant and wrote with great rapidity, and as a rule she was so absorbed in her work that even if we made a noise she would never stop, or so much as say that we were disturbing her."

Contemporary accounts deemed such speed miraculous. She was writing, they suggested, in a state of rapture. But the true miracle was her ability to move so naturally between two worlds that for most people are contradictory: the outer world of negotiation, tension, and stress, and the inner world of the progress of the soul to God. For the subject of this book is nothing less than that. It is an account of a journey written by one who has traveled, often painfully, every inch of the way and knows every hazard, every reward. She understands the soul's instinct for God, its constant yearning Godward, but she knows, too, that every person progresses through different stages and that understanding is limited by the point an individual has reached on his or her own journey. Experience is speaking to experience, deep calling to deep. So the book rings with authenticity and certainty, yielding new truths on every reading as the reader progresses on his or her personal journey toward greater knowledge.

Though Teresa writes from a pinnacle of mystical experience, she never ceased to be fully human. "We are not angels and we have bodies," she had written many years earlier. Unworthy though she feels, she cannot escape the knowledge that few have been granted her experience and that she must try to communicate it to others.

Nevertheless she undertook the task unwillingly. We have two firsthand accounts of the origins of the book, from Gracián and from Diego de Yepes, one of her earliest biographers. Gracián records how they were talking one day about spiritual matters, when Teresa exclaimed how well a particular point was put in her *Life,* at the time in the hands of the Inquisition. Gracián promptly suggested she should write a new book expounding her teachings in a less personal way, adding that she should first consult her current confessor, Don Alonso Velázquez. Once again she was writing under obedience and insisted on her inadequacy for the task:

> Let learned men, who have studied, do the writings; I am a stupid creature and don't know what I am saying. There

> are enough books written on prayer already. For the love of God, let me get on with my spinning and go to choir and do my religious duties like the other sisters. I am not meant for writing; I have neither the health nor the wits for it.[1]

Whatever her conscious mind thought, her unconscious drew her remorselessly toward the idea. A few days later she had a vision, which she later confided to Yepes. She saw

> a most beautiful crystal globe, made in the shape of a castle, and containing seven mansions, in the seventh and innermost of which was the King of Glory, in the greatest splendor, illumining and beautifying them all. The nearer one got to the center, the stronger was the light; outside the palace limits everything was foul, dark and infested with toads, vipers and other venomous creatures.[2]

The very next day she sat down to write.

Such is the archetypal power of this symbol, such is the inevitability with which it unfolds in Teresa's hands that *The Interior Castle* has been compared and contrasted with other great metaphors for the inner journey such as the Eightfold Path of Buddhism culminating in *nirvana,* to the Yogic path with *samadhi* as its goal, to Jewish and Sufi-Islamic models, and to Jung's psychological theory of individuation. Within Teresa's own writings on the spiritual life commentators have tried to draw parallels between the Seven Mansions of *The Interior Castle* and her earlier image of the Four Waters of prayer, but this comparison has not proved easy to work out in detail. It is best read in the light of what we know of Teresa's own spiritual journey.[3]

The primary image, the castle, represents the soul. Teresa immediately sees the apparent paradox: Is she talking nonsense, she asks rhetorically, in telling someone already in a room to enter it? "But you must understand," she continues, "that there are many ways of 'being' in a place." In a clear reference to John's Gospel ("In my Father's house are many mansions"), she says that this castle contains many rooms, "some above, some below, others at each side; and in the center and midst of them all is the chiefest mansion where the most secret things pass between God and the soul." This central room is the soul's destination; it is both already there and to be discovered. As she wrote, Teresa herself was in that room, in the center of the castle. How else could she write with such clarity?

The key to the castle is prayer and meditation, but even with these weapons the journey through the rooms of Teresa's metaphor is hazardous. It is beset by snakes and vipers, her image for the enemies of the soul such as irrelevant thoughts, worldly temptations, and aridity, but these perils must be overcome if the soul is to arrive at its ultimate destination. Using the image of a shrub common in parts of Spain whose thick layers of leaves conceal a succulent kernel, she says, "Think of a palmito, which has many outer rinds surrounding the savory part within, all of which must be taken away before the center can be eaten. Just so around this central room are many more." The soul must be allowed to roam freely, never remaining long in any room "unless it is the room of self-knowledge."

The First Mansions (Teresa always uses the plural as at each stage there is scope for endless variety) are the rooms of self-knowledge and humility. A reader today, tending to assume that psychological understanding began with Freud, may be surprised at the emphasis she put on self-knowledge; she was adamant about its importance:

> However high a state the soul may have attained, self-knowledge is incumbent upon it, and this it will never be able to neglect even should it so desire. . . . Self-knowledge

> is so important that, even if you were raised right up to the heavens, I should like you never to relax your cultivation of it.[4]

This need for self-knowledge was not new in her thinking. Her early life was a long cry of anguish at her own imperfection; everything she wrote, even in her letters, is infused with the need for self-understanding. In one of her long digressions in *The Foundations* she wrote: "I think it is a greater favor if the Lord sends us a single day of humble self-knowledge, even at the cost of many afflictions and trials, than many days of prayer." She advises her nuns that "however sublime your contemplation may be, take care both to begin and to end every period of prayer with self-examination."

Teresa is ruthless in applying these criteria to herself, even in the smallest details of behavior. She admitted to Gracián that she did not have "charity enough to nurse sick nuns," and to María de San José she wrote that her own easily given gratitude was "not in the least a sign of perfection: it must be my nature — I could be suborned with a sardine." We are all tarred with the same brush of ignorance about our own motivation: prioresses, she affirms, "never think they are not telling the truth, but such is our self-love that it is the rarest thing for us to blame ourselves or to understand ourselves either." Even seeking affection is put under the microscope of meticulous honesty. "We always seek it because of some interest, profit or pleasure of our own." And her inner voice supported her. Once, when she was thinking how it distressed her to eat meat and to do no penance, she heard these words: "Sometimes there is more self-love in such a thought than a desire for penance."

We can never wholly succeed, however, in the search to understand ourselves. The time comes when we should stop analyzing and let the soul "soar aloft in meditation upon the greatness and majesty of its God." Even in these matters Teresa's common sense and practicality do not desert her. In any case, knowledge of self and knowledge of God are indivisible: "we shall never succeed in knowing ourselves unless we seek to know God."

Linked to self-knowledge and so closely identified with it that Teresa sometimes uses the two words synonymously is humility. "Nothing matters more to us than humility," "Humility must always be doing its work like a bee making honey in the hive: without humility all will be lost." At last she is explicit about her own humility, her constant, almost irritating, self-abasement. "Let us think of His greatness and then come back to our own baseness: by looking at His purity we shall see our foulness." White looks even whiter when set beside black; black even blacker beside white. This is why she considers herself such a sinner. It is not merely a matter of the perpetration of actual sins, whether of commission or omission, but the stark contrast between the nature of the Creator and the created. True humility means facing the truth about oneself; it is about reality. Humility is truth.

Teresa had once been told that souls without prayer are like people whose limbs are paralyzed; these "paralyzed souls" do not, she writes, even gain entry to the castle. However, the desire for prayer is enough to unlock the door, and those who are aware of their capacity for God, even if they pray only a few times a month, may enter the first room. But so busy are they with worldly matters that evil forces, the "reptiles and snakes and venomous creatures," that lurk in the moat and the outer court of the castle come in with them. The light from the center of the castle is there, but the clouded eyes of those in the first Mansions are too preoccupied by themselves and their own affairs to see it. Nonetheless, they have at least taken the first step, and Teresa assumes that a soul once in the castle will not leave it.

By the time a soul arrives in the Second Mansions the longing for God has been crystallized by some form of conversion experience. There is less danger, for now worldly preoccupations are less absorbing and the voice of God can be heard through the clatter of self-interest. Even so the road is hard, for the soul is torn between the temptations of the world and messages of truth coming through sermons, books, conversations, sicknesses, and suffering. And if the ears are open to God, so too are they open to the call of the devil. It it still a fight between good and evil, but now it is a *conscious* fight. "The understanding is keener and the faculties are more alert, while the clash of arms and the noise of cannon are so loud that the soul cannot help hearing them." Here it is helpful to be in the company of others on the same path, better still with those who have entered the rooms nearer the center. Any desire for spiritual graces must be resisted in favor of hard work and perseverance; the important thing is "to labor and be resolute and prepare oneself with all possible diligence to bring one's will into conformity with the will of God." Yet again Teresa stresses the importance of self-knowledge: "It is absurd to think that we can enter Heaven without first entering our own souls—without getting to know ourselves." The second Mansions are a place of confusion and change, as Ruth Burrows puts it, "more like a railway station than a chamber of a castle made for living in."[5]

The Third Mansions have been called "the mansion of the complacent."[6] On similar lines Rowan Williams identifies it as the place of the professionally religious, where good deeds and prayer are over-familiar. It is too comfortable. To stop there is to regress, because the roots of sin are deeply hidden, buried under outward displays of virtue.

In tackling this sensitive area of the spiritual life Teresa begins positively. Unless the one who enters these mansions strays from the path, he or she is on the straight road to salvation. There are many such:

> They are most desirous not to offend His Majesty; they avoid committing even venial sins; they love doing penance; they spend hours in recollection; they use their time well; they practice works of charity toward their neighbors; and they are very careful in their speech and dress and in the government of their household if they have one.[7]

While writing about this stage Teresa could not forget the young man in Matthew's Gospel who, when he asked Jesus what he should do to have eternal life, was told to sell all his possessions and give the money to the poor. She is speaking here of the importance of detachment, "for if this is carried out perfectly it includes everything else." With her outgoing, passionate nature, detachment was not something she found easy. When writing *The Way of Perfection* she expressed her longing for this virtue in a moving *cri de coeur:* "May I not depart this life till there is nothing that I desire, till I have forgotten what it is to love anything but Thee and till I deny the name of love to any other kind of affection."[8]

We must detach ourselves not only from our possessions but even from our good works; we must learn to *be* and learn to listen to God's voice rather than our own wishes. The outward forms of faith are not enough; by now they should be taken for granted. Again she stresses the need for self-knowledge: "Enter, then, enter within yourselves, good daughters; and get right away from your own trifling good works, for these you are bound, as Christians, to perform." People in this room of the Castle tend to think that their own lives are so well ordered that they can allow themselves to be shocked by the behavior of others, even critical of it. We must stop interfering, consider our own shortcomings and leave other people to make their own journey in their own way.

Here, as in so many places on the spiritual journey, travelers will experience aridity, but this is something Teresa insists should not be a source of worry. Aridity can be a blessing, it should teach humility. The Third Mansions are a time of testing, a time to master the passions, a time for *determinación* to continue the journey.

When Teresa begins to write of the Fourth Mansions she begs the Holy Spirit to speak for her. We now begin to touch places of exquisite beauty, which even she finds difficult to describe "without being completely obscure to those devoid of experience." The Fourth Mansions are a place of transition, where human effort gives way to God's grace, action is replaced by passivity. The higher states of mystical contemplation defy communication. This room is very near the center of the castle, where God dwells; how can words describe such an encounter?

Nevertheless Teresa's gift for vivid communication is such that there is much in the three chapters she devotes to this stage that clarifies and enlightens the path to God. She calls the first state usually experienced in these Mansions "the Prayer of Passive Recollection." People who experience this, she writes, "are sometimes in the castle before they have begun to think about God at all":

> They have become markedly conscious that they are gradually retiring within themselves; anyone who experiences this will discover what I mean: I cannot explain it better. I think I have read that they are like a hedgehog or a tortoise withdrawing into itself; and whoever wrote that must have understood it well. Those creatures, however, enter within themselves whenever they like; whereas with us it is not a question of our will — it happens only when God is pleased to grant us this favor.[9]

Here "the person who does most is the one who thinks and desires to do least." We should not try to reason, but simply wait "in humble expectation." The soul is safe from the reptiles and poisonous creatures, who seldom reach this place. Worldly temptations are no longer a serious impediment, but perseverance in prayer becomes even more important, "For as yet the soul is not even weaned, but is like a child beginning to suck the breast. If it be taken from its mother, what can it be expected to do but die?"

From this state the soul may progress to "the Prayer of Quiet," where it is no longer restlessly seeking and searching, but quieter, more passive, waiting for God to take the initiative. Teresa illustrates this with her favorite metaphor — water. She suggests we think of two fountains, whose basins can be filled with water in different ways. It can come from a long way off, conducted by human ingenuity and intricate engineering, or it can come directly from its source, abundant and overflowing. This reminds her of a phrase from the psalms: *Dilatasti cor meum* (thou didst enlarge my heart). She suggests, however, that this happiness has its source deeper than the heart: it comes from the very center of the soul as if (here she uses another metaphor) "in those innermost depths there were a brazier on which were cast sweet perfumes; the light cannot be seen, nor the place where it dwells, but the fragrant smoke and the heat penetrate the entire soul, and very often, as I have said, the effects extend even to the body." For anyone wishing to progress along this royal road the important thing is not to think much, but to love much: *No está la cosa en pensar mucho, sino en amar mucho.* She follows this, the key to so much of her teaching, with the advice, "Do, then, whatever most arouses you to love," and with the question, do we know what love is? Teresa is not talking about a sentimental love, the test of which is the immediate happiness it produces, but a love which is shown in its determination to do the will of God.

The soul is not yet in complete union with God. However great the love and peace which it experiences at the deepest level, however much it is in the hands of God, it is still, at a conscious level, subject to distractions. Teresa describes this state vividly: "Yet the soul may perhaps be wholly united with Him in the Mansions very near His presence, while thought remains in the outskirts of the castle, suffering the assaults of a thousand wild and venomous creatures and from this suffering winning merit."[10]

She herself had for years been oppressed by those "venomous creatures," the turmoil of distracting thoughts. "It exasperated me to see the faculties of the soul, as I thought, occupied with God and recollected in Him, and the thought, on the other hand, confused and excited." But she has now learned something of great encouragement to all who experience problems with irrelevant thoughts — to accept them. She says we simply cannot restrain our thoughts "just as we cannot stop the movement of the heavens." So we must not let ourselves be disturbed or upset because we experience this distraction. Sometimes we worry over the wrong things; we must be further along the road than we think.

In the last three Mansions, in which the soul is in various degrees of union with God, description becomes virtually impossible. Teresa, always unconfident of her ability to communicate, admits endearingly: "I do not mind if I write any amount of nonsense, provided that just once in a way I can write sense."

In the Fifth Mansions the soul is asleep, totally abandoned to God; it is a "delectable death," a "heaven on earth." The soul in this state can, at the time, neither see nor understand; only afterward can it see what has happened and then it is sure. "If anyone has not that certainty, I should say that what she has experienced is not union of the whole soul to God but only union of one of the faculties or some one of the many other kinds of favor which God grants the soul."

In her attempt to communicate the joys of the Fifth Mansions, Teresa changes her image. Needing a living and growing metaphor, she describes the silkworms emerging from seeds like tiny peppercorns:

> When the warm weather comes, and the mulberry trees begin to show leaf, this seed starts to take life; until it has this sustenance, on which it feeds, it is as dead. The silkworms feed on the mulberry leaves until they are full grown, when people put down twigs, upon which, with their tiny mouths, they start spinning silk, making themselves very tight little cocoons, in which they bury themselves. Then finally, the worm, which was large and ugly, comes right out of the cocoon a beautiful white butterfly.[11]

Just so the soul feeds on Christ and is transformed; it is no longer bound by possessions or even relationships, now it has wings, it is free and can fly. It no longer cares for its former state. In seeing and beginning to share the new life ahead it can more easily die to the old.

This is a place of extreme passivity; there is no longer any temptation to take the initiative in prayer. The soul is as wax in God's hands. "In reality, the soul in that state does no more than the wax when a seal is impressed upon it — the wax does not impress itself. . . . It merely remains quiet and consenting."

Teresa finally compares this state with two people considering becoming engaged to be married:

> It seems to me that this union has not yet reached the point of spiritual betrothal, but is rather like what happens in our earthly life when two people are about to be betrothed. There is a discussion as to whether or not they are suited

> to each other and are both in love; and they meet again so that they may learn to appreciate each other better. So it is here.[12]

In these Mansions the experience of union is short, "never, I think, for as long as half an hour," but the contract has been drawn up and "the soul sees Who this Spouse is that she is to take."

In the Sixth Mansions God "confirms this betrothal" by bestowing raptures, ecstasy, and trances, which by now are almost continuous. Teresa is, as always, anxious to distinguish the genuine from the false, but here she also identifies another phenomenon that she calls "the flight of the spirit."

> But now this great God, Who controls the source of the waters and forbids the sea to move beyond its bounds, has loosed the sources when water has been coming into this basin; and with tremendous force there rises up so powerful a wave that this little ship — our soul — is lifted up on high. And if a ship can do nothing, and neither the pilot nor any of the crew has any power over it, when the waves make a furious assault upon it and toss it about at their will, even less able is the interior part of the soul to stop where it likes, while its senses and faculties can do no more than has been commanded them: the exterior senses, however, are quite unaffected by this.[13]

It is as if the soul had left the body, as if the person who experienced this flight (which begins as quickly as "a bullet leaves a gun") had been in another world. There the person knows, without words, things he or she had for years been trying to understand. But, though joy has reached a peak, so too has suffering, for living on earth has become painful. These flights of the spirit, these "meetings with the Spouse" make an indelible impression, but as it is not yet a permanent state there is constant frustration at not being in complete union. To continue with the nuptial imagery, the lovers are still living in separate houses and have, periodically, to part.

Only in the last Mansions is the union complete and permanent. The "marriage" has taken place and the two who are united can no longer be separated. "It is like rain falling from the heavens into a river or spring; there is nothing but water there and it is impossible to divide or separate the water belonging to the river from that which fell from the heavens."

Those who reach the last Mansions live in a permanently altered state. No matter how occupied they may be with worldly concerns, the soul never leaves that place where it is united with God. It is not a mystical experience, but a way of living. Teresa, who spent the last years of her life in this state, is quite clear about the effects.

There is a strange forgetfulness. There is no more fear of death than of a gentle rapture; in fact there is a curious indifference to either living or dying except when there is something to do in response to God's will. So intense is this longing to do God's will that no suffering disturbs the soul's interior peace and joy; it lives in a state of total acceptance. Occasionally "Our Lord leaves such souls to their own nature," and a flash of the old self appears as a reminder of humility. For the most part there are no periods of aridity, no turmoil, no loneliness, no fear, no doubt as to the source of this tranquility. The devil cannot enter here. It is the place where God dwells, the end of our exploring.

18

Back on the Road
1579–1581

By the time peace had been declared between the Calced and the Discalced Teresa was sixty-four and describing herself as "an old crone." She was stout now, leaning heavily on the ebony stick Lorenzo had sent her from the West Indies; her teeth were black, her skin "the color of earth," her three moles, once adding piquancy to her face, now sprouted hairs. She felt old and tired, her left arm was useless, and her health so poor that to feel even tolerably well was sufficiently unusual to deserve mention to her correspondents. Yet in June 1579 she was on the road again, visiting her convents at Medina del Campo, Valladolid, Alba de Tormes, Salamanca, and Malagón. "Just think," she wrote to her friend María Bautista, "of a poor old body like me being packed off to Malagón! It really makes me laugh — and yet I have the spirit to do more even than that."

There was indeed plenty for her to do, for she had been sorely missed. She found the state of the Convent of the Incarnation "a matter for weeping: the poor creatures spend their time trying to divert each other." Once again, inevitably, Teresa came within a hair's breadth of being made prioress. At Malagón, too, they wanted her as superior, though perhaps there was an ulterior motive here? "One may suspect," she wrote to Gracián, "that the needs of Malagón have less to do with it than my Calced brethren's desire to get me sent far away from them."

Despite her age, her health, and her three years of virtual imprisonment, Teresa was still very much in control. She had lost none of her shrewdness and was still forthright and outspoken. Her bracing mixture of realism and kindheartedness had always been particularly evident over the decisions to be made concerning the acceptance of novices. Now, eighteen years into her Reform, these first postulants were becoming her prioresses, influencing the choice of the next generation of nuns, at the receiving end of the foundress's blunt advice.

Sometimes Teresa was so pragmatic that her judgments seem harsh; for instance, though she did not like girls with any kind of facial scarring, she could be tempted by a good dowry. She advised one of her prioresses thus: "They say she has some kind of mark on her face: if this is very disfiguring, do not take her. But I was very much attracted to the chance of getting some money which you could have whenever you wanted it. . . . " Yet often she welcomed the disadvantaged and was repelled if social or worldly reasons caused discrimination. It was more typical for her to tell a prioress to accept "the little slave girl" and "to take the little black girl without hesitation, and her sister too." In short she does not cling to rules, but lets circumstances affect her judgment. She knows it is sometimes difficult to accept a postulant without a dowry, but the guide must be suitability. "If nuns are of the sort we really want, we have no need to trouble so much about their dowries."

On this round of visits, after the years of persecution, she showed the same spirit. Soon after she arrived at Valladolid she wrote forcefully to Gracián about a difficult nun:

> I have never wanted to tell your Paternity how insufferable that daughter of the Licentiate Godoy, now at Alba, is, in case you should be distressed about it. I have done all I can to see that she is given every kind of opportunity, but none is of any use — she is quite intolerable. Not being very intelligent, she cannot be appealed to by reason, and she must be extremely unhappy, for she keeps breaking into loud cries. She says she has heart trouble, but I don't believe it.[1]

So much for the notion that a saint is someone too gentle to criticize, too full of ideals to face hard truths. She was also realistic in facing the danger of families being together in the same convent, for she had seen at the Incarnation how cliques could easily result. She advises the prioress at Seville that she must take one girl, because they are deeply indebted to her father, but not the other two, "because it is never a good thing to have three girls who are sisters in one convent at the same time, especially in one of our communities, which are so small."[2]

She could be outspoken, too, about her prioresses, handpicked though they generally were. For instance, she wrote to Gracián of her irritation "to see how such nuns rise to positions of seniority." She was even critical of her beloved María de San José:

> I am extremely sorry about the foolish behavior of the Seville prioress: she has gone down a great deal in my opinion. . . . I find a puerility about that house which is intolerable, and the prioress is shrewder than befits her vocation. . . . I assure you I had a lot to put up with from her while I was there. . . . I have written her some terrible letters, but you might as well talk to a stone wall.[3]

If so harsh a judgment of a close friend comes as a surprise, it is worth remembering that it was when this difference was patched up that she admitted to María de San José herself that she "knew it was silly," but the more she loved someone, the less she could bear them having faults.

Teresa was not to be allowed to spend her old age simply visiting the convents she had already founded. Such was her fame that offers were flooding in for new foundations from Zamora, Madrid, Valencia, and Lisbon. However, the site of her thirteenth foundation was to be a tiny, remote village to the east of Malagón, Villanueva de la Jara. The possibility of a convent there had been mooted intermittently since 1576, before the persecution of the Discalced had put a temporary stop to Teresa's foundations. It was a curious suggestion, coming as it did complete with a ready-made community. Nine *beatas*, much influenced by Catalina de Cardona, the eccentric hermit who had so impressed both Teresa and the friars of Pastrana over a decade earlier, were already living a life of strict enclosure, but Catalina had died in 1577, so the *beatas*, now with no leader and no Rule, wished to join the Discalced Carmelites.

Teresa's first reaction was that it would be too difficult for women already living their own contemplative life to adapt to another Rule, that Villanueva de la Jara was so small they would have no means of subsistence, that they had no house, were a long way from the other foundations, and that in any case they were unknown to her. The case against was substantial. Nevertheless Teresa followed her usual course of consulting her confessor, who told her to accept, and of commending the matter to God, who reproved her severely, asked her what resources she had had when making previous foundations and told her "it would be greatly to His service and to the profit of souls."

Immediately, like light filling a darkened room, Teresa's faint-heartedness turned to resolution, her poor health became a state of well-being of which she could say, "I felt as if I had never been ill," and even the winter weather responded by showing its gentlest face. On February 13, 1580, a party of seven set out. It was a triumphant journey. Teresa was by now so well known that as they passed through the villages of La Mancha people turned out to greet the famous foundress, offering hospitality and bringing their cattle for her blessing. On the way the party stayed with some friars from the nearby village of La Roda, who greeted them barefoot in their frieze mantles. Teresa was deeply touched by the sight. "It was as if we were back in the great days of our holy Fathers. In that lonely field they seemed like fragrant white flowers." The church had an underground entrance representing the cave of Elijah. Moved as she always was by a reminder of the roots of the Carmelite Order, she was filled with joy.

Long before they reached Villanueva they heard the church bells pealing in welcome. When they arrived, the whole village turned out to meet them, and the new foundation was inaugurated with music and rejoicing on the very day of their arrival.

Strange stories about Teresa — her holiness, even her saintliness — were beginning to circulate. Two such tales date from this time in Villanueva. One took place on the journey. Teresa was sharing a room with two of the nuns, when one of them heard the sounds of strange, celestial music bearing no resemblance to any earthly music she had ever heard. She woke her companion and the two listened as Teresa, who was, they were sure, the source of the divine sounds, slept.

Then there was the time, during recreation one day, when a poor woman came to see Teresa, lamenting that all her children had been born dead. The nuns complained, disappointed that Teresa had left them to comfort the unfortunate woman. "My recreation is to comfort the afflicted," Teresa told them. She gave the woman her belt and, from then on, that belt was said to be a remedy for women with problems in child-bearing.

After the triumphal foundation in Villanueva Teresa left for Toledo, where she spent some time with Gracián discussing her plans to make a foundation in Madrid, a cherished ambition which was not fulfilled in her lifetime. After another round of visits — Segovia, Avila, and Medina — she went to Valladolid at the request of the bishop of Palencia, Don Alvaro de Mendoza, the man who as bishop of Avila had helped her start her reform. Now he wanted Teresa to found a convent in Palencia, just north of Valladolid, but she was indecisive, almost indifferent.

At the time an influenza epidemic known as the "universal cold," *catarro universal,* was sweeping the whole of Europe. It carried off Teresa's Jesuit confessor, Baltasar Álvarez; one of her nuns testified that Teresa cried uncontrollably for a whole hour when she heard the news. Her old friend Francisco de Salcedo, the *Caballero santo,* died of it, as did her beloved brother Lorenzo, leaving her responsible for his three children. Predictably Teresa herself caught it; in fact, she became so gravely ill that it was feared she would die. She became weak and listless, and felt she had lost "even the confidence which God had been wont to give me when I was about to begin a foundation. I felt that everything was impossible."

Teresa was no *malade imaginaire;* she was infuriated when her health prevented her from doing what she wanted. When writing about this latest illness Teresa reveals (as she came more and more frequently to do) an interest in the relationship between mind and body which approaches what today would be called psychosomatic. Many years earlier she had written that "the devil does his best to incapacitate [our bodies] when he sees that we are getting fearful about them," adding that her own poor health made her particularly aware of these fears. She admitted that since she had been "less self-regarding and indulgent" her health had been much better and crucially that it always improved when she was confident she knew what God wanted her to do. Did indecision make her ill or illness cause her to be indecisive? There is no doubt of the connection, nor that inner conviction frequently brought about an outer improvement.

Toward the end of her life she goes further, wondering whether her present apathy and indifference toward the next foundation was directly due to illness or whether "the devil wanted to hinder the good that was afterward done." "The fact is I am as amazed as I am distressed — and I often complain to Our Lord about this — to see how the poor soul has to share in the frailty of the body: it really seems as if it has to observe the same laws and participate in its needs and in things which cause suffering."[4]

Teresa knew all too well the trials of illness and pain, but if "the soul is awake," she writes, suffering and illness become as nothing; we must have the "spirituality with which to control it." As always, Teresa speaks from experience, indeed as she was wrestling with this indifference over the Palencia foundation (and her worry over another at Burgos, also under discussion) she again had the experience of certainty of purpose banishing illness. Irresolute and filled with doubts, she begged the Lord for light. In a reproachful tone he said to her, "What dost thou fear? When have I ever failed thee? I am the same now as I have always been. Do not give up either of these foundations."[5] Immediately her courage and resolution returned, and her health improved. "The whole world would not have been sufficient to put any obstacles in my way. So I set to work on the matter at once and Our Lord began to provide me with the means."

It was less than thirty miles from Valladolid to Palencia, so they set out on December 28 and the monastery was inaugurated the following day. Apart from a fog so dense that they could barely see each other on the journey, all went well. Indeed, the part Teresa played in the harmonious founding of the convent was commemorated in a tribute that has passed into Teresian mythology: "Mother Teresa must have in her bosom some authorization from the Royal Council of God, which makes us do whatever she wants whether we like it or not."

Don Alonso Velázquez, bishop of Osma-Soria, had been of great spiritual help to Teresa and she was very attached to him, so, when he asked her to make a foundation at Soria, she was delighted; it would give her plenty of opportunity to talk to him. Tradition has it that, as they set out, Teresa said, "Daughters, when we get to Soria, which is the end of the world, there must be no turning back; you must go on working for God." She was by then far too well traveled to think that Soria, a city about a hundred miles east of Valladolid, was really "the end of the world"—she must have been speaking of her own end. She was saying that, when she died, the nuns must be ready to go on without her.

She took seven nuns, a lay sister, and her companion Ana de San Bartolomé, who, since Teresa had broken her arm, had looked after her faithfully. At the beginning of the summer of 1581, they set off on a journey quite unlike her usual travels; in fact, Teresa found it so refreshing it was "like an outing." The weather was fine, the terrain was flat, and all the practicalities were arranged for her convenience: Doña Beatriz de Beaumont, who was financing the convent, sent her a carriage and her own chaplain; Don Alonso provided a servant and a policeman to prepare rooms at the inns on the way; and the bishop of Palencia told the cathedral bursar to see that the party had all they needed. It was a far cry from the interminable, uncomfortable journeys to which, however unwillingly, she had become accustomed.

More of the anecdotes which were accumulating around Teresa attesting to her saintliness date from that journey from Palencia to Soria. Small children remarked on the sweet smell coming from her habit. Diego de Yepes, later her biographer and less innocent, also noticed a mysterious odor and was at first scandalized — surely the holy nun did not use scent? Then there was the curious story of her power over the elements. At one stop the country folk told her they were badly in need of rain for their crops — would she please have a word with God on their behalf? Teresa began to recite the Litany of the Saints. It rained immediately.

When they arrived at Soria, Doña Beatriz was awaiting them. There were no contractual problems, and the next day the convent was inaugurated. There was, however, one fly in the ointment: Teresa had expected Gracián to be with her. He was not and she was heartbroken. She did not hesitate to let him know her feelings; before she left Palencia she wrote him:

> So I must remind you, my Father, that, after all, the flesh is weak, and that what has happened has made me sadder than I could have wished to be: it has been a great blow to me. Your Paternity might at least have postponed your departure till you could have left us in our house: a week more or less could have mattered to you very little. I have been very lonely here: please God he who was the cause of your Reverence's departure may have hurried you off to better purpose than I suspect.[6]

The contradictions and paradoxes in Teresa's nature seem never-ending. In the same month that she made this petulant complaint, she wrote to the bishop of Osma-Soria in very different vein: "I firmly believe that no strong attachment to any creature or to all the glory of Heaven has any dominion over me. My one attachment is to the love of God." Her inner state had reached a pitch when she could say: "I think no more of Teresa of Jesus than if there were no such person." One of the few things which depressed her was that she was increasingly being called a saint.

Which is one to believe, the querulously demanding Teresa or the detached, selfless Teresa? The answer must be both. Despite her advanced spiritual state, she still operated, as we all do, at different levels. In her depths she might feel serene, but her humanity, that "extraordinary ordinariness," still breaks out. We cannot disbelieve her, she is too honest to make false claims; indeed it is her very honesty that allows her to admit her need to Gracián. Few could doubt her sincerity as, within days of complaining of Gracián's absence, she wrote of the inner serenity she was experiencing:

> Oh, if only I could give Your Lordship a clear idea of the quiet and calm in which my soul now finds itself! For it is now so certain that it will have the fruition of God that it seems to be in possession of it already, though not yet enjoying it.... All I want is to serve, even if service means great suffering.... In some respects my soul is not really subject to the miseries of the world as it used to be: it suffers more but it feels as if the sufferings were wounding only its garments; it does not itself lose its peace.[7]

Later in the same letter Teresa makes one of her most astonishing claims. She no longer needs to "go in search of reflections" to know that God is there. Her normal state now is of a great interior peace; she even says that her understanding of the Trinity and the humanity of Christ have become a constant state. "It is so impossible for me to doubt the presence of the three Persons that I seem clearly to be experiencing the truth of those words of Saint John, that He will make His abode with the soul. . . . Sometimes it seems to be God's will that I should suffer and have no interior comfort, but never, even for a single moment, does my will swerve from the will of God."

19

The Last Foundation
1582

Teresa left Soria in mid-August of 1581, traveling by way of Osma and Segovia. The journey was hot, tiring, and dangerous. The guides were, to put it kindly, unfamiliar with the route; when the roads became too bad they would simply leave the party, saying they had business elsewhere. Teresa and her two companions often had to alight, watching as the carriage hung in the air over steep precipices.

She arrived at Avila ill and lonely, complaining that she had no one to turn to for comfort. "God help me — the farther I journey in this life, the less comfort I find." She was further distressed by the state in which she found her "little dove-cot," St. Joseph's. It was in a poor way materially, having lost its three main benefactors, one through promotion and two through death. The rapid deterioration and loss of morale were also due — in a sense almost more painfully — to the chaplain, Julián of Avila. Teresa's faithful traveling companion and chronicler of the early journeys was, she wrote to Gracián, troublesome: "God deliver us from elderly confessors." In old age he had allowed his always easygoing nature to fall into indulgent laziness; his excessive benevolence was not suitable for an enclosed convent.

In spite of her protests, in these circumstances it was inevitable that Teresa should be made prioress. "Kiss the floor, accept the office," said Gracián firmly. Teresa wrote to María de San José (their recent disagreement entirely and lovingly healed) that they had made her prioress out of sheer hunger. "Pray to God for me, all of you, that I may find enough for the nuns to eat, or I don't know what I shall do."

In November John of the Cross arrived in Avila with a petition to make a foundation in Granada. It would have been a formidable journey, especially for one of Teresa's age and in such poor health. In any case she was too occupied with her current plans for Burgos to give the matter her usual attention. She simply delegated the sixteenth foundation to John of the Cross and one of her nuns, Ana de Jesús.

She had not seen John since his arrest four years earlier and she cannot have realized that this was to be their last meeting. On November 28, after agreeing that John should look after the Granada foundation, he set out for Andalusia. The convent was founded at the beginning of the following year. Though it boasts many Teresian relics, including her cross and walking stick, her *Renunciation of the Mitigated Rule* and even fragments of her flesh, she was not present at its inauguration, nor does she describe it in *The Foundations.*

In contrast to the smooth passage of the convents at Palencia and Soria, the inauguration of Teresa's last convent, at Burgos, was to be full of conflict and suffering. Yet human and divine, Teresa and God, were interwoven in almost inextricable cooperation: she so frail in body that she frequently directed operations from her bed; God, in the words of Tomás Álvarez, "at once the leading character and a spectator."[1] Teresa and her God are now engaged in a constant dialogue. His instructions no longer surprise her; his presence and help are as natural to her as breathing.

Burgos, then the home of some eight thousand souls, was the most important city in old Castile, its ancient capital. It was a splendid and famous city, its people having a reputation for being devout, honorable, and hospitable. For some time Teresa's Jesuit friends had been urging her to make a foundation there. With their encouragement, with the backing of the new archbishop, Don Cristobel Vela, and with several friends in the city, all the signs were favorable. "Everything would be plain sailing," thought Teresa.

She was, however, worried about the journey. It was mid-winter, in her old age the cold weather had a bad effect on her health, and the climate of Burgos was even more notorious for its extremes than Avila. She was considering this problem, when God said: "Make no account of the cold, for I am true heat." The snow on the ground no longer deterred her; once more the situation was flooded with light. Besides, Gracián was insisting on coming: "He was anxious to go so that he might look after my health on the journey, because the weather was so severe, and I was so old and ill, and they apparently think my life of some importance."

On January 2, 1582, they set off in sleet and snow, the rivers swollen, the roads flooded. By the time they reached Medina del Campo, Teresa was not only tired and ill but had also developed a large sore (believed by some to have been cancerous) in her throat, and could only ingest fluids and gruel. Nevertheless it is said that, while she was there, though so ill herself, her presence healed the prioress of a fever and cured one of the sisters of cancer of the nose. When they arrived in Valladolid her throat was so bad she could barely speak, but, as soon as she was well enough, the party took to the road again, arriving to a rapturous welcome in Palencia. There they were told that the roads to Burgos were impassable, they would be mad to go. But the Lord told Teresa it would be all right, he would be with her.

It was all right—just—but the last fifty miles were among the most perilous of all her travels. The men had to walk ahead to find the best path, often helping the muleteers drag the carriages out of the mud; at one point Teresa suggested that, to lighten the load, the women should walk too. There are stories of carts skidding, drivers being pitched under the mules, Gracián falling into the mud, and Teresa's wagon being carried away by the current. But the most dramatic incident occurred just before they reached Burgos, where they had to cross a ford known as the Pontoons:

> Here, in many places, the water had risen so high that it had submerged these pontoons to such an extent that they could not be seen; and we could not find any way of going on, for there was water everywhere, and on either side it was very deep. In fact it was very rash of anyone to travel that way, especially with carriages, for, if they heeled slightly, all would be lost.[2]

According to one of her traveling companions, Teresa laughed at the danger and offered to go first; if she drowned they were under strict instructions not to try to save her, but to turn back. However, writing about this dramatic incident in *The Foundations,* she admitted her true feelings: "When I saw we were entering a regular sea of water, with no sign of a path or a boat, even I was not without fear, despite all the strength Our Lord had given me." She was delighted, though, to suffer under obedience, and after the danger was passed they all found it great fun to talk about.

One of the most famous, though probably apocryphal, stories about Teresa has its origins in this journey. Afterward, it is said, she was complaining to God about the perils they had endured, when he said, "But that is how I treat my friends!" "Yes, Lord," she replied, "that is why you have so few of them!"

Later on the same day, the rain still sheeting down, they arrived at Burgos. The exhausted group went first to see the famous crucifix, then housed in the church of the Augustinian Fathers. This detour was at Gracián's particular wish, for he wanted to commend their task to Christ, but there was another reason. They thought it prudent to delay their arrival until nightfall, so that they might, as they had done before, steal a march on the sleeping city and make the foundation the next morning before anyone could stop them. Teresa showed her potential as a public relations consultant when she later noted that "this place is the capital of a kingdom, and if we had entered quickly no one might have heard about us, so this turmoil and opposition will do us no harm."

They stayed that night with Teresa's friend, the rich and noble Doña Catalina de Tolosa. She cosseted them with motherly love, lighting a huge log fire to dry their soaking clothes, but Teresa was exhausted, sick, and spitting blood. The next day she was unable to raise her head. "So to those who came to see me I could only speak lying down: I spoke to them through a barred window over which we draw a curtain. As it was a day on which there was essential business to be done, this was a great trial to me."

It was indeed a busy day, for they had not succeeded in arriving unnoticed. Far from inaugurating the convent, Teresa was kept fully occupied by the civic authorities, who came to see her "in a body." They were pleased to see her and eager to know how they could help. Meanwhile, Gracián was seeing the archbishop, thinking that little more remained to be done. He returned with a very different story.

The archbishop had quite simply changed his mind. He had been in Avila when the founding of St. Joseph's *sin renta* had caused such turmoil, and he had no wish to witness a similar situation in Burgos. Far from being prepared to put the final seal to the arrangements, he was annoyed with Teresa for coming without his knowledge, and told Gracián so in no uncertain terms.

Gracián, in his gentle way, reminded the archbishop that it was he who had told Teresa to come. The response was that he had wanted to see her alone to discuss possibilities, not with a bevy of nuns in the assumption that it was a *fait accompli.* He dismissed Gracián, telling him that unless they had an income and a house he would never give his consent; they might just as well go back to Avila again. "The roads, of course, were charming, and it was such nice weather," added Teresa ironically.

Her friends rallied round — by now there were many. One was Dr. Pedro Manso, a canon of Burgos cathedral, with whom Gracián was staying. He had become Teresa's confessor and from initial skepticism had come to respect her deeply. Many years later he recounted that, as he approached Teresa, "his limbs began to tremble and his hair to stand on end, so strong was the impression that he was entering into the presence of a saint."[3] Manso did his best, but the archbishop was not moved by his intervention, nor did Teresa's usually irresistible charm soften his heart. He was adamant. He would not even allow Mass to be said in Doña Catalina's house, where they were staying. The most he would grant was that they could remain in Burgos.

Doña Catalina, who emerges from this story as something of a heroine, then offered her own house and an endowment. The archbishop sent his representatives, who managed to fault this too: the house was damp, they reported, and the situation too noisy. At this Gracián lost heart and decided they should leave, but Teresa could not forget that God had told her to make this foundation. And at that point her voice encouraged her again: "Now, Teresa, hold thou fast."

Gracián's instinct to give up was not simply faintheartedness; he had preaching commitments to honor. Yet, despite Teresa untypically begging him to depart, he did not feel he could leave the nuns homeless and almost hopeless, so he first made arrangements for them to stay in the attic of a hospital. It was far from ideal. The one good room was occupied by a widow who resented their presence, Gracián and Teresa had to sign a document promising to leave the moment they were ordered to, and it was smelly, rat-infested, and haunted. But it was somewhere to live, somewhere from which Teresa could continue the search for a permanent house acceptable to the archbishop. When she was not house-hunting, she was comforting the patients in the hospital, sharing a bag of oranges which Doña Catalina had brought for her.

Eventually they found a house. There was some doubt about its value, but once again God guided Teresa's decision. "Art thou hesitating on account of money?" he asked her. Teresa knew this meant that the house was quite suitable — an instinct confirmed by the speed with which the agreement was finalized. It was later considered miraculous, for the price was, in fact, very reasonable, and no one could understand why it had not been snapped up by one of the other religious communities looking for a house in Burgos at the time. The grilles and turns were installed, and on March 18 the community moved in.

Still the archbishop would not give them a license. This time he was annoyed that Teresa had installed the grilles and turns without consultation. Searching to understand his intransigence, Teresa wondered if he might feel she was trying to be independent of his jurisdiction. The archbishop would not even allow them to have Mass said, so the nuns had to go to a nearby church. This might seem a small thing to these nuns, accustomed as they were to traveling great distances, but the degree of enclosure they observed on their travels must never be forgotten; few of them were used to going outside their enclosure and being the subject of curious scrutiny. Teresa says she bore this better than the others, "but there was one nun who would tremble with the distress it caused her to find herself out in the street."

Friends and supporters were enrolled, letters were dispatched, and, on April 15, 1582, a full three months after their arrival — by which time the sisters had reached the depths of depression and the valiant Doña Catalina was inconsolable — the license was at last granted. The archbishop, once again the benevolent well-wisher, preached at the dedication ceremony. He even asked the nuns' forgiveness for the trials he had caused them.

Teresa's delight is recorded in one of the most moving passages she has written about the need for a life of enclosure:

> Only those who have experienced it will believe what pleasure we get from these foundations when we find ourselves at last in a cloister which can be entered by no one from the world. For, however much we may love those in the world, our love is not enough to deprive us of our great happiness when we find ourselves alone. It is as when a great many fish are taken from the river in a net: they cannot live unless they are put back in the river. Even so it is with souls accustomed to live in the streams of the waters of their Spouse: if they are drawn out of them by nets, which are the things of the world, they can have no true life until they find themselves back again. This I always observe in all these sisters and I have discovered it to be so by experience.[4]

Shortly after the house was founded Teresa began to worry that Doña Catalina might face difficulties, even lawsuits, over the endowment she had provided for them. This was a real possibility, because Catalina had promised to bequeath her considerable fortune to the Jesuits, and their displeasure at the prospect of losing the estate to the Carmelites was such that at one point they had even threatened to withhold absolution from her. Teresa would not risk Doña Catalina's kindness leading her into serious trouble, so in the presence of a lawyer they renounced the bequest and returned the legal documents. Teresa's last foundation was, after all, made in poverty.

This temporary enmity between Teresa and the Jesuits, in no way reflecting their true relationship, was followed by a natural disaster. On Ascension Thursday the River Arlanzón flooded and the waters surged round the convent, threatening to fill the lower rooms. The wind howled round the house and cracks appeared in the roof. Neighboring houses were destroyed, trees uprooted, and the nuns even saw dead bodies washed from graves. All around them people were fleeing to safety, but Teresa took the Blessed Sacrament to an upper room and there, for six hours, the nuns said litanies for their safety. The next day divers broke the doors and windows, letting the waters pour out as the floods subsided.

Teresa was anxious not to leave Burgos until the flood damage was put right and the convent was running smoothly, but once again the decision was made for her. The Lord said, "Why dost thou doubt? This is all over now: thou canst quite well go."

20

The Joy of God

"Go! You have yet to suffer greater things!" According to Ana de San Bartolomé, the faithful lay sister who nursed her in her last years, Teresa heard these words from God just before she left Burgos. Like Christ at Gethsemane, at the end of her life she was to face suffering of a particularly poignant kind: the disloyalty and ingratitude of some of her closest friends.

Teresa was glad to be going home. "Please God," she had written a few weeks earlier, "I shall not have to go traveling any more, for I am very old and tired." Accompanied by Ana and Teresita, she left Burgos on July 26, 1582, intending to see to business affairs in connection with her convents, return to Avila, and prepare for the foundation at Madrid. They stopped at Palencia, one of her favorite foundations, where she rested for three weeks before they pressed on to Valladolid.

There Teresa was plunged into family problems arising from her brother's will. Lorenzo had left a bequest to the Discalced Carmelites at Avila, but his son, Don Francisco, had his eyes on the money and Don Francisco's mother-in-law was trying to have the will proved invalid on the grounds that it was found open on Lorenzo's death. She threatened Teresa with a lawsuit, finding an ally in the Valladolid prioress, María Bautista, who, as María de Ocampo, was the young cousin with whom Teresa had first discussed the reform. María Bautista had become an opinionated, bossy woman, and she persuaded some of the other nuns, even the devoted Teresita, to side with her against Teresa.

An acrimonious discussion between the interested parties took place in the convent parlor in the presence of a lawyer. The exchanges must have been lively, to say the least, for the lawyer accused Teresa of behaving in the most unladylike fashion, quite unbefitting a nun. Teresa, at her most ironical, responded, "May God reward you, Señor, for your charity." In her last extant letter to Gracián, Teresa told him about this legal wrangle:

> I have had a dreadful time here with Don Francisco's mother-in-law. She is a strange woman. She is absolutely bent upon going to law to discuss the validity of the will. She is not in the right, of course, but is well thought of, and some people support her, and have advised me to come to an agreement with her, in case Don Francisco should be completely ruined and we should have to pay for it. This will mean a loss to St. Joseph's, but I trust in God that, as its claim is sound, it will eventually inherit everything. I have been pestered to death with it all.[1]

In fact Doña Beatriz did win the case, but as her son-in-law Don Francisco died childless the estate eventually reverted to St. Joseph's. Teresa was, however, far more hurt by her old friend María Bautista's extraordinary parting words. According to Ana, she said to her departing guests: "Get out of my house, both of you, and don't ever come back."

Painful though this squabbling among family and friends was to Teresa, even more hurtful was that Gracián, against her wishes, had gone to Andalusia. She was bitterly lonely:

> Your frequent letters to me do not suffice to alleviate my distress, though it was a great relief to me to know you are well.... The reasons you gave for your decision to go did not seem to me sufficient.... You could have postponed going to the houses in the south for another two months.... I cannot think why your Paternity decided to go. So keenly did I feel your being away at such a time that I have lost the desire to write to you.... I do not know what purpose your Reverence can have in staying for so long in Seville. I am told you will not come north before the chapter, and that news greatly increased my distress.[2]

She was disappointed, too, in the way one of her most impressive prioresses, Ana de Jesús, was handling the foundation at Granada. Teresa had written to her from Burgos, complaining of her negligence in sending news, criticizing her for having favorites and thus fostering rivalries, and disapproving of her extravagance. Despite her failing health, she wrote with regal authority: "I declare and command that, with the exception of the mother prioress, Ana de Jesús, all the nuns who came from Beas shall return there as soon as facilities can be found for sending them. This order holds even if they have gone into a house of their own...."[3]

Ana de Jesús took note of the sharp reproof—this letter does not reflect the affectionate respect the two women normally had for each other. In fact, while it seems that Teresa would have preferred María de San José, it was Ana de Jesús, the friend and spiritual confidante of John of the Cross, who was to become Teresa's successor.

At Medina del Campo, the last stop before Avila, more humiliation awaited her. The prioress there, Alberta Bautista, was an austere woman, who Teresa had in the past encouraged to be gentler. There is a story, too, that on her last visit, Teresa had miraculously cured the prioress. Resentment outweighed gratitude. On arrival at the convent Teresa was given a cool reception and ushered into the parlor, where the acting provincial, Antonio de Jesús,[4] had news for her.

Relations between Teresa and Antonio had never been easy. He did not like women, he resented Teresa's preference for Gracián, and he still nursed a grievance that it was John of the Cross, and not he, who had the distinction of being the first Discalced friar. He had come with an order which shattered Teresa. She was not to go straight to Avila, but to make a detour to Alba de Tormes, where she was to attend the election of a new prioress and support the duchess of Alba during the last days of her daughter-in-law's confinement.

It was, Teresa told Ana, the hardest act of obedience she had ever had to make. Her friends urged her not to go, reminded her that her health fully justified her desire to go with all speed to St. Joseph's, where she longed to be. She would not even consider it. Obedience was, for her, the greatest virtue and, in Gracián's absence, Antonio was her superior. She would not use any excuses or justifications, however valid, to avoid an order simply because it was not convenient. She had expressed just this danger in *The Foundations,* suggesting that it was the devil who, "seeing there is no path which leads more quickly to the highest virtue than that of obedience, suggests all these objections and difficulties under the guise of good."[5]

Before leaving for Alba — the ducal coach was already waiting for her — she finished her last extant letter, a businesslike communication to the prioress at Soria. As if she was in full health she wrote of the affairs of the Reform — a nun's profession, a possible foundation at Pamplona, her hopes for the house at Madrid, the repugnance she felt if worldly considerations enter into the choice of postulants. But her short stay at Medina was to be bitter to the very end. An uneasy exchange between Teresa and the prioress led to the prioress taking offense and going to her cell without even offering the foundress of her convent a meal. Teresa's last night at Medina was passed in hunger, pain, and loneliness. She had been snubbed by two of her prioresses and coldly forced into obedience by her acting superior; she was missing John of the Cross and her beloved Gracián, both far away.

It was September 16 when Teresa, accompanied by Ana and Teresita, climbed into the duchess of Alba's rudimentary coach. The journey was a serious risk to Teresa's life for the coach was quite unsuitable for the bumpy roads and there was nothing to eat. That night they reached a village near Peñaranda de Bracamonte, but still they could find no food. Teresa, already looking like a corpse, was so weak and in such pain that she fainted. Ana records her anguish at her own helplessness:

> I had nothing but some dry figs, and she was suffering from fever. I gave the servants four reals to get some eggs for her, whatever they might cost. When I saw that nothing could be had for the money, which they gave back to me, I could not look at the saint without weeping, for her face seemed half dead. I can never describe the anguish I felt then. My very heart seemed to be breaking and I could only weep when I saw the plight she was in, for I saw her dying and could do nothing to help her, but she comforted me and told me not to be grieved — the figs were extremely good and there were many poor people who would have less.[6]

The night was spent in a miserable hovel. The next day all they could find to eat was some herbs and onions. Throughout this agonizing journey Teresa had been praying in her traveling cell for the safe delivery of the duchess's grandchild. Her reaction must have been mixed when they arrived at Alba to be greeted by the news that the duchess's daughter-in-law had safely given premature birth to a son. Teresa had made her last great act of obedience on a duchess's whim and her presence turned out to be unnecessary. "God be praised," exclaimed Teresa, apparently without resentment, "there will be no need for this saint now!"

On September 20 the coach stopped outside the Alba convent doors with Teresa so weak that she could not even speak to the nuns. She told Ana she felt "as if she hadn't a single sound bone left in her body." The nuns put her straight to bed in the clean linen sheets reserved for the seriously ill and called a doctor. Teresa no longer attempted to conceal her pain and exhaustion. "God help me, how tired I feel. In twenty years I never had to go to bed as early as this." Nevertheless, the next morning she insisted on getting up to hear Mass and receive Communion; she even inspected the convent and looked after a few business affairs. There was, too, the election of the new prioress to be attended. Again she met disloyalty among her prioresses. The newly elected prioress sided with an interfering benefactress against Teresa and treated the foundress with off-hand coolness.

Teresa longed to be at home. She was worried about St. Joseph's and eager to see her niece Teresita professed there. "As soon as you see me a little better, do something to please me, daughter!" she begged Ana. "Find some carriage or other and take me back with you to Avila!" But it was not to be. On September 29 she went to bed, never to rise from it again.

All her life the thought of death preoccupied Teresa, though her attitude to it changed as she grew older. When she was young, she was terrified of death, as she admitted years later to Gracián.

Even in her early sixties she felt an instinctive revulsion to some of its manifestations, for instance, when she wrote to her brother Lorenzo asking for her own seal, "For I cannot bear sealing my letters with this death's head. . . ."

This natural fear is reflected in her childhood chant *Para siempre, siempre, siempre . . .*, speaking of a yearning for eternal life far beyond her years. Her constant search was for that which does not change:

> We did not come here to seek rewards in this life, but only in the years to come. Let our thoughts always be fixed upon what endures, and not trouble themselves with earthly things which do not endure even for a lifetime. For today some other sister will be in your superior's good books; whereas tomorrow, if she sees you exhibiting some additional virtue, it is with you that she will be better pleased — and if she is not it is of little consequence. Never give way to these thoughts, which sometimes begin in a small way but may cost you a great deal of unrest. Check them by remembering that your kingdom is not of this world, and that everything comes quickly to an end, and that there is nothing in this life that goes on unchangingly.[7]

Her desire was for God, the unchanging. And the only way to be always with God was, she believed, to die.

> [The soul] seeks nothing but the Creator, yet sees that without dying it is impossible for it to have Him, and, as it must not kill itself, it is dying for death, in such a way that there really is a risk of its dying. It sees itself suspended between heaven and earth and has no idea what to do.[8]

Often she longed for death, knowing that she should not and that while on earth it is our duty, not to mention our instinctive desire, to live fully. She understood this ambiguity well, for she had written of it to María de San José several years earlier when a pious old lady had died: "It is right for me to be glad that she has gone to taste the joy of God; but it is wrong of Beatriz to want to do the same, and she should beware of falling into sin by saying such a foolish thing."[9]

Teresa loved life, she was convinced she had plenty to do on earth, and in any case she knew that the matter was not in her hands nor should it be. Nonetheless she longed to be united with God in death. By the time she was sixty-five she had resolved this ambivalent position into true detachment and could write to Gracián:

> I have had a dreadful month, though I have been on my feet most of the time, for I thought I could keep about, however ill I felt, as I am used to the constant suffering. I really believed I was dying, though I was by no means sure I was, and I hardly cared whether I lived or died. This is a grace which God gives me now, and I consider it a great one, when I remember how terrified [of death] I used to feel in the past.[10]

Now Teresa knew she was dying and she was not afraid.

Many witnesses wrote about Teresa's final illness and death. Inevitably some accounts were exaggerated and some could have been the result of devout, overkindled imaginations. Nevertheless a vivid picture emerges.

Her Gethsemane was over. For her last few days on earth she was surrounded by loving nuns, constantly attended by Ana de

San Bartolomé. Even the duchess came frequently to see her, trying to tempt her poor appetite with bowls of soup. One day she arrived just as some particularly vile-smelling medicine had been spilt on the sheets. The fastidious Teresa was greatly upset and one of the sisters said, to console her, that she need not worry, for the medicine would seem to the duchess to be mixed with a delicious perfume. And so it was. The duchess noticed nothing amiss, merely remarking on the fragrant smell of water-of-angels, a scent fashionable at the time.

After a heavy hemorrhage Teresa was taken to a cell near the chapel, so she could hear Mass from her bed. The sisters claimed that all summer they had seen strange lights and heard hushed sighs billowing round the convent. Now they knew why. The foundress was dying.

On October 2 she asked Antonio to hear her confession. Under the shadow of death, his responsibility and, no doubt, his guilt for her last, terrible journey were forgotten. He implored her not to leave them. She answered gently, "I am no longer needed in this world." Then the nuns pleaded for some words to carry them through the days to come, when she would no longer be with them. Vehemently and sometimes in tears, she responded:

> My sisters, my daughters and my ladies; pardon the bad example that I have given you, and do not learn from me, who have been the worst sinner in the world, and have observed the Rule and Constitutions worse than anyone. I pray you, for the love of God, daughters, to observe them with the greatest possible perfection, and to obey the superiors.[11]

She repeated this combination of confession and advice over and over again, asking for the message to be given to the other convents. The memory of her sins still afflicted her; her consolation lay in a phrase she was frequently heard to say as she became weaker: "After all, Lord, I am a daughter of the church."

On October 3 Antonio gave her Extreme Unction. He asked her where she wanted to be buried, in Alba or in Avila. "Do I have to have anything of my own?" she replied. "Won't they give me a little bit of earth here?" All night she was heard to murmur, in her native Castilian, "A broken and a contrite heart, Lord, thou wilt not despise.... Cast me not away from thy face." Later, according to a nun who was present, she turned to the host, which Antonio was bringing her, and exclaimed:

> O my Lord and my Spouse! This is the longed for hour, it is time now that we should see each other, my Beloved and my Lord, it is time now that I should go to Thee; let us go in peace, and may Thy holy will be done. Now the hour has arrived for me to leave this exile, and to enjoy Thee Whom I have so much desired.[12]

Many strange things are said to have occurred during these last days. Brilliant stars were noticed over the church, rays of light passed the window of Teresa's cell. One of the sisters saw a white dove come from Teresa's mouth; another heard a joyful noise as a throng of white-robed people came into her room. Ana saw Christ, attended by angels and the Ten Thousand Martyrs, standing at the foot of Teresa's bed.

All this while Ana had stayed faithfully by Teresa's bed, but the next day Antonio sent her to fetch something. Hardly had she left the room when Teresa looked anxiously round. The old priest asked if she wanted Ana? With the smallest of signs she indicated "Yes." Quickly they called Ana. "As soon as she saw me, she smiled, showed me gratitude and love, touched my hands, laid her head between my arms, and thus I held her until she died."

Epilogue

The gruesome story of the indignities to which Teresa's mortal remains were subjected is one of the more shameful episodes in the church's long and checkered history. The body of one whose dying claim was that she was "a daughter of the church" was, for many years, prevented by many of its most devout members from resting in peace.

The race to possess her body started as soon as she had died. Lest the people of Avila claim her, she was buried the next day, in due solemnity but without embalming, near the convent. Teresa de Layz, the woman who had endowed the Alba foundation, insisted that the coffin should be covered with stones, bricks, and quicklime (to ensure the body would be quickly consumed). Then two cart-loads of earth were piled upon the grave to impede the efforts of anyone trying to take the body away. The grave looked, said one of the nuns, as if workmen were laying the foundations for a building.

The nuns, who often prayed beside the grave, began to notice a curious thing; that the delightful fragrance which had emanated from Teresa in her last sickness and wafted round the corridors at her death was still present near her body. They further remarked that this was particularly strong on the days of saints to whom Teresa had formed a particular devotion. Curiosity overcame them and, nine months after her death, when Gracián arrived on a visitation, they asked him to open the tomb. Eager to see his beloved Teresa's face once more, he did not take much persuading.

Francisco de Ribera records how they stealthily removed the earth and rubble from her grave — it took four days. On July 4, 1583, they opened the coffin:

> They found the coffin lid smashed, half rotten and full of mildew, the smell of damp was very pungent. . . . The clothes had also fallen to pieces. . . . The holy body was covered with the earth which had penetrated into the coffin and so was all damp too, but as fresh and whole as if it had been buried the day before.[1]

So perfectly preserved was the body that the men discreetly retired while the nuns undressed and washed her. When they had finished, they covered her and called Gracián back. "Uncovering her breasts," he wrote, "I was surprised to see how full and firm they were." Before they clothed her in a new habit and closed the coffin he cut off her left hand, wrapped it first in a coif and then in paper, and took it to Avila. There he left it in a sealed casket, but first he severed her little finger, which, for the rest of his life, he always wore round his neck.

Two years later, in November 1585, the Discalced fathers, meeting at a chapter, decreed that the body should be returned to Avila. A party of grave robbers, Gracián, Julián of Avila, another priest, Gregorio Nacianzeno, and the chancellor of the cathedral at Avila, met at Alba the following day to steal the body. They were fortunate, for the town was untypically quiet and the duchess away. Gregorio and Gracián took the body from the coffin, and called the sisters to see it. Gregorio, "with extreme repugnance," then drew a knife from his belt and inserted it under the left arm, from which the hand was already missing. Ribera's account is horribly graphic: "Wonderful to relate: without using any more effort than in cutting a melon or a little fresh cheese, as he said, he severed the arm at the joints as easily as if he had spent some time beforehand trying to ascertain their exact position."[2] Again they found the body was incorrupt. Fresh blood flowed from the wound; the smell was wonderfully fragrant, reminiscent of clover.

Three years after her death, Teresa was traveling again. Early in the morning after they opened her grave they took her home to Avila. She was laid on a carpet and the nuns, the bishop of Avila, and various town dignitaries came to pay homage. Two doctors examined the body and reported that there was no natural explanation for the perfect state of the body.

Still she was not allowed to rest. The duke of Alba, furious at the theft, appealed to Rome. The pope, fully aware of the duke's power, gave in. The following August the mutilated body was returned to Alba. Even then the exhumations were not over. Ribera saw the body in 1588, Diego de Yepes in 1594, and Julián of Avila two years later. All reports agree that the body remained incorrupt.

The butchery continued. Now most of her remains are in Alba, though her transverberated heart and her right arm are preserved separately as sacred relics. Her right foot and a piece of her jaw are in Rome, her left hand in Lisbon and her right hand, her left eye, and fragments of flesh are treasured over the whole world.

Those who carried out these mutilations would claim they were carried out in love and respect. Nevertheless they are, to the twenty-first century, shameful. But though her body was treated in so fearful a fashion, her memory at least has been honored.

Six years after her death the first collected edition of her writings was published under the editorship of the writer and mystic

Luis de León. Such was its reception that the following year it was reprinted. Though this wider dissemination of her thought caused some critical outcry — for instance, a historian called for the banning of her books and a few friars branded her a heretic — their voices were drowned by demands for her canonization. In 1614 she was beatified, and eight years later she was made a saint. Spain rejoiced, but wanted her to be in some special way their own: in 1812 she was declared Patroness of Spain.

In her lifetime Teresa greatly disliked being regarded as a saint; one can imagine her embarrassment at the idea of formally joining such a company. But surely her reaction to a more recent honor bestowed on her would be amusement? On September 27, 1970, Teresa was solemnly proclaimed Doctor of the Church, the first woman ever to be so honored. Teresa, who constantly belittled her own sex as having no learning, who in her lifetime was, as a woman, excluded from the humblest teaching office in the church and denied any participation in theological discourse, was awarded the church's highest theological honor.

Teresa, the nun from Avila, had become an international figure. One of the reasons she was made a Doctor of the Church was that her teaching had bridged ecumenical divisions. Her works are studied not only by Roman Catholics but by those of every denomination and faith, from Lutherans and Calvinists to Buddhists, Hindus, and Shintoists. They even find appreciative readers among atheists and unbelievers, who find in her writings a serious witness to the existence of God.

Teresa's legacy has as many facets as her personality: the reform of the Carmelite Order, the convents she founded and those founded later in her name; her detailed and painfully honest charting of mystical experience; her personality, ringing through her writings with its humility, humor, forthright common sense, and faith; her attractive, determined, yet unaggressive, feminism;

and the emphasis she places on experience rather than dogmatic teaching. Her spirit is as alive today as it was over four hundred years ago.

Perhaps most of all Teresa deserves honor and gratitude because, in finding her own true center, she gives hope to others. While fortunate in her gifts and in her beauty, she spent much of her sixty-seven years on earth taming a complex and difficult temperament, reconciling a mass of opposing characteristics, tossed between heaven and earth. Grateful though she was for the "favors," the visions, locutions, and raptures which she experienced, she knew that this was not where holiness lay. The highest perfection, she wrote, lies in "the bringing of our wills so closely into conformity with the will of God that, as soon as we realize He wills anything, we desire it with all our might, and take the bitter with the sweet, knowing that to be His Majesty's will." For anyone struggling to sort out the true from the false in their own natures, to find the still center in seemingly irreconcilable opposites, Teresa remains an example of one who succeeded in this most heroic task. She could even refer to the challenge as "the joy of doing something which brings our will wholly into opposition with our nature."

So, too, does Teresa make God more real, more concrete. God is both part of her world and yet utterly different. Growing up in a society which valued honor so highly, Teresa would give honor only to God. Finding so much of her pain and her anguish in relationships, God was her greatest friend. Enjoying communication and excelling at it whether in conversation, by letter, or in her books, she communicated with God through prayer, which for her was "nothing but an intimate conversation between friends." To anyone asking for proof of the existence of God, anyone saying, "Is God there?" Teresa's whole life offers a resounding "Yes."

Chronology

1515	March 28. Birth of Teresa.	
		1519 Luther breaks with Rome.
1522	Teresa's attempted flight to the Moors with Rodrigo.	
c. 1528	Death of Teresa's mother.	
c. 1531–33	Teresa enters Augustinian Convent of Our Lady of Grace.	1532 Pizarro conquers Peru.
		1534 Henry VIII breaks with Rome.
1536	Enters Carmelite Convent of the Incarnation.	First suppression of monasteries in England.
		Death of Erasmus of Rotterdam.
1537	Makes profession.	
1538	Breakdown of health.	Excommunication of Henry VIII.
1539	"Drastic remedies" at Becedas. Attack of catalepsy. Nearly dies. Helpless for eight months.	
1540	Returns to the Incarnation, seriously ill until 1542.	
		1542 Birth of John of the Cross.
		Death of Copernicus.
1543	Teresa gives up prayer. Death of Teresa's father.	
		1545 Council of Trent opens.
		1547 Birth of Cervantes.
1554–55	Teresa's "second conversion."	1554 Jesuits in Avila.
1555	First contact with Society of Jesus.	

c. 1556–57	Teresa begins to experience visions.	1556 Accession of King Philip II.
1558	People declare her to be possessed.	Destruction of Spanish Protestantism.
	Discussions about reform of Carmelite Order begin.	Archbishop of Toledo tried by Inquisition.
		Accession of Queen Elizabeth I.
1559	Álvarez becomes Teresa's confessor.	Index of forbidden books published by Inquisition.
	Transverberation of Teresa's heart.	
1560	Teresa makes vow of greater perfection.	Inquisition at Toledo and Seville.
1562	Stays with Doña Luisa de la Cerda at Toledo.	
	Foundation of St. Joseph's, Avila.	
1563–67	Teresa at St. Joseph's.	1563 Council of Trent closes.
		1564 Rubeo elected general of the Order of Carmel.
1565	Completes her *Life*. Begins *The Way of Perfection*.	
1567	Carmelite general authorizes Teresa to found further convents of the Reform.	Duke of Alba fighting in the Netherlands.
	Foundation at Medina del Campo.	
	First meeting with John of the Cross.	
1568	Foundation at Malagón.	
	First Mass said at Duruelo.	
	Foundation at Valladolid.	

1569	Foundation at Toledo.	
	Foundation at Pastrana.	
1570	Foundation at Salamanca.	Excommunication of Elizabeth I of England.
1571	Foundation at Alba de Tormes.	Naval Battle of Lepanto.
	Teresa formally renounces Mitigated Rule in favor of Primitive Rule.	
	Prioress of Incarnation at Avila (until Oct. 1574).	
1572	John of the Cross becomes confessor to the Incarnation.	Massacre of St. Bartholomew's Day.
1573	Teresa writes to Philip II imploring his protection for the Reform.	Cardinal Quiroga becomes Inquisitor-General.
	Begins to write *The Foundations.*	
1574	Foundation at Segovia.	c. 1574 Inquisition becomes more moderate.
	Returns to St. Joseph's as prioress.	
1575	Foundation at Beas de Segura.	
	First meeting with Gracián.	
	Foundation at Seville.	
	Harsh measures adopted toward the Reform.	
	Teresa ordered back to Castile.	
	Writes to Philip II asking for Discalced to be a separate province.	
1576	Foundation at Caravaca.	
	Measures taken to suppress Discalced foundations.	

1577	Writes *The Interior Castle.*	
	Election of prioress at Incarnation.	
	Violent scenes; nuns voting for Teresa excommunicated.	
	John of the Cross imprisoned by Friars of the Observance.	
1578	Persecution of Reform at its height.	
1579	Teresa authorized to continue visiting convents.	Union of Utrecht.
1580	Foundation at Villanueva de la Jara.	Portugal united with Spain.
	Discalced Carmelites recognized as a separate province by a bull of Pope Gregory III.	
	Foundation at Palencia.	
1581	Gracián appointed provincial of the Discalced.	
	Foundation at Soria.	
1582	Foundation (in Teresa's absence) at Granada.	
	Foundation at Burgos.	
	Completes *The Foundations.*	
	Leaves Burgos for Avila. Though ill, travels to Palencia, Valladolid, Medina del Campo. Arrives at Alba de Tormes.	
	October 4. Teresa dies at Alba de Tormes.	

Notes

1. Castilian Childhood

1. *Life*, 1.
2. Brenan, Appendix 1, 90–91.
3. *Life*, 29.
4. Ibid., 13.
5. *Letters*, 34.
6. *Life*, 262.
7. *Letters*, 97.
8. *Life*, 14.

2. The Convent of the Incarnation

1. *Life*, 20.
2. Auclair, 50.
3. *Life*, 21.
4. E.g., Victoria Lincoln, *Teresa: A Woman.*
5. Ribera, *Vitae B. Matris Teresae de Jesu*, 1620, trans. John F. X. Harriott.
6. *Life*, 46.
7. V. Sackville-West, *The Eagle and the Dove*, 33.
8. Osuna, *The Third Spiritual Alphabet*, 349.
9. *Life*, 23.
10. Ibid., 32.
11. Ibid., 35.

3. "That Stormy Sea"

1. *Life*, 140.
2. Ibid., 45.
3. Ibid.
4. *Letters*, 767.
5. *Life*, 51.
6. Ibid., 54.
7. Ibid., 56.
8. Ibid., 54.
9. Ibid., 55.
10. Ibid., 58.

4. "Another and a New Life"

1. *Life*, 145.
2. Ibid., 84.
3. Ibid., 84–85.
4. Ibid., 90.
5. Ibid., 105.
6. Ibid., 106.
7. Ibid., 110.
8. Ibid., 115.
9. Ibid., 155.
10. Ibid., 170.
11. Ibid., 174.
12. Clissold, 55.

5. Delectable Torments

1. *Life*, 179.
2. Ibid., 180.
3. Ibid., 192.
4. From St. John of the Cross, *The Living Flame of Love.*
5. Psalm 102:7.
6. *Complete Works*, vol. 1, *Spiritual Relations*, 320.
7. Ibid., vol. 2, *The Interior Castle*, 315.
8. Ibid., 310.
9. Ibid., 321.
10. *Life*, 287.
11. Ibid., 157.
12. Ibid., 162.
13. Ibid., 124.
14. *Complete Works*, vol. 2, *The Interior Castle*, 314.
15. *Life*, 204.
16. Ibid., 276.
17. Ibid., 165.
18. Ibid., 216.

6. St. Joseph's — Secret Preparations

1. *Life*, 224.
2. Ibid., 226.
3. Ibid., 229.

4. Ibid.
5. *Complete Works*, vol. 1, *Spiritual Relations*, 307.
6. Ibid., vol. 2, *The Way of Perfection*, 181.
7. *Life*, 242.

7. St. Joseph's — Victory

1. *Life*, 249.
2. Ibid., 250.
3. Ibid., 251.

8. "The Most Restful Years of My Life"

1. *Complete Works*, vol. 3, *Foundations*, 3.
2. *Life*, 250.
3. *Complete Works*, vol. 3, *Constitutions*, 222.
4. Ibid., 237.
5. Ibid., vol. 2, *The Way of Perfection*, 89.
6. Ibid., 82.
7. Melia, v.
8. *Complete Works*, vol. 3, *Constitutions*, 227.
9. Ibid., vol. 2, *The Way of Perfection*, 18.
10. Ibid., 35.
11. *Life*, 266.
12. Ibid., 198.

9. "Restless Gad-about"

1. J. H. Elliott, *Imperial Spain: 1469–1716*, 244.
2. *Complete Works*, vol. 3, *Foundations*, 7.
3. Silverio, *Vida de Santa Teresa*, 5:352–53.
4. *Complete Works*, vol. 3, *Foundations*, 11.
5. Ibid., vol. 2, *The Way of Perfection*, 147.
6. Ibid., vol. 3, *Foundations*, 12.
7. Mrs. Cunninghame Graham, 289.
8. Silverio, *Ana de San Bartolomé*, 2:301.
9. Ibid., 285.
10. Silverio, *Gracián*, 5:xi–xii.
11. *Complete Works*, vol. 3, *Foundations*, 47.

10. "A Friar and a Half"

1. *Complete Works,* vol. 3, *Foundations,* 66.
2. Ibid., vol. 2, *The Way of Perfection,* 6.
3. Ibid., vol. 3, *Foundations,* 66.
4. Clissold, 160.
5. Ibid., 161–62.
6. There are now, worldwide, some 3,500 friars in 460 communities who regard Teresa as their foundress.
7. "*En una noche oscura,*" vv. 1 and 8, trans. Roy Campbell in *St. John of the Cross — Poems,* ed. E. V. Rieu, Penguin Classics, 1960.
8. Quoted in Crisógono de Jesús, *The Life of Saint John of the Cross.*
9. Ibid.
10. Peers, *Studies of the Spanish Mystics,* 199.
11. Antonio Machado quoted in Peers, *Studies of the Spanish Mystics,* 199.
12. *Letters,* to Don Francisco de Salcedo, September 1568, vol. 1, no. 10, 82.
13. *Letters,* to M. Ana de Jesús, December 1578, 2:625.

11. Toledo and Pastrana

1. *Letters,* to Doña Juana de Ahumada, December 1569, 1:70.
2. *Complete Works,* vol. 3, *Foundations,* 71.
3. Ibid., 72.
4. Auclair, 207–8.
5. *Life,* 289.
6. Álvarez and Domingo.
7. Ibid.

12. Salamanca and Alba

1. *Complete Works,* vol. 2, *Exclamations,* 406.
2. Silverio quoted in Peers, *Mother of Carmel,* 97.
3. Ibid., 96.
4. *Obras de Santa Teresa de Jesús,* 9th ed., Editorial Apostalado de la Prensa S.A., 1964.
5. *Complete Works,* vol. 2, *Exclamations,* 402.
6. Ibid., vol. 3, *Foundations,* 94.
7. *Life,* 27.
8. *Complete Works,* vol. 3, *Judgment,* 267–68.

9. Ibid., vol. 3, *Foundations*, 98.
10. *Letters*, to Ambrosio de San Benito, 1576, vol. 1, no. 121, 309.
11. Álvarez and Domingo.
12. *Complete Works*, vol. 1, *Spiritual Reflections*, 344.
13. Address given by St. Teresa at Convent of Incarnation, *Complete Works*, 3:337.

13. Reluctant Prioress

1. *Letters*, to Doña María de Mendoza, March 7, 1572, vol. 1, no. 34, 100.
2. Sonya A. Quitslund, "Elements of a Feminist Spirituality in St. Teresa," *Carmelite Studies Centenary of Saint Teresa* (Washington D.C.: ICS Publications, 1984).
3. *Letters*, Gracián, October 1580, 2:778.
4. Ibid., to Don Antonio Gaytán, March 28, 1581, 2:834.
5. Ibid., to Discalced Carmelite nuns of Soria, December 28, 1581, 2:258.
6. Ibid., to Doña Juana de Ahumada, September 27, 1572, 1:109.
7. Ibid., to a benefactor at Toledo, December 16, 1576, 1:379.
8. Ibid., to M. Ana de San Alberto, July 2, 1577, 1:465.
9. Ibid., to M. María de San José, February 1577, 1:440
10. *Complete Works*, vol. 1, *Spiritual Relations*, 339.
11. *Letters*, to M. María Bautista, June 1579, 2:657.
12. *Complete Works*, vol. 1, *Spiritual Relations*, 250.
13. Ibid., 352.
14. Auclair, 245.
15. See chapter 11.
16. *Complete Works* vol. 3, *Foundations*, 107.

14. Gracián

1. Álvarez and Domingo.
2. *Letters*, to M. Inés de Jesús, May 12, 1575, 1:175.
3. *Complete Works*, vol. 1, *Spiritual Relations*, 355.
4. *Letters*, to Gracián, September 5, 1576, 1:266.
5. Ibid., to Gracián, October 23, 1576, 1:316.
6. Ibid., to Gracián, March 2, 1578, 2:531.
7. Ibid., to Gracián, October 4, 1579, 2:683.
8. Melia, 49.

9. *Letters,* to Gracián, November 1576, 1:345.
10. Ibid., to Gracián, January 9, 1577, 1:401.
11. *Life,* 46.

15. Andalusia

1. *Complete Works,* vol. 3, *Foundations,* 123–24.
2. Julián de Avila quoted in Álvarez and Domingo.
3. *Complete Works,* vol. 3, *Foundations,* 124.
4. Ibid., 126.
5. Ibid., *Spiritual Relations,* 1:358–59.
6. Ibid., *Foundations,* 3:133–34.

16. Persecution

1. *Complete Works,* vol. 3, *Foundations,* 149.
2. Quoted in Walsh, 465.
3. *Complete Works,* vol. 3, *Foundations,* 147.
4. *Letters,* to María de San José, October 1577, 1:488.
5. Ibid., to King Philip II, December 4, 1577, 1:497.
6. Ibid., to Discalced Carmelite nuns at Seville, January 31, 1579, 2:629.
7. Silverio quoted in Álvarez and Domingo, 121.

17. "In My Father's House"

1. Quoted in *Complete Works,* 2:189.
2. Ibid., 188.
3. *Within You He Dwells: Rediscovering St. Teresa's Interior Castle,* ed. Philip Boyce, OCD (Teresian Press, 1984), 10–12.
4. *Complete Works,* vol. 2, *The Interior Castle,* 208.
5. Burrows, 26.
6. Joseph Glynn, OCD, *The Eternal Mystic* (New York: Vantage Press, 1987), 168.
7. *Complete Works,* vol. 2, *The Interior Castle,* 221.
8. Ibid., *The Way of Perfection,* 177.
9. Ibid., *The Interior Castle,* 241.
10. Ibid., 234.
11. Ibid., 253.
12. Ibid., 264.
13. Ibid., 294.

18. Back on the Road

1. *Letters,* to Gracián, July 7, 1579, 2:671.
2. Ibid., to M. María de San José, July 22, 1579, 2:675.
3. Ibid., to Gracián, October 4, 1579, 2:684.
4. *Complete Works,* vol. 3, *Foundations,* 166.
5. Ibid., 167.
6. *Letters,* to Gracián, May 24, 1581, 2:838.
7. *Complete Works,* vol. 1, *Spiritual Relations,* 334.

19. The Last Foundation

1. Álvarez and Domingo, 155.
2. *Complete Works,* vol. 3, *Foundations,* 190.
3. Clissold, 235.
4. *Complete Works,* vol. 3, *Foundations,* 203.

20. The Joy of God

1. *Letters,* to Gracián, September 1, 1582, 2:965.
2. Ibid.
3. Ibid., to M. Ana de Jesús, May 30, 1582, 2:938.
4. Previously Antonio de Heredia.
5. *Complete Works,* vol. 3, *Foundations,* 23.
6. Clissold, 248.
7. *Complete Works,* vol. 2, *The Way of Perfection,* 119.
8. *Complete Works,* vol. 1, *Spiritual Relations,* 331.
9. *Letters,* to María de San José, December 13, 1576, 1:377.
10. Ibid., to Gracián, May 5, 1580, 2:746.
11. Silverio, *Gracián,* 155.
12. Ibid.

Epilogue

1. Auclair, 420.
2. Ibid., 432.

Selected Bibliography

Teresa's Own Writings

The Life of Saint Teresa by Herself. Trans. J. M. Cohen. London: Penguin Books, 1957.

The Complete Works of St. Teresa of Jesus. Trans. and ed. E. Allison Peers. London: Sheed & Ward, 1944–1946.

The Letters of St. Teresa of Jesus. 2 vols. Trans. E. Allison Peers. London: Sheed & Ward, 1951.

The Collected Works of St. Teresa of Avila. Trans. Kieran Kavanaugh, OCD, and Otilio Rodríguez, OCD. Washington, D.C.: Institute of Carmelite Studies, 1976–1985.

Early Biographies

Yepes, Diego de. *Vida de Santa Teresa.* Madrid, 1587.

Ribera, Francisco de. *La Vida de Santa Teresa de Jesús.* Salamanca, 1590.

Julián of Avila, *Vida de Santa Teresa.* Ed. Vicente de la Fuente. Madrid, 1881.

León, Luis de. *De la vida, muerte y virtudes y milagros de la Santa Madre Teresa de Jesús.* Burgos: Biblioteca Mistica Carmelitana, 1915.

Other Relevant Works

Ahlgren, Gillian T. W. *Teresa of Avila and the Politics of Sanctity.* Ithaca, N.Y.: Cornell University Press, 1996.

Álvarez, Tomás. *Living with God: St. Teresa's Concept of Prayer.* Trans. Christopher O'Mahony and Dominica Horia. Carmelite Centre of Spirituality, 1980.

Álvarez, Tomás, and Fernando Domingo. *Saint Teresa of Avila: A Spiritual Adventure.* Trans. Christopher O'Mahony. Burgos: Editorial Monte Carmelo, and Washington, D.C.: ICS Publications.

Auclair, Marcelle. *St. Teresa of Avila.* London: Burns & Oates, 1953.

Barry, Gabriel. *Historical Notes on the Carmelite Order.*

Bilinkoff, Jodi. *The Avila of Saint Teresa: Religious Reform in a Sixteenth-Century City.* Ithaca, N.Y.: Cornell University Press, 1989.

Brenan, Gerald. *John of the Cross — His Life and Poetry.* Cambridge: Cambridge University Press, 1973.

Burrows, Ruth. *Interior Castle Explored.* London: Sheed & Ward, 1981.

Clissold, Stephen. *St. Teresa of Avila.* London: Sheldon, 1979.

Crisógono de Jesús, OCD. *The Life of Saint John of the Cross.* Trans. Kathleen Pond. London: Longmans, 1958.

D'Souza, Gregory, OCD. *Teresian Mysticism and Yoga.* Pub. by the author, India, 1981.

Efrén de la Madre de Dios and Otger Steggink. *Tiempo y vida de Santa Teresa.* Biblioteca de Autores Cristianos. Madrid: Editorial Católica, 1968.

Egan, Keith J. *Carmelite Prayer: A Tradition for the 21st Century.* Mahwah, N.J.: Paulist Press, 2003.

Elliott, J. H. *Imperial Spain 1469–1716.* Harmondsworth: Penguin Books, 1963.

Francis of Osuna. *The Third Spiritual Alphabet.* Toledo, 1527.

Glynn, Joseph. *The Eternal Mystic.* New York: Vantage Press, 1987.

Graham, Gabriela Cunninghame. *Saint Teresa.* London, 1894.

Hamilton, Elizabeth. *The Great Teresa.* London: Chatto & Windus, 1960.

Heliodore of the Child Jesus, OCD, Father. *The Work of St. Teresa and Her First Monastery.* Buffalo, N.Y.: Discalced Carmelite Nuns, 1967.

Hoornaert, R. *Saint Teresa in Her Writings.* Trans. J. Leonard. London: Sheed & Ward, 1931.

Jiménez-Duque, Baldomero. *Convento de San José; Primera Fundación de Santa Teresa de Jesús.* Avila: Monjas Carmelitas de San José.

Lincoln, Victoria. *Teresa: A Woman.* Albany: State University of New York Press, 1984.

Melia, Nora. *St. Teresa and Friendship.* Melbourne: Carmelite Communications, 1988.

Peers, E. Allison. *Mother of Carmel.* London: SCM Press, 1945.

———. *Studies of the Spanish Mystics.* London: SPCK, 1951.

———. *Saint Teresa of Jesus.* London: Faber & Faber, 1953.

———. *Handbook to the Life and Times of St. Teresa and St. John of the Cross.* London: Burns & Oates, 1954.

Poulain, A. *The Graces of Interior Prayer.* London: Kegan Paul, Trench, Trübner & Co., 1928.

Sackville-West, V. *The Eagle and the Dove.* London: Michael Joseph, 1943.

St. John of the Cross. *Poems.* Trans. Roy Campbell. Harmondsworth: Penguin Classics, 1960.

———. *Collected Works.* Trans. K. Kavanaugh and O. Rodriguez. Washington, D.C.: ICS Publications, 1976.

Silverio de Santa Teresa, P., OCD. *Procesos de beatificación y canonización de Sta. Teresa de Jesús.* 5 vols. Burgos: Tipografía "El Monte Carmelo," 1935.

———. *Vida de Santa Teresa.* Burgos, 1935–37.

———. *Saint Teresa of Jesus.* London: Sands & Co., 1947.

Slade, Carole. *St. Teresa of Avila: Author of a Heroic Life.* Berkeley: University of California Press, 1995.

Walsh, William Thomas. *Saint Teresa of Avila.* Milwaukee: Bruce Publishing Company, 1943.

Weber, Alison. *Teresa of Avila and the Rhetoric of Femininity.* Princeton, N.J.: Princeton University Press, 1990.

Welch, John. *Spiritual Pilgrims: Carl Jung and Teresa of Avila.* New York: Paulist Press, 1982.

Williams, Rowan, *Teresa of Avila.* London: Geoffrey Chapman, 1991.

The Making of a Doctor. Exeter: Catholic Record Press, 1970.

Carmelite Studies, ICS Publications, Washington, D.C.: *Spiritual Direction; Centenary of St. Teresa,* 1984; *Edith Stein Symposium and Teresian Culture.* 1987.

Acknowledgments

My thanks to the many Carmelite convents I visited in Spain, where I was always received with courtesy and where I learned much. To two members of the Teresian Association, Pilar Campos, who helped me with Spanish, and Elsie Sebastian, who checked the Spanish spelling and accents. To Professor Keith J. Egan for his comments. To the Carmelite Priory at Boar's Hill, Oxford, in particular Father Iain Matthew, for their generosity as regards their excellent library, for allowing me working space and giving much help. To Archbishop Rowan Williams for reading the typescript and making valuable comments. Any errors remaining are, of course, my responsibility alone.

All quotations from Teresa's writings are taken from *The Complete Works of St. Teresa of Jesus,* translated and edited by E. Allison Peers, published by Sheed & Ward, London.

Index

Please note: Spanish surnames which include the prefix *la* are indexed under L; those including two surnames are under the penultimate name. Saints are under their forenames; T stands for Teresa of Avila herself. Her family surname is Cepeda y Ahumada, indexed under C.